ONCE
UPON A
WISH

ONCE
UPON A
WISH

True Inspirational Stories of Make-A-Wish Children

by RACHELLE SPARKS

BENBELLA BOOKS, INC.

DALLAS, TEXAS

The stories in this book were told from the perspectives and recollections of the families involved.

BENBELLA
BenBella Books, Inc.
10300 N. Central Expressway, Suite 530
Dallas, TX 75231
www.benbellabooks.com
Send feedback to feedback@benbellabooks.com

Printed in the United States of America
10 9 8 7 6 5 4 3 2 1
Library of Congress Cataloging-in-Publication Data is available for this title.
978-1-937856-12-0

Editing by Marite Hart
Copyediting by Cortney Strube
Proofreading by Christine Koch and Amy Zarkos
Cover design by Kit Sweeney
Text design and composition by Neuwirth & Associates, Inc.
Printed by Berryville Graphics, Inc.

Distributed by Perseus Distribution
(www.perseusdistribution.com)

To place orders through Perseus Distribution:
Tel: (800) 343-4499
Fax: (800) 351-5073
E-mail: orderentry@perseusbooks.com

Significant discounts for bulk sales are available. Please contact Glenn Yeffeth at glenn@benbellabooks.com or (214) 750-3628.

"While we try to teach our children all about life, our children teach us what life is all about."

—*Angela Schwindt*

For my boys,
Bobby, Andrew, and Evan

★ CONTENTS ★

IN APRIL 1980, I met a seven-year-old boy named Chris Grei-cius, who would change my life and, to date, the lives of more than two-hundred fifty thousand children worldwide.

Chris had leukemia and was not going to win his battle. At the time, I was a motorcycle officer with the Arizona Highway Patrol. When I learned that Chris had a wish to become a highway patrol motorcycle officer, like his heroes Ponch and John from the TV series *CHIPS*, I became part of a group of officers that would make his wish come true. We turned Chris into the first and only honorary Arizona Highway Patrol officer in the history of the patrol and presented him with a custom highway patrol uniform, complete with hat, badge, and his most prized possession, his uniform motorcycle wings.

While Chris's wish came true, this little boy forgot about his illness, hospitals, and chemotherapy treatments. He once again became a typical seven-year-old boy, running, laughing, and hopping up and down with excitement. I remember the tears in his mother's eyes as her son was having fun again, laughing and living, for the moment, like a child.

Chris passed away a few days after we granted his wish. After his passing, I couldn't stop thinking of how happy Chris and his mother were during and after his wish. I knew that this happiness needed to be spread to other children with life-threatening illnesses, so I became involved with helping to start a nonprofit foundation that would make their wishes become true. In November 1980, the Make-A-Wish Foundation became official. The first official wish was granted in March 1981.

The stories included in this book will give you a firsthand look into the lives of eight "Wish" children and their families as they journey through a frightening world of doctors, hospitals, operations, and anxieties. You will feel the power of a simple question—"If you could have one wish, what would it be?"—and find inspiration in the answers.

You will learn how wishes granted by the foundation give both the children and their families a new focus as they reconnect and have fun together once again, forgetting about illnesses, doctors, and hospitals. Many children go into remission following the granting of their wish, a phenomenon that doctors cannot even explain; a phenomenon many believe can only come from the power of a wish. Not all children survive their illness, but many have lived for several months and years following their wish. All of this because of the Make-A-Wish Foundation and a seven-year-old boy named Chris, who inspired it all.

FRANK SHANKWITZ, COFOUNDER
MAKE-A-WISH FOUNDATION

A NOTE FROM THE AUTHOR

Dear Reader,

It is my greatest wish and deepest hope that you will be forever touched by the journeys you are about to embark on as you read the stories of the families featured in this book; these families are some of the strongest, most inspirational in the world. They truly make us realize just how precious life is, and through their optimism, they remind us of the importance of family and friends. These stories inspire us to find light in the darkness and spread it any way we can. I wholeheartedly believe that connectivity between people—the relationships we have, the bonds we share—bind us all together, and I would love to share this with you. I personally invite you to visit and connect with me on my website, www.onceuponawishbook.com.

SINCERELY,
RACHELLE SPARKS

* INTRODUCTION *

NEARLY TEN YEARS ago, I sat with a man in a cowboy hat at a coffee shop table. With a leg crossed over his knee, he sat back, settled in, and drifted back in time thirty years, taking me with him. Pen in hand, I was ready—ready to scribble blue ink across the pages of my notebook, ask the right questions, and put the pieces of his story together in my mind as he told it. After all, listening to someone else's story, capturing it in just the right words, printing it in a newspaper's black-and-white columns, was my job as a reporter at *The Daily Courier* in Prescott, Arizona. But when this man, Frank Shankwitz, cofounder of the Make-A-Wish Foundation, took me back to 1980, to when it all began, his words became more than a story; they became windows to the soul of humanity.

As a reporter in that small, northern Arizona town, I had seen glimpses of the human spirit through stories I had written about local Wish children. I had sat in the living rooms of countless families, tears in my eyes, as they took me on their journeys to places even the most creative of minds could not imagine—dark places of emotional torment, where death was waiting while the rest of the world was living. Places that I, whose life had never been touched by something so unthinkable, could not fathom. In the midst of their stories, my pen would inevitably stop in disbelief. The strength of these families, the maturity of these children, was something that, no matter how many times I heard it, touched and inspired me so deeply. Every story I heard, every glimpse into these families' lives that I was so graciously given, was a reminder of how deserving they were of the wishes they received—truly life-changing gifts.

I tried with all my might to capture in words what I took away in my heart—an indescribable sense of hope—but the space I was allotted in the confines of a newspaper was never enough. The stories I wrote became summaries of these families' lives, small glimpses into their struggles, their determinations, their unwavering strengths, and unthinkable optimisms. I was forced to break down their stories and water down the details, capturing only a fragment of the faith, courage, and hope that pulled them through. I wanted my readers to feel the true impact that wishes had in these families' lives and learn the whole stories leading to those wishes.

These families changed me. And when Frank's watery eyes looked at me from beneath the brim of his hat, unashamed to let his tears fall, I knew the little boy he spoke of from thirty years before had changed him, too. The boy's name was Chris Greicius, a spirited, seven-year-old fighting leukemia; the day he became a highway patrol officer was a bright point in his dark battle. In 1980, Frank and a few other officers made Chris's dream come true, changing his life, short as it was, by granting his wish of becoming an officer. When Frank told me about the seamstress who stayed up all night to make a small uniform for Chris, the wings a jeweler cast in one evening, the autographed photo from the actors who played Ponch and John—Chris's heroes—on *CHIPS*, I was filled with the same hope I was filled with every time I sat down with a family that had received a wish just like Chris's.

But that was just the beginning of the story. When Chris passed away, Frank and fellow officer Scott Stahl traveled to Illinois to conduct a police funeral for their fallen officer, and they had to come up with $1,600 for travel costs in two days. A hat was passed, police agencies across the state were contacted, and they had half of the money in one day. A friend of Frank's who heard of their mission donated the rest. Trying to keep up, I scribbled fast as Frank continued with stories of how officers in Illinois, who had heard about Chris's funeral, escorted Frank and Scott to the funeral; how fifteen local police officers who had never even met Chris were there to attend the service; how two strangers lent them their motorcycles to lead the procession; and finally, how Frank and Scott flew home first class when a flight attendant recognized them from local news coverage.

The generosity continued nine months later when Frank, Scott, Chris's mother, Linda Bergendahl-Pauling, and two others—the department's Public Information Officer Allan Schmidt and Kathy McMorris, wife of motor officer Jim McMorris—decided to start the Make-A-Wish Foundation. News coverage around the state of Arizona about Make-A-Wish resulted in the organization receiving envelopes stuffed with checks and piles of money. The first official wish was granted in March 1981 to a child named Frank "Bopsy" Salazar. "He knows he has leukemia, and he has no fear of death," Bopsy's mother told Frank. "He knows what's coming, so he lives life to its fullest."

My pen stopped, goosebumps crawling down my arms, as the tears behind Frank's voice paused the story. That's when the window opened, exposing that raw, honest, undeniable, aforementioned element of humanity. In that moment, I realized Frank's story was about much more than a little boy becoming an officer. It was a story revealing the thread that ties us all together—the strength, power, and resilience of the human spirit. It was a story of compassion and generosity, about people coming together to help other people.

It was also in that moment that the idea for *Once Upon A Wish* was born. People needed to hear these families' stories—the heart and guts and truth of them—not just the stories in nutshells. They needed to know that the Make-A-Wish Foundation no longer changes only the lives of *terminally* ill children, but the lives of those fighting life-threatening medical conditions. These stories are not about death and sadness; they are enlightening stories of love, compassion, determination, and inspiration.

Frank's story—the story of the world coming together for the sake of children—and the stories of those featured in this book, unexpectedly became a journey of self-discovery for me, leading me to a world where nothing should be taken for granted and every moment should be lived like it's the last. The stories in this book will mean something different to every reader, will motivate and offer insight in different ways, but my mission in writing them was to ignite the spark of hope and inspiration that will forever live inside of us.

Tatum Null

"My wish was like a true miracle to me."

—Tatum Null

STANDING IN A corner of the enchanted Castle of Miracles at Give Kids The World Village in Central Florida, tiny hands cupped around the pointy edges of a shiny star, seven-year-old Tatum Null covered her lips with her hands as though telling a secret to her best friend.

"I wish for all the other children's wishes to come true," she whispered to the star before glancing up at the gleaming, dome-shaped ceiling sprinkled with stars. Her parents, David and Sherry, and younger sister, Hannah, watched as she then dropped her star, initialed with "T.C.N." for Tatum Chloe Null, into a gold-painted box lined with red velvet. Lights twinkled as Tatum's star vanished magically into the depths of the box.

"What did you wish for?" Sherry asked playfully, hunching childlike toward Tatum.

"Mom, I can't tell you that," she said with a grin. "Then it won't come true!"

A Give Kids The World Village volunteer explained that the star fairy would retrieve all of the children's stars and place them into the castle sky that night, adding to the thousands of stars already pinned to the ceiling from previous children who had stayed at the village.

David looked down at his two daughters. "Okay, girls, what's next?" he asked.

Hannah looked up at her sister with big, blue, four-year-old eyes lined with face paint and glitter. The pink and blue swirls on Tatum's face creased as a smile spread across her face.

"The carousel!" she yelled, and Hannah squealed, jumping up and down.

"We'll catch up with you," David said, and the girls were off, sprinting down the cobblestone road toward the red and white polka-dotted mushroom covering a handcrafted carousel imported from the Netherlands.

"I'll race you, Dad!" Tatum hollered to David as they hopped onto the wooden platform of the carousel.

"But we'll be going the same speed, Tate," he said logically.

"You have to use your imagination!" Tatum yelled before hopping onto the back of a rainbow-colored rooster.

Sherry placed Hannah on a nearby horse and hung on.

"Oh, well in that case, you're on!" David yelled, straddling the back of a rooster next to Tatum's. The music fired up, and they began their dizzying circles. David scrunched his face to match that of a competitive derby rider, and Tatum did the same.

"I'm beating you, Dad!" she yelled.

"You sure are!"

It was the perfect way to end their first day at Give Kids The World Village, a nonprofit resort in Kissimmee, Florida, that partners with 250 Wish-granting organizations and children's hospitals to house children with life-threatening illnesses and their families. The Nulls had six more days ahead of them, with meals at the Gingerbread House Restaurant, shows at Julie's Safari Theater, bedtime tuck-ins by a six-foot-tall rabbit named Mayor Clayton, laughs from talking wishing wells, and banana splits for breakfast.

Sherry filled the girls' tub with bubbles that night, and as Tatum carefully smeared a beard and mustache of white suds across Hannah's face, Sherry asked, "What park would you girls like to visit tomorrow?"

With free passes to Disney World, Universal Studios, MGM

Studios, Disney's Animal Kingdom, and SeaWorld, Sherry thought it would take longer than a split second to decide.

"Disney World!" Tatum shouted as she perfected the pointy tip of a foamy cone on Hannah's head that was slowly taking the shape of a wizard's hat.

The decision was made, and the next day, the girls, with their parents trying to keep up with them, spent most of the day dashing from one ride to the next, skipping to the front of each line after Tatum flashed her Make-A-Wish button.

"Welcome, Princess" was the common greeting at the front of every line, and this expedited service allowed the girls to enjoy each ride in the park multiple times. Halfway through the day, Tatum's skips and sprints gradually turned into slow walks.

"You okay, sweetie?" Sherry asked.

"Yeah, I'm okay. I'm just a little tired," Tatum said.

"Let's take it easy for a while," David said, and they relaxed watching light shows and parades before Tatum's energy increased and she could happily frolic once again toward the next ride. That night, for her eighth birthday, they went to Akershus Castle in The Norwegian Pavilion at Epcot Theme Park.

"Welcome to our castle," Ariel from *The Little Mermaid* said sweetly as Tatum and Hannah looked up at her with wide, star-struck eyes. Ariel bent down and left the girls with bright-red, heart-shaped kisses on their cheeks that they later refused to wash off before going to bed.

Each morning for the rest of the trip, Tatum and Hannah woke to taps on the door and musical voices of volunteers chiming "gift givers" before presenting them with piles of gift shop toys like key chains and stuffed animals. On Thursday night, two days before they left Give Kids The World Village to return home to Dallas, Texas, it was Christmas in the Castle of Miracles. Children at the village piled onto the laps of Santa and Mrs. Claus and shared their secrets and wish lists. Excited to meet with Santa in January, less than a month after they had met him for Christmas, Tatum and Hannah pranced in circles as they followed their parents back to their villa.

As their energy dwindled, David scooped Hannah into his arms and she plopped her tired head onto his shoulder. Tatum grabbed Sherry's hand and, as they walked together, said, "Mom, I found a lump under my armpit."

Those words nearly stopped Sherry in her tracks.

"Does it hurt, sweetie?" she asked, keeping calm.

"A little," Tatum admitted as she looked up at her mom.

Sherry could see the concern in her daughter's eyes, so she gave a reassuring smile before stopping to take a look.

"Lift your arm up and let me see," Sherry said, and David bent down next to Sherry with Hannah asleep in his arms.

They each felt the lump under Tatum's right arm.

"It's probably just a clogged sweat gland from all the running around you've been doing," Sherry said with a teasing tone. "I've had that happen before."

"Okay," Tatum said, and they finished their walk to the villa in silence.

During the last two days of Tatum's Wish trip, the Null's spent their time exploring nearly every theme park in Florida, swimming at the village, playing miniature golf at Marc's Dino Putt, and living in a fantasy world that could have been taken straight from the pages of a fairy tale.

"Are you girls ready to go home tomorrow?" Sherry asked on the last night of their trip.

"I wish we could live here!" Hannah said, and Tatum agreed.

"Well, get a good night's sleep tonight and we'll see you in the morning," David said before slowly shutting the bedroom door, leaving a crack for light to seep in.

For fear of the girls overhearing, David and Sherry had spent the past couple of days avoiding a discussion about the lump under Tatum's arm. After tucking them into bed, David gave Sherry a tight hug, kissed her on the forehead, and smiled slightly before heading to the rocking chair on the front porch of their villa. Sherry watched as he sat down with heavy shoulders and glistening eyes.

She curled up on their bed with a glass of wine and her journal, and barely touched the pen to the page when an orange flame caught her eye and made her look up. The intensity of the small blaze dissipated quickly and smoldered into a red glow with each puff that David took. It was a weakness he hid from the girls; a nerve-calming secret he kept for times like these. Sherry watched as he sat in the dark, gray swirls dancing around her husband's head. That was David's release, and she needed hers. As she began to write, her throat, swollen from seized tears, opened the moment she let them fall.

I don't want to go to back to the hospital. It hurts my heart to think of Tatum enduring more procedures and possibly cancer. I'm scared about this lump under her arm, but I'm hoping it is just a swollen sweat gland. That is what I am telling her for now. She is feeling terrible, but she is still having the time of her life. Thank you, Make-A-Wish. I look around and see all these wonderful children and their families, and I realize the intensity of the world we've entered—a chronically ill one.

Sherry closed her eyes and let her pen rest on the page. Like a movie in fast-forward mode, images of what Tatum had been through less than a year before entered her mind uncontrollably as she opened her eyes and stared at the page.

⋆ 2 ⋆

TEN MONTHS EARLIER . . .

One March morning, Sherry's dad, or "Granddad" as the girls called him, stopped by the house for breakfast.

"What are your plans when you get to San Antonio?" he asked. It was almost spring break, and the Nulls were planning a vacation in San Antonio, Texas, about five hours south of their home in Dallas.

"We're taking the girls to SeaWorld and having dinner with Shamu, which they're really excited about," Sherry said. "We'll take them to the Alamo, and … "

She stopped and stared at her father. "What's the matter, sweetie?" he said.

"Did you hear that?" She turned her head toward the back of the house. The faint sound of coughing and gasping came from the hallway.

"It sounds like Tatum has a cough," David started, but Sherry had already jumped from her chair and was racing to the bathroom.

She found Tatum curled around the toilet, hair hanging toward the front of her face as her little body jolted and released with violent waves. Sherry held her hair and rubbed her back, which was damp with sweat.

"It's okay, baby," she repeated until Tatum finished.

She helped her up, put her back into bed, and joined her father at the table.

"The flu has been going around her school," Sherry explained.

She and David spent the rest of that Saturday afternoon keeping a close eye on Tatum, feeding her crackers and Sprite, but nothing stayed down. If it was a twenty-four-hour stomach flu, she would be fine by Sunday morning. After a long Saturday night, Tatum woke up Sunday feeling better.

"I guess we'll head out tomorrow," David said, and on Monday afternoon they shoved the last suitcase into their Toyota Sequoia.

"We're all set," he said, and Sherry strapped Hannah into her car seat in the center of the second row. Tatum crawled into the "way back," a third row of seats that made her feel independent. David watched as she slowly swung one leg over and rested on the top of the seat for a moment before flopping into the back.

"You okay, Tate?" he asked.

"Yeah," she managed, and then rested her head on the pillow she had taken from her bed, reached for her portable DVD player, and turned on *Bambi*, her favorite movie at that time.

"You still feeling a little weak?" he asked, and she nodded a small yes. "Well, just take a little nap and you'll feel better when you wake up, okay?"

"Okay," she said, slowly blinking her eyes to fight falling asleep.

Sinking into the layers of pillows, Tatum disappeared and remained quiet. Hannah snacked, Sherry dozed, and David drove in the welcomed silence, listening to the radio. A few hours down the road, Tatum spoke for the first time.

"My tummy hurts again," she said, holding her stomach with both hands.

David looked back at her through the rearview mirror and saw the top of her head. A few wisps of blond curls blew gently in the breeze of the air conditioning. He angled the mirror down to get a closer look at her face, which had turned white. She proceeded to throw up all the way to San Antonio.

They pulled up to the hotel around 5:00 p.m. and checked in. David and Sherry hoped Tatum was just suffering from the flu and it would pass by morning. Sherry tucked Tatum into bed while David made three trips to the car for their luggage—they had never been light packers. Exhausted, David and Sherry climbed into bed a few hours later and slept until 1:00 a.m., when David woke to hear Sherry in the bathroom with Tatum.

"Is she sick again?" he asked, growing very concerned. His eyes adjusted to the glow of the bathroom light pouring into the pitch blackness of the hotel room. He sat up and watched Sherry lift Tatum and carry her back to bed. She knelt and flicked on the lamp on the nightstand.

"She's not doing very well. She's . . . "

Sherry's words hung in the silence. She quickly cupped Tatum's face with both hands, gently turned her head toward the light, and held her eyes wide open. She bent down toward Tatum's face and looked up at David, terrified.

"The whites of her eyes are yellow."

"Why don't we drive home?" David asked, feeling the seriousness of the situation pound through his veins. He suggested taking Tatum to her regular pediatrician, Dr. Leslie Moore, the next morning. "If we leave in the next hour, we'll get home right around the time his office opens in the morning."

By 2:00 a.m., they were packed and on the road back to Dallas. Tatum continued throwing up every ten minutes until a few hours passed and they were in Austin. When she finally fell asleep, David thought to himself, *Now watch, she'll sleep and wake up wanting to have dinner with Shamu.* He smiled at the irony. The thought of her waking up and feeling better also made him smile.

They made it home shortly after 7:00 a.m. and put the girls to bed while they waited for Dr. Moore's office to open. When it did, they were able to receive the first available appointment at 9:00 a.m.

When Sherry went to wake Tatum, there was no response.

"C'mon sweetie, it's time to go," she said softly. "Tatum, we're going to the doctor now. It's time to get up."

Tatum's entire body moved fluidly beneath Sherry's fingertips with every gentle nudge she used to try and wake her.

"C'mon, baby, wake up!" she said in a louder voice, growing more urgent with panic. She shook her shoulders and pulled at her arms. "Tatum, wake up!"

David came running into the room.

"Oh, God, she won't wake up!" Sherry nearly screamed as David yelled, "Tatum! Wake up ...! Wake up!"

He felt for a pulse and shouted, "She's breathing!"

"We've gotta go!" Sherry said, and David scooped little Tatum into his arms and carried her to the car, her limp body dangling and bouncing with every long stride until he laid her on the back seat next to Hannah, whom Sherry had just strapped into her car seat.

David hit the gas pedal and skidded from the driveway. Homes in their quaint neighborhood whirled by as he tore through the quiet streets, zipping with precision, turning stop signs into suggestions. Freeways leading to Dr. Moore's office were full but moving as car horns blurred behind them and streetlights, red, yellow, and green, blended to gray with everything else.

Dr. Moore always writes "She's fine" on Tatum's charts, David reassured himself as his eyes searched frantically for the closest parking spot when they got to the office. *That's what he'll do this time. He'll wake her up and make everything okay like he always does.*

"You need to get her to Medical City," was the unexpected response of Helen, a friendly nurse at Dr. Moore's office who took one look at Tatum when they ran through the front doors. "They have an excellent pediatric center there."

They got back into the car, and David sped through red lights, swerved through traffic, and challenged speed limit signs before plunging into the parking lot of Medical City Dallas Hospital a few minutes later. Pulling up to the front doors, he jumped from the car, lifted Tatum carefully from the back seat, and told Sherry to park. With Tatum over his shoulder, David ran, plowing through the front doors.

"My daughter needs a doctor!" he pleaded.

"Follow me," said a triage nurse as she grabbed his shoulder.

She took him to a large room in the emergency room, where he lay Tatum down on a bed with white sheets. The nurse pulled a curtain around the bed and asked David to come with her.

God, what's happening? he wanted to shout. *I need to stay with my baby!*

Not knowing what else to do, he followed the nurse's orders and left Tatum there with the doctors. They found Sherry, and the nurse led them into a small, private waiting room and asked them to sit.

"Someone will be right with you," she said gently before closing the door.

Moments passed and time stood still. Sherry pushed her face into David's chest as they waited for what came next.

★ 3 ★

An hour later, there was a tiny tap on the door.

David and Sherry turned to see a doctor enter the room.

"Your little girl is very sick," said the doctor, who introduced himself as Dr. Mark Miller. "We're setting her up in the intensive care unit right now and we'll be running some tests."

They wanted answers so desperately, but waiting was all they could do. David had already started a chain of phone calls that resulted in family, friends, and members of their church coming to visit. Dan Stevens, their friend and church pastor, and his wife,

Kelli, one of Sherry's best friends, came to visit. They said they would take Hannah for however long David and Sherry needed them to watch her, and Sherry looked at Kelli with grateful eyes.

Sherry went to greet those who had come to offer support, indicating David could stay and wait for the doctor.

He smiled nervously and said, "I can't just sit here. I'm going to walk around for a minute."

David wandered into a long, lonely hallway and sat. He imagined it as one of those empty hallways on TV shows that groups of doctors run the length of while surrounding a gurney, trying to save a dying person's life. He shook the vision from his mind. That was the last thing he needed to think about. In real life, doctors were surrounding his own daughter at that very moment, trying to wake her up, testing to see if she was going to live.

God, this can't be happening, David thought as he held his eyes tightly shut. It was the first quiet moment since returning to Dallas that he had to actually think about what was happening. *This can't be real*, he said to himself.

He needed to feel Tatum's touch, to hear her voice. He reached into his pocket, grabbed his cell phone, and listened to a message she had left just a couple of weeks before. He thought it would somehow give him hope.

"Hi, Daddy! Thank you so much for the playroom. I really, really love it! Thank you!"

David stared at the white wall in front of him, arms crossed, lips curling into a small smile as tears filled his eyes. Tatum's arms had stretched as wide as they could reach, chin pointed toward the ceiling, when he had announced that the room was finally finished and asked if she'd like to come in and see it. Sitting on the floor in the long, quiet hallway of the hospital, he closed his eyes and pictured how she had stepped through the purple door with a gaping mouth, stood in the middle of the room, and spun, letting colors of the freshly painted walls blur to rainbows until she was nearly too dizzy to stand. Before David had finished the room, Tatum spent countless hours circling the newly installed hardwood floor on her scooter with Hannah in tow on her tricycle. They had placed a pile of their favorite stuffed animals in the center and circled like a carousel before serving tea and sitting down with the animals for a picnic.

When the room was complete, the furniture, old and new, was placed neatly and the bright yellow walls were decorated with handcrafted pictures, pink shelves, and giant flowers painted in the brightest colors. Hot pink curtains hung over windows lined with green trim and were swooped and tied to the side, letting bright Texas sunlight into the room every morning.

Tatum and Hannah had always shared a room, so as Tatum got a little older and needed her own space, David and Sherry decided to squeeze the home office into their bedroom and give each of the girls a room of their own—a place to create, to share, and to imagine. David scraped the popcorn ceiling, tore out the twenty-year-old carpet, replaced the doors and moldings, added a ceiling fan, and painted the retextured walls with colors like "forest sunrise" and "enchanted coach ride." Tatum loved that room, and she was never shy to wrap her arms around her parents' waists and tell them how grateful she was.

Silence around him, alone, David watched as the long, skinny arms of a round, starch-white clock with black numbers ticked loudly. Each tick felt like an hour. He let out a long, breathy sigh and stood.

Then he paced.

He pressed the button on his phone to hear Tatum's message again.

"Hi, Daddy! Thank you so much for the playroom. I really . . . "

he slapped the phone shut and squeezed it. Her voice was too real; the images of her face too clear. The thought of her leaving that message made the feeling of wanting her to be okay too overwhelming. So he sat with his eyes closed, praying that when he opened them he'd be somewhere, anywhere, but in that hallway.

"Dan is asking that we go and pray with Tatum," Sherry said, and David's eyes shot open to the reality of their situation. He hadn't even heard her coming. The thought of seeing Tatum, of touching her hand, of being in her presence, filled him with hope as he followed Sherry to where Dan and Kelli waited.

⋆ 4 ⋆

The girl whose personality drew people to her when she walked into a room lay there quietly, eyes closed. David and Sherry stood in disbelief. Pale and fragile, with attached IVs draped over the rails of her bed, Tatum seemed like somebody else's little girl lying there. But no, she was theirs, and this was real.

Sherry reached for Tatum's hand and stared at her face, thinking of the time the two of them spent together in New York City when Tatum was five. The thought made her smile through her tears. While dancing in circles down the streets of the city, Tatum sang songs from *The Lion King*, a Broadway musical they had seen the night before. People stared; some laughed, most applauded.

"Is she in a show?" they rightfully asked. She belonged on stage.

"No, not exactly," Sherry said, laughing. "She's just in a world of her own."

"Well, she should be," one woman said. Her wise eyes creased when she smiled. "She just glows with joy."

The same face that served as a canvas for an artist in Central Park to create a brilliantly colored butterfly with a wingspan stretching from one side of it to the other was now white and nearly lifeless.

"Everybody, join hands," Dan said, jolting Sherry from her thoughts. The four of them formed a circle around Tatum and tightly held hands. Dan began to pray, and Tatum's chest, which had remained so still, suddenly lifted with his words. Her breaths, which had been so quiet, sounded like whispers filling the room. As Dan finished the prayer, Sherry leaned toward her daughter's face and said, "It's okay, baby, calm down. Just rest." The prayer filled them with strength, and they knew they were not in this alone.

"Okay, you can come with me," said a short Indian man who introduced himself as Dr. Patel a few minutes later.

David and Sherry followed him into another small conference room where Dr. Patel sat them down and asked, "Do you have a faith?"

Before Tatum was born, David would have proudly answered "no." He had chosen to fall away from the Christian beliefs he was raised with—until seven years ago when Tatum was born. He looked into her eyes that day, and she had turned him back into a believer.

"Yes, we are Christian," he told Dr. Patel. With a slightly tilted head and questioning eyes, David stared.

"Now would be a good time to start praying," the doctor said gently. "All we know is that it looks like her organs are shutting down."

"Shutting down?" Sherry cried. "Everything was fine a few days ago! She's never been sick in her life!"

She wanted so desperately for her reasoning to be enough to change what the doctor was saying, but she knew it wasn't. Her hands shook and tingled and she fell to her knees, gasping for air between sobs. For David, a solid hit to the chest with a baseball bat might have felt better than the pain he experienced when he heard the doctor's words. He knelt beside his wife and hugged her tightly with both arms. The brief silence gave Sherry's mind a quick chance to clear, and she managed to ask, "What do we do next? How do we save her?"

Dr. Patel had perfected the necessary calm in a voice that still had hard news to deliver.

"We've done all that we can do," he said softly. "We're sending her to Children's Medical Center."

The critical nature of the moment, the shock, the reality, deepened—Children's Medical Center of Dallas was a place for very sick, and often dying, children.

"What can they do for her there that you can't do here?" Sherry asked. She felt as though Dr. Patel was telling them that they had given up. That there was nothing left for them to do.

"They have techniques to try that we don't have here," Dr. Patel explained.

The heaviness in David's chest sunk slowly toward his heart. How could this be happening to their little girl?

The transport team placed Tatum into the ambulance, and Sherry looked at her husband as he wrapped his arms around her and whispered, "Everything's going to be just fine." Tucking a blond curl behind Sherry's ear, he pulled away, touched her cheek, and smiled down at her. She let out a long breath, stared into the eyes that made her strong, and nodded.

David drove their car, and Sherry climbed into the front seat of the ambulance. When they arrived at Children's, the driver threw the ambulance into park, the back doors were ripped open, and by the time Sherry stepped out, she was surrounded by people in white. Doctors and nurses, she guessed, but her mind was spinning. Her heart pounded violently in her chest, and one of the EMTs said, "You sign her in, we'll take her."

Take her? Take her where? Where do I go?

She needed David. She frantically looked around, and there, in the blur, stood Dan and Kelli. The three of them followed a nurse to the ICU waiting area, where family and friends had already started to gather.

Sherry took a moment to step away from the crowd and look out the window, where she saw that the longest day of her and David's life was slowly coming to an end. The sky was turning charcoal, and stars were beginning to poke through. The three hours of sleep they had gotten the night before on their drive home from San Antonio was somehow enough, and she knew she wouldn't get much more until they knew whether or not their baby girl was going to live. That was something they still didn't know, and as her thoughts started to make her feel sick, she joined the crowd. By then, David had found his way to the room.

"Hopefully someone will come in soon and tell us what's going on," Sherry said, and no sooner, a doctor dressed in white with small glasses, black hair, and a contagious smile walked into the waiting room.

☆ 5 ☆

"Hi, I'm Paul Shore," the doctor said to David, giving him a firm handshake and a reassuring squeeze on the shoulder with his other hand. David noticed right away that Paul Shore left the "doctor" out of his introduction.

"It's so nice to meet you," David said, hoping he would turn out to be the man who finally had some answers. He didn't yet, but he came back later with results of tests they had been running on Tatum.

"Her liver is failing," he said gently.

Devastated by the news but relieved that doctors had identi-
fied *which* organ was failing, Sherry and David listened. Dr. Shore
explained that toxins were taking over Tatum's body and her brain
was beginning to swell. He performed a successful procedure to
keep the swelling down and started Tatum on dialysis.

Testing and the distribution of medications continued into the
late hours of the night and left David and Sherry pacing the waiting room and the hallways. They wanted nothing more than to
see their little girl, but that was not an option. She needed them to
remain patient and strong.

The friends and family who had come to join David and Sherry
surrounded them and filled them with encouragement. After four
hours of dialysis, Dr. Shore told them that the level of ammonia
was decreasing in Tatum's body, but the levels of other toxins,
equally as dangerous, remained.

"Dialysis isn't enough," he said, letting out a long breath. "She
needs a liver transplant."

"Let's do it. Where do we get a liver?" David asked immediately and hopefully, thinking there had to be some sort of organ
bank with an abundance of livers for situations just like theirs. He
crossed his arms over his chest and shifted impatiently, ready to
follow the doctor into the room with the livers.

"It doesn't really work that way, unfortunately," Dr. Shore said.

"How *does* it work?" Sherry asked.

"We put her on a donor list and wait."

"How long will that take?" David asked.

"You never know. It took one little boy two weeks before a match
came in," Dr. Shore said, trying to expose the reality of the situation
without scaring them.

"But we don't have two weeks," Sherry said, her voice pushing
past a lump forming in her throat.

"You're right, we don't," he said, "which is why we need to get her on the list and start testing everybody in the family to see who is a potential donor."

Sherry would have died to give Tatum her liver, but she had one concern. "I have scar tissue on my liver," she told Dr. Shore, then shared the story of how a painful childhood bicycling accident that sent a blow to her abdomen had lacerated her liver. "Will that be a problem?" Sherry asked.

"It shouldn't be," Dr. Shore said. "We'll test you to see if you're even a match. In the meantime, let's keep our fingers crossed that we get a liver." The doubt in their faces triggered the doctor to add, "Sometimes miracles happen."

★ 6 ★

When Sherry and David received news the next day that they found a liver matching Tatum's blood type and that it was in transport to Children's Hospital, they knew it was true—miracles did happen.

The morning the new liver arrived, seventy-five of David and Sherry's family, friends, and church family were at the hospital to show their love and support. They were piled into the waiting room and wandering the halls, available for needed hugs and words of encouragement. The news of Tatum's illness had spread like wildfire to people they didn't even know throughout the United States and into other countries.

Dan had given Sherry a "prayer pager"—a beeper for people to send the number 143 (common code for "I love you," as the amount of letters in the phrase is one, four, and three, Dan explained)—to receive reminders of the love and support from family and friends. Emails requesting prayer and "143" to be paged to David and Sherry were sent to Sherry's missionary friends in

Sweden and Africa, and those emails reached across the globe, through other countries, and into Mexico. The prayer pager buzzed in Sherry's pocket every minute or so with "143"—reminders of how much Tatum was loved.

Sherry was encouraged that people everywhere were praying for her little girl. She felt as if she could see those prayers floating to Heaven, and after news of the liver, she was sure they had landed right in God's lap and brought about a miracle.

As David and Sherry broke away from the group to meet with Dr. Shore and Dr. Goran Klintmaulm, a world-renowned transplant surgeon from Baylor University Medical Center at Dallas who would perform the transplant surgery, David felt hesitant excitement rush through him. Tatum was going to live.

It was a bittersweet feeling since he knew that a liver for his daughter meant someone had just died to give it.

"The liver is sixty years old," Dr. Klintmaulm explained, and panic that had momentarily subsided within Sherry resurfaced.

Is the only option to save our daughter a liver that is sixty years old? she thought.

David vocalized her concern. "Is that okay?" he asked without hesitation. "How long do livers last?"

"There is nothing to indicate that this liver won't last a hundred years," Dr. Shore said, slowly easing their minds.

But he was wrong.

Thirty minutes later, he and Dr. Klintmaulm walked side by side toward David and Sherry, their faces announcing bad news before their words could.

"I found a tumor on the liver," Dr. Klintmaulm said in a kind but matter-of-fact tone. "We can't use it."

He paused momentarily, and then continued, explaining that it would be best to take her liver out before it poisoned her.

"You're going to take it out and not put anything back in?" David asked, feelings of desperation bubbling in his gut. "How long can a person live without a liver?"

"Thirty-six hours," Dr. Klintmaulm said. "We need another option."

David and Sherry knew what that option was. Among the family members tested earlier that day, Sherry's brother-in-law Jim had proved to be a perfect match. "Take mine," he ordered.

Sherry, who, along with her sister, Gay, was also a perfect match but could not donate because she was too thin, looked at her brother-in-law of nearly ten years.

"You don't have to do this, Jim," she said sadly, knowing the risk he'd be taking to give a portion of his liver to Tatum. It would be a major surgery, and though the portion remaining inside of him would rejuvenate itself within weeks and the healthy, left lobe portion he would give to his niece would also rejuvenate and save her life, Sherry wanted him to know he had a choice. "You can change your mind."

His unfaltering stance gave Sherry combined hope and fear. Doctors sent Jim to Baylor University Medical Center-Roberts Hospital for further testing to make sure his body was indeed ready for such a major surgery.

"We'd like to do an exploratory procedure in the meantime to see if there's any chance of Tatum's liver revitalizing itself," Dr. Klintmaulm said. "As the body's most resilient organ, rejuvenation is not at all impossible. It's a low-risk surgery that should just take a couple of hours, and that will tell us, for sure, whether or not Tatum needs a transplant."

Sherry and David gave consent for the exploratory surgery and then joined their family and friends in the waiting room. Nerves crawled through Sherry's body and grabbed at her stomach with each passing second as she and David made their way into the hallway that led to the operating room before the doctors wheeled Tatum by. Though low-risk, they knew that with any surgery, there was never a 100 percent guarantee of her coming out alive. Holding on to each other for support, they watched as Tatum neared, the clinking sound of metal from her hospital bed echoing between quiet walls. Sherry pursed her lips together and swallowed the burning in her throat as the bed came to a halt at their feet. Tatum remained in the coma that had started on their trip back from San Antonio. Sherry and David stared down at their beautiful daughter, whose skin had yellowed and sunk around her closed eyes. They bent over the rails of the bed, kissing her cheeks and whispering quick messages into Tatum's ear.

"Keep living," Sherry managed, her voice shaking. "We love you *so* much, baby."

"Stay strong, Tate," David said softly into her ear. "You're going to be just fine. Just stay strong."

With that, Tatum was wheeled through the double doors, into the unknown.

As the doors swung closed, David and Sherry slumped to the floor, shaking with the agonizing reality that they may have just told their daughter good-bye.

After minutes that felt like hours, they finally stood, hugged, and walked back into the waiting room, hand in hand. They mingled nervously for the next few hours, praying with friends and family, finding strength in their presence. With no food or sleep in two days, they needed it.

The hands of the clock on the wall ticked nonchalantly past midnight before they heard the distinct sound of an opening door. David and Sherry shot their heads toward the entrance of the room, where gastroenterologist Dr. Naveen Mittal and transplant surgeon Dr. Henry Randall stood in their scrubs and booties. Dr.

Randall used a large, wooden desk at the front of the waiting room as a podium, and everyone stood and rushed to surround him, David and Sherry at the front of the group.

A pin drop would have sounded like a shattering vase.

"There is more healthy liver than not," Dr. Randall began. "We can't tell yet if Tatum's liver will be able to heal itself, but there is enough healthy liver to leave it in for the night."

With that, the room erupted. Hugs and cheers were tossed around the room, but David and Sherry stood in that moment simply looking at each other, the celebration surrounding them a blur. They didn't cheer or clap or shout. There was a shared and silent understanding between them that, while it was great news, this didn't mean Tatum was going to live. Though both natural optimists, wanting to rejoice, they pushed that urge aside. They were learning that a moment of good news meant only that—a moment. Nothing more. And moments like these could pass as quickly as it takes for good news to spread.

⋆ 7 ⋆

When the excitement died down and the hour hand on the clock passed one, Sherry and David walked groups of dedicated visitors to their cars in the parking lot and made their way back into the hospital and up to Tatum's room in the ICU. As they pushed open the door, familiar, panicked shouts of doctors' orders escaped the room and four nurses surrounded Tatum's small body. Beeps of every machine collided, mockingly, as alarms sounded and blended to chaos. David and Sherry backed to the far wall of the room, eyes wide, mouths covered, petrified. They watched as they were hit with pieces of words thrown from the nurses who were trying to fill them in on her condition.

Her heart rate is dropping. Blood pressure, increasing.

None of it made sense, but they had learned already what numbers to look for on what machines—how to tell if her intracranial pressures (ICPs) were increasing—and what numbers indicated a steady heartbeat and a healthy blood pressure. The green line revealed Tatum's ability to breathe on her own and the yellow line showed breaths the ventilator took for her. Their eyes darted between machines as Sherry felt the urge to scream, *What the hell happened? She was fine a few minutes ago! How does this keep happening, where's she's fine one minute and dying the next?*

David's internal voice seemed to be the one Tatum heard.

Fight, Tatum, fight! he shouted in his mind.

Her fight was the reason those nurses got her stabilized once again, and Tatum was calm. When the fire died and the room was quiet, Sherry and David sat across from Tatum on the small hospital couch, letting their hearts find a normal beat while their eyes remained intently on the machines working to keep her alive. By now, they could have interpreted those beeps with their eyes closed. Ears perked and eyes dancing, Sherry let them stop for a moment on a picture of Tatum that nurse Erin had asked them to bring and hang in her room.

Just three months earlier, Sherry had taken the girls to get a portrait taken as a Christmas gift for David. Captured in black and white, Tatum and Hannah flashed their radiant smiles from the steps of a beautiful staircase, and it was this image that let Sherry fall asleep for just a little while with a smile on her face.

She awoke to news that they had received the liver of a three-year-old child who had just passed away. With deep, familiar, and agonizing pains of sympathy for the family that had just lost their child, Sherry and David also knew that this was their chance to save Tatum.

As doctors explained, cadaveric donors are always preferred

over living donors due to higher success rates and only one person having to undergo surgery. After news of receiving a liver for Tatum, doctors told Jim, who was still at Baylor getting tested for possible surgery, that he was no longer needed to give half of his liver to Tatum. A great sense of relief washed over him and the rest of their family.

David and Sherry spent the afternoon by Tatum's side, watching the silent rise and fall of her chest, praying for a successful transplant the next day. As reds and oranges from the sun's setting colors streamed and glowed into Tatum's room, David's mother, Betty, called to tell him that she and David's dad, Gary, had arrived. They had been on a road trip from Texas to Arkansas when they received the phone call about Tatum, and they had finally made the long drive back.

David took Betty to visit Tatum, and twenty minutes later, she and David appeared in the waiting room to join the rest of the group. As Sherry went to greet them, the door burst open and a young, male nurse they had seen only in passing shouted, "Sherry, we need you and David immediately!"

The panic in his voice sent them running toward the door, and they followed him quickly out into the waiting room with the stained glass. He didn't waste any time.

"They're performing CPR on Tatum right now," he said.

"What?!" Sherry nearly screamed. *No, no, no, no, no, no,* she thought to herself. She was certain that screaming it enough times in her head would make God finally listen and jump-start Tatum's heart.

David sprang from his seat and ran from the room. He went to get the one person he knew could help.

"Oh, God, noooooooooooo," Sherry sobbed as the door swung closed behind David. She dropped her head into her sister's lap. "This can't be happening! Not now!"

"They'll get her back on track," Gay promised, over and over, as she cried with her sister.

"Is God not hearing all our prayers?" Sherry asked angrily. "Where is He?"

"Excuse me, Sherry?" said an elderly man who introduced himself as the hospital's chaplain. "Is there anything I can do to help you? Would you like to pray?"

She looked up at him through stained, swollen eyes and went against her sweet, patient nature.

"I don't know you," she said. "I really don't want you in here."

Her patience was gone. Her hope was gone. If Tatum died, part of her soul would be gone. Sherry stared at the man above her, who gave her a gentle, apologetic smile.

"I'll leave you alone," he said nicely. "That's all I needed to hear."

"I *would* like to see Larry," she told Gay after the chaplain left the room. Larry was their church's minister and the man who had married Sherry and David nine years before. Sherry grew up in his church, and he had known and loved Tatum from the time she was born. Sherry had always felt a sense of peace in Larry's presence, a reassurance that everything would be okay.

"You've got to pray for us," she said, hugging him tightly when he came into the room with David. "Pray that God's will be done; pray that we stay strong, no matter what happens."

Sure that the words "she's gone" were waiting just around the corner, Sherry bowed her head and closed her eyes, praying harder than she had ever prayed, crying more than she had ever cried, believing deeper than she had ever believed.

Larry finished the prayer, and within moments, Dr. Shore plunged through the waiting room doors with a shining smile.

"She's okay!" he blurted, explaining that either during the exploratory surgery or during intubation at Medical City, a small hole was poked into Tatum's lung. Her chest cavity had slowly filled with air, pushing her heart to the side and causing it to beat irregularly.

"I inserted a catheter under her left armpit to release the air," Dr. Shore said. "We've got her stable now."

David and Sherry's hearts were still racing and settling when Sherry wiped her eyes and smirked.

Okay, God. I will not doubt you again, she said in a silent prayer for Tatum's transplant the next day. Sherry and David said goodbye to friends and family that night and made their way to the ICU to see Tatum.

⋆ 8 ⋆

Exhaustion had settled into every bone and muscle in Sherry and David's bodies and the air around them became thick as they pushed their way down the long hallway. It had only been a matter of minutes since the chaos of the group dissipated, but the silence left Sherry's eyelids free to fall, and they did. It had been three days since either of them had slept.

"I can hardly stay awake," she said as they neared the ICU.

"Me, too," David said, suddenly feeling the weight of his head as he struggled to keep it upright. "We've just got to hang in there a little longer. Tomorrow is the big day."

Sherry smiled and leaned into him as he reached for the door to the ICU.

"Her meds are maxed out! Call the team in! David and Sherry, we need you to stand back!"

Shouts from a roomful of doctors and nurses hit them from every direction.

God, you've got to be kidding me! Sherry screamed in her mind. *When is this going to end?*

She and David backed up slowly, their strength gone, as their daughter's stable condition crashed before their eyes, once again. Alarms sounded, switches were flipped, and buttons were pressed on every machine hooked to their little girl, and all they could do was watch. They plopped helplessly onto a short couch by the window at the opposite end of the room, took each other's hands, and bowed their heads.

"God, until now I have been asking," David prayed out loud, angry, his voice shaking. "But now I am telling you. You will keep her through the night. One more night is all she needs before her surgery tomorrow."

His prayer became a plea.

"Just give her that."

They silently understood that there was nothing more they could do or say. The turmoil in the room continued, with beeps turning to whispers and shouts dimming to hums, as David and Sherry's bodies uncontrollably faded and shut down.

There is nothing more we can do, they reminded themselves again before falling fast asleep. The tears they knew they had left were too weak to fall.

One calm, steady beep invaded David's dream three hours later and shot him straight up.

"What's going on?" he asked, rubbing his eyes, letting them focus from the bright light of the room. He couldn't believe he had fallen asleep.

His voice jolted Sherry from her sleep as he threw a question at a nurse who was calmly checking on their daughter. "How is she doing?"

"She's stable and hardly on any meds," said the nurse, who had apparently taken over the calm of the storm that had occurred just a few hours before. "She's ready for her transplant today. They'll take her back to surgery around 3:00 p.m."

David just looked at Sherry, any hope of understanding gone. "It was that prayer," he said quietly.

"It sure was."

They spent the day by Tatum's side, talking to her though they knew she couldn't hear, stroking her hair though they knew she couldn't feel, until 3:00 p.m., when doctors arrived to take her to surgery. David and Sherry kissed Tatum's face as many times as they could before she was wheeled through the doors of the operating room.

Seven hours later, they got the news from Dr. Randall that the transplant was over, it was a perfect fit, and the new liver was already producing bile.

Rumble and boom from a furious lightning storm would have gone unnoticed in the wake of the thunderous applause that escaped the waiting room.

When Sherry and David finally got to see Tatum, Sherry whispered, "It's almost time to wake her up." Her eyes uncontrollably filled with tears and in the peaceful quiet of the room where Tatum lay, perfectly still and just as perfectly healthy, the ordeal somehow seemed as though it had never happened.

After a few hours, David, Sherry, and Gay stood over Tatum as her eyes fluttered open for the first time in several days. Watching his daughter's eyes open filled David's with tears, and he wasn't ashamed to let them fall. Sherry, on the other side of Tatum, held her hand tightly and cried with her husband as their little girl looked between them, her wide eyes searching for answers. A single tear dropped and slid slowly down her right cheek.

"It's okay, baby," Sherry managed. "You're at the hospital. You were very sick, but you're okay now. Mommy and Daddy are here. There's nothing to be afraid of. Everything is okay."

"Don't talk, sweetie," she continued as Tatum tried to open her mouth to spit out a million questions. "The machine is breathing for you. You can talk later. You're okay, though, I promise. You're going to be just fine."

David took over and Sherry called her friend Karen, who was now watching Hannah. Sherry told Karen that Tatum was awake and asked her to bring Hannah to the hospital to see her sister. Sherry sat the prayer pager, which buzzed every five minutes, next to Tatum, who stared at it with confusion. Sherry explained that the world had been praying for her. The pager continued buzzing "143" for the next three days. During those three days, David and Sherry did not leave Tatum's side. They took turns sleeping on the couch while the other sat on a stool next to her bed, holding and rubbing her hand.

"How long have you been a teacher?" one nurse asked Sherry while filling Tatum's IV with meds.

"Seven years," she said.

"What grade do you teach?"

"Sixth-grade math and science."

"I bet it's a lot of fun," the nurse said.

"Yes, I love it. It keeps me young," Sherry replied.

The small talk comforted Tatum. It brought normalcy to her hospital room, to her life. Confined to a bed with metal rails in a place that smelled like ammonia and Band-Aids made her cry.

"Are you in pain?" Sherry asked.

Tatum moved her head back and forth slightly. The nurses made sure to keep her pumped with as much morphine as necessary.

"It won't be long until you can tell us what's wrong," Sherry said, comforting her daughter. Unable to move, eat, or breathe on her own, Sherry knew that waking to a body that, essentially, no longer worked, had to be the most terrifying thing for her daughter.

The next day, after determining that Tatum's lungs were strong enough to breathe on their own, a group of doctors and nurses came to remove the tube from her throat.

"Can you talk?" the respiratory therapist asked once the tube was gone.

"Ouch" was all she said.

Breathy whispers were all Tatum could manage for several days, and she had to go through the painful process of relearning to swallow. After two days in the ICU, she was moved to the fifth floor of the hospital, where she spent the next ten days undergoing tests and therapy to regain her strength.

One evening, as Sherry and David watched Tatum sleep, enjoying welcomed quiet time between frequent nurse and doctor visits, Jennifer, a friendly member of Tatum's transplant team, tapped on the door, walked in, and smiled as she passed Sherry and David. She peered down at Tatum, hoping to find her awake, and decided to share her exciting news with Tatum's parents instead.

"You know," Jennifer said, smiling with childlike excitement, "Tatum qualifies for a wish from the Make-A-Wish Foundation."

Was there some sort of miscommunication? Sherry thought. *Is Jennifer here to tell us our daughter is dying? Make-A-Wish is for terminal children.*

"Oh, no, no, no," Jennifer said with one long breath, sensing the worry pouring from David and Sherry's eyes. "Tatum is just fine," she reassured them. "The Make-A-Wish Foundation grants wishes for children with life-threatening illnesses. Tatum can wish for anything she wants."

"Oh," Sherry said, letting out an equally long sigh of relief. "Oh, good. That'll give her something to look forward to!"

Anything she wants, Sherry thought, repeating Jennifer's words in her mind. She wondered what their daughter, a little girl full of ideas and imagination, would wish for. When Tatum woke a few hours later, Sherry gave her the good news, and Tatum spent the day thinking about it. She considered shopping with her favorite celebrity, Raven-Symonè, meeting the cast of one of her favorite TV shows, *Full House*, or meeting the President of the United States.

"I'd like to meet George W. Bush," she declared a few days later when a volunteer from the Make-A-Wish Foundation came to visit her at the hospital. She wanted to spend the weekend in the White House, sharing breakfasts and dinners with George and Laura Bush, sleeping in the Blue Room, playing in the gardens, enjoying fancy tea parties.

But when she learned that a wish to meet the president would involve waiting up to two years for a three-minute meet and greet, Tatum quickly decided on a Disney wish. She would leave this hospital and visit a world where everything was perfect—a world with castles, rides, princesses, and candy.

For the next few days before Tatum was discharged, she closed her eyes during blood draws and procedures, letting the magic of Disney consume her imagination. She grew stronger every day, with thoughts of riding rides and meeting her favorite princess, Tinkerbell—who Tatum always liked best because "she's sassy like me"—pulling her through.

A few nights after Tatum told her parents what she was going to wish for, David, asleep in a sleeping bag on the tile floor, woke up to quiet sobs from Sherry, who was curled up in the foldout chair above him.

"What's the matter, baby?" he said, sitting upright.

"She just looks like a little concentration camp victim," she said, looking at Tatum, who was sound asleep in her hospital bed. The look of her daughter tore Sherry apart—lethargic, bony, pale. She didn't deserve to be any of those things. Sherry knew they would be leaving soon, and though filled with hope and faith that Tatum would continue to recover until she was well enough to meet

Tinkerbell, the quiet of the night, the moon's glow on her daughter's tired face, made everything real.

"She's alive," David reminded his wife with a playful grin. "She's been clinging to life. We've come this far. She's going to get better. Just give it some time."

"I know," Sherry said through cries. "It's just so hard to see her this way."

"I know," David assured her. "But things will only get better from here."

⋆ 9 ⋆

Back at Give Kids The World Village, Sherry continued writing in her journal.

> *I find myself feeling angry at the idea of Tatum suffering anymore. She looks panicked at the idea of going back to the hospital and stressed about the idea of knowing what to expect. She almost knows too much now. I watch her sleep and I just cry. I'm so thankful she's still alive and that we're still a whole family. I think we're still in shock at all that's happened, and we feel so uncertain about our future.*

They had lived the past week worry-free, doctor-free, and carefree. It was the first time in nine months that they felt like a "normal" family again. After Tatum's transplant surgery, the rollercoaster ride doctors predicted was scarier and more intense than anything they ever could have imagined.

Her body's rejection of its new liver three different times, a severe *C. difficile* infection that resulted in damage to her digestive tract, and a constant battle to regulate meds and keep her body from rejecting the liver once again, were the deepest dips; exhilarating climbs came only from rare days spent between hospital stays.

With physical and occupational therapy, Tatum relearned to breathe on her own, swallow, and walk, and when she was discharged from the hospital after her transplant surgery, her first-grade education continued at home, where she was able to be until her health declined and she was readmitted to the hospital again.

After eight months of that terrifying ride, spending more time in hospital rooms than at home, Tatum and her family were finally able to start thinking about taking this trip to Florida—a trip they had to cancel once before when Tatum's health had made yet another turn for the worse.

This trip was supposed to be the beginning of their happily ever after. It was everything Tatum and her parents needed after what they had gone through, and it was the greatest blessing of their lives. As a family, they had escaped death, stepped off the roller coaster that tested their endurance, proved their determination, and landed safely on solid ground.

The lump Tatum had found under her armpit shook that solid ground, opening an abyss to the unknown yet again. After her transplant surgery, doctors had warned Sherry and David that post-transplant cancer was always a possibility—not likely, but a possibility. Sherry had told Tatum that the lump was probably a clogged sweat gland, but she knew in her gut, in the deepest part of her soul, that it was cancer.

Letting the pain Sherry felt drip from her face onto the pages, she continued writing in her journal and ended with a written prayer.

Dear God, protect Tatum's health and her liver. Bring Hannah peace and a sense of security. Thank you for this trip and the healing it has brought to our family.

They left the fairy tale they had been living in Florida and returned home to Dallas, where they scheduled an appointment immediately at Children's Hospital to get the lump checked out.

A few days later, on their drive to see Dr. Mittal at Children's, Sherry wondered what she would fix for dinner that night; it was the only worry she felt she could handle. She pushed the possibility of Tatum getting admitted to the hospital out of her mind, letting herself focus only on the fun and freedom she and her family had just experienced at Give Kids The World Village. She wasn't ready to let go of the idea that life could remain that way. But when doctors admitted Tatum that very day, Sherry knew it was time, time to let go of their trip as the start of their "happily ever after." Instead, she would look at it as a reminder of what life would be like after they beat cancer. It was time, once again, to fight, as the whirlwind they had escaped pulled back, circling and suffocating them.

"Did you pack your bags?" Dr. Mittal asked.

Sherry nodded. "They're always in our car."

A few days later, after extensive testing and agonizing hours of waiting, Dr. Mittal's mouth moved in slow motion, his words a useless hum, as fancy medical terms fell and landed upon unwilling ears.

"Is she going to live or die?" Sherry interrupted, her eyes like stone.

"She has PTLD—post-transplant lymphoma disorder," the doctor said, referring to lumps they had found in Tatum's armpit, in her ribcage, and along the walls of her rectum. "This could be serious."

Ten days after being admitted, Tatum sunk into her hospital bed and remained there. "How are you feeling, baby?" Sherry asked. Nothing.

"Is there anything I can do for you?" Silence.

"C'mon, Tate, you need to talk to us."

For two weeks, Tatum looked out her window and rolled or closed her eyes when nurses came in to take her blood, change her IV, or give her the medicine she needed to fight the cancer.

She was defeated, and it frightened Sherry. The spirit of her lively, energetic daughter was dead.

"Wooooo-wooooo-woooo," Tatum heard from down the hall. She gave the first smirk Sherry had seen in weeks as she turned her head toward the doorway.

Nurse John skidded to an imaginary halt and pretended to put his ambulance into park. He got his needles and gloves ready and attempted to make a breakthrough with his young patient.

"Done anything cool lately?" he asked playfully.

Tatum gazed at the pink princess tiara hanging in her hospital room. "Yeah," she started, then sat up a little and didn't stop. She told Nurse John stories of the princesses she had met on her Wish trip, the lines for the theme park rides where she and her family had been escorted to the front, the banana splits they ate for breakfast, the six-foot-tall rabbit, the carousel, her eighth birthday party with the princesses, and the free pizza they could order at any time, day or night.

"One time, the delivery guy had on a crystal watch and a three-piece suit!" Tatum exclaimed excitedly.

She was back.

From that point on, she made every nurse and doctor sit in her room's rocking chair for pre-poke, pre-test, or pre-procedure story time. She was reliving her wish and taking the rest of the family there with her. It was the only normalcy she had experienced in nearly a year, and the mere thought that life could become the healthy, fun-filled destination she had experienced on her Wish trip made her fight for it.

And she did.

Tatum and her parents left the hospital nearly two months later, cancer-free, with hope they had never felt before. So grateful for what the foundation had given to her family, Sherry spoke to the Make-A-Wish Foundation board the day after their return home.

"You've literally turned our girls' lives into Wish trips," she said, her voice heavy with threatening tears. "When they see bad in this world, we can point to you to remind them that there is still so much good. Your work and example is what brings it alive and makes it real for the kids. You guys are a light in the darkness. A city on the hill. We're grateful for a wonderful wish come true for Tatum and thankful for all you've done for us."

She paused and finished with, "It's our prayer that God makes our family useful to your cause."

✱ Epilogue ✱

Seven years have passed since Tatum's Wish trip, and her mother's prayer is still being answered. After her bout with cancer, Tatum immediately became involved with the foundation, and David started to see the impact that one spunky, curly-haired little girl can make.

That year, during the North Texas chapter's Wish Night, a signature event that raises close to $1 million a year for the foundation, Tatum and Hannah, in fancy little dresses, felt like princesses mingling with guests in gowns and black tuxedos. The room around them, filled with music and twinkling lights, became their castle as they floated through a sea of millionaires.

As the chapter's largest annual fundraiser, the most dedicated donors and the city's biggest moneymakers flood the event to become inspired by the stories they hear and the children they meet.

When a Dallas businessman and millionaire shook hands with Tatum that evening and listened to her story, he pulled out his checkbook and her eyes grew wide as she watched the motion of his hand complete circle after circle on the small piece of paper, giving a total of $60,000.

She looked up at him in silence. No words were needed to accompany her big eyes and wide smile.

She had just made a difference.

I wish for all the other children's wishes to come true, she recalled whispering into that star seven years before, on the very first day of her Wish trip at Give Kids The World Village. The check in her hand was proof that she could make that wish come true on her own.

She started attending local Wish parties, gathering with other Wish children to create mosaics, jewelry, pottery, and other art to donate for Wish Night. One painting that Tatum helped create was auctioned for $15,000.

She started speaking at countless fundraising events and began selling Wish bears at Christmastime.

"Talk to anybody you make eye contact with," David told Tatum the very first time she volunteered to sell the bears.

Tatum left with her arms full of bears and, chatting and laughing with every person she encountered, returned with fistfuls of money. She has helped every year since, raising thousands of dollars.

Over the years, Tatum's bubbly personality has had golfers laughing at tee time during fundraising golf tournaments. Her voice, promoting the foundation, has poured into home, car, and office radios throughout the Dallas area, and her ability to tell her Wish story has left audiences in tears.

"My wish was like a true miracle to me. I felt like a princess," the now 15-year-old said during a 2008 fundraising event. "After returning from my Wish trip, I was diagnosed with lymphoma and that was a hard and dark time in my life. While going through that in the hospital, I had my wish to think about and tell everyone about."

She continued, "When I think of the people at Make-A-Wish, I think of miracles, and love, and giving, because that is what they have shown me. I can't imagine a life without them, and I am eternally grateful."

Katelyn Atwell

"St. Jude healed Katelyn physically. Make-A-Wish healed her spiritually."

—Sharon Atwell

★ 1 ★

SHARON'S TEARS OF joy blurred the crisp, December morning—the bright blue sky dripped into the crowd of thousands lining the streets of downtown Memphis, Tennessee, bled into the streets and onto the buildings—as she watched for flames of orange and red turning the corner, dancing wildly.

She blinked the world back into place when she saw her daughter proudly holding the Olympic flames aloft; her smile radiant as the flames, and her spirit fierce as fire.

"Katelyn! Katelyn! Katelyn!" the crowd chanted, voices of soldiers in her battle against illness—her doctors, nurses, family, friends, church family, even strangers—marching victoriously alongside her wheelchair as she glided down Memphis's famous Beale Street. She waved like a beauty queen, soaked in the praise, and lived in that moment, which stood still like a photograph for Sharon.

A committee member wheeled Katelyn toward her mother, who waited on the corner of Beale and Third streets with a dark torch, untouched by her daughter's light. Cheers and shouts slowly disappeared into that suspended moment, clapping hands froze, faces faded.

In Sharon's mental photo, there was Katelyn, smiling behind the dancing flame she was carrying as a 2002 Olympic torch bearer. Like a movie flashback, Sharon couldn't help but think of the moment she and her husband, Ray, realized their daughter's determination to one day compete as a swimmer in the Olympics.

It was six years earlier, when Katelyn was ten, that she, her parents, and her older sister, Crystal, traveled from their Florida home to an early morning swim meet three hours away in Kings Bay, Georgia. It was 5:00 a.m. and the only other cars on the highway surrounding them were packed with sleeping kids from Katelyn's swim club team, part of USA Swimming. Crystal, also a competitor, snored lightly beside her sister, who sat as stiff as someone wearing a back brace, eyes focused as if she were about to breaststroke through water. Ray could see the tip of her hot pink swimmer's cap—the rest of the team wore gold—in the rearview mirror. He tilted his head up a few inches to see her eyes covered in goggles. It was hours before the meet, but she was ready. Katelyn stayed frozen in that position as Ray nudged Sharon with his elbow. She peeked from the passenger's side mirror at their daughter and grinned proudly.

Their swim coach greeted them when the team arrived. "If you guys were all as intense as Kate, you'd be undefeated!" her coach said.

The coach had passed Katelyn and her family on the highway, seen her focus, smiled at her dedication, and admired her commitment.

Voices of a chanting crowd seeped into Sharon's mind, invaded her memory, snapping her back to the moment she was in—a moment that defined the new chapter in her family's life. She knew that carrying a torch wasn't the same as competing, but after everything Katelyn had been through, it was better than winning a gold medal. The fact that she could hear shouts from her family and friends, could see them as they cheered, and could carry a blazing torch in the cool, Tennessee air, was a far greater accomplishment—one worth more than gold.

As Katelyn approached her mother, Sharon wiped her eyes and tried to keep past images in her mind alive—smiles that came from victorious swim meets, laughter on the lake where Katelyn grew up, Punky Brewster-style outfits she had put together as a kid—but when the reality, so fresh in her mind, of doctors' words, hospital smells, and threats of death took over, Sharon cried again.

But Katelyn was here and she was alive.

As she was wheeled toward her mother, she looked up with a smile that Sharon could only have dreamed about just a few short months ago. Katelyn reached up and ignited her mother's torch, uniting their spirits. Sharon continued with a jog, continued their journey, down the streets of Memphis, her daughter's light leading the way.

*　2　*

The sky in all its rage swirled black and hovered, threatening Ray as he raced down the open highway, hoping and praying it wouldn't rip loose, drenching the road and his spirits.

"Dad, God gave us this storm to slow you down," Crystal said a few hours later when the sky finally tore open, sending down blinding rain, exposing brutal thunder and lightning. At sixteen years old, Crystal had just started driving, but it didn't take a license to understand the power of this storm, the advantage it had over her father's determination to push through it. "So, please, slow down!"

If Crystal had seen the way Ray had driven to catch up to the bus she was on just a few hours before, she would have been even more persistent.

Katelyn has cancer.

Ray had repeated those words in his mind as he made his way down Mississippi's Highway 49 in an effort to stop the bus bringing Crystal home from a church camp in Panama City, Florida. They worked as the force behind his determination to track down his oldest daughter and get her to Jacksonville, Florida, where they could all be together as a family.

Waiting around for a slow-moving bus to return his daughter had not been an option for Ray. He could not sit at home calmly with the word *cancer* stirring in his mind—the road, the changes of scenery, the chase, had given him something to do and allowed him to proactively deal with the situation.

On his way out the door, scrambling for anything he might need on the road, Ray had grabbed the first thing he saw that would catch all the tears he knew he was about to cry—a dirty dishrag.

Those tears drenched the road before the rain even had a chance. He looked through them to the other side of the blurred highway, eyes skipping between every northbound car he passed, ready to make a U-turn at the first sight of seven white charter buses.

After a few hours, the wide, four-lane highway narrowed and a wall of pine trees suddenly crept between Ray's lane and the other side of the road. He stiffened with panic and grabbed the steering wheel, leaning as close to the windshield as possible with false hope that it would somehow allow him to see through the trees.

Great! he thought.

The pines blurred to a solid line of green as his eyes searched desperately for a small gap, a miraculous break. And there it was. Through the trees was a sudden flash of white.

Ray found an illegal turning point in the median and sped in the other direction. He punched the gas and zoomed up beside the first of the seven buses, honked his horn, and leaned against the passenger seat to make eye contact with the driver, who looked down at him as if he were a road-raged maniac.

"Pull over!" Ray screamed, swinging his arm and pointing his finger toward the side of the road. "Pull over!"

He swerved in front of the bus, touched his breaks, and pulled to the shoulder with hope that seven white charter buses would pull up neatly behind. Instead, they buzzed by, leaving Ray's tiny Mazda rocking in their breeze.

Unbelievable, he thought, and pulled back onto the highway. It was time to try another bus.

Pulling up beside the second in line, Ray honked his horn once again, flashed his lights, and kept pace with the driver until the bus slowly pulled to the side of the road. Ray tossed his tear-soaked rag onto the floor and got out of his car. Crystal's eyes were wide and terrified as she got off the bus and saw her father. He was the last person she expected to see on an empty highway in the middle of Mississippi. The youth pastor, who knew Ray was on his way but lost touch after hours of patchy cell phone reception, stepped off the bus as well.

"I'll say a prayer for you," the youth pastor said kindly. "I'll tell everyone on the bus what's going on, and we'll all be praying for you."

Ray smiled thankfully.

"Come with me, sweetie," he said.

Crystal gave the pastor a weak, confused smile, followed her father to his car, and crawled inside.

Ray looked down at the steering wheel, studied it, picked at its leather, as the buses pulled back onto the highway.

"Sweetheart, Katelyn has cancer," he said, choking over the last word as his daughter sat stiff in the silent car, waiting for more. "That's all they know. We don't know yet what kind of cancer we're dealing with, but we'll find out soon. We've gotta get to Jacksonville."

The next ten hours were spent in darkness that seeped from the black sky and pounded from their heavy hearts, but Crystal became Ray's light.

"Katelyn is going to be all right," she said, over and over, of her twelve-year-old sister. "God is in control."

She had felt His strength, His presence, His will during church camp, and her faith stopped Ray's tears. But thoughts of possibly losing his youngest daughter pulled selfishly at his hope, stripping away his faith.

"Dad, we need to talk about something else," Crystal said when he brought it up again, and after telling him about camp, she passed the time by reading Bible scriptures aloud and helping Ray find the highway's lines through thick sheets of black rain.

"I told Katelyn I would get there tonight," Ray said, glancing at the clock on the dash. "It's almost eleven."

They pulled into the hospital at midnight, and when Ray found Sharon in the halls, he broke down once again.

"She stayed up to see you," Sharon said. Ray buried his face in his wife's neck and sobbed until there were no tears left to fall.

"When you go in there, you can't be crying," Sharon said, almost warning. "You will scare her to death."

"I know, I know," he said, wiping his face.

"No matter what we're dealing with, she's gonna be fine," Sharon reassured him, wiping away his tears.

They had been each other's strength for the past twenty-one years, but Ray had never needed Sharon the way he did now. The storm he had just maneuvered through was nothing like what they were about to face, and rather than black asphalt and white dotted lines, Sharon's intuition, her mother's instinct, would be leading the way.

"From now on, I'm not gonna get upset until you tell me I need to get upset. I trust you completely," Ray said, wiping his eyes before leaving Sharon's side.

★ 3 ★

Two days earlier, Sharon had returned from a missionary trip in the Dominican Republic to Florida, where her mother lived. Katelyn had been staying with her grandmother for the past week and had complained of an aching back since before she arrived.

"Don't be picking her up, twirling her around when you see her," Sharon had warned her mother, Veda, before dropping Katelyn off. "She pulled a muscle in her back lifting a heavy two-year-old little boy the other day."

"Darlin', you need to be careful while I'm gone," she told Katelyn when they arrived at her mother's house. "You need to let that muscle heal."

During the week she was there, Veda took Katelyn twice to see Dr. Gary Soud, her pediatrician from the time she was born until a year before when she and her family moved from Florida to Tennessee. After ruling out a sore muscle, Katelyn's doctor tried antibiotics for kidney or bladder infections, but by the time Sharon returned from the Dominican Republic, Katelyn was crawling on her hands and knees.

The night Sharon arrived, Katelyn was asleep in the spare bedroom of Veda's house, and Sharon curled up beside her.

"I'm here, sweetie," she whispered.

Katelyn, lost in a dream, whispered, "No, you're not. You're not here." She knew her mother was out of the country.

"Yes, I am, baby. Mom's right here," Sharon said.

In the darkness of the room, Katelyn reached out her hand to Sharon's arm and caressed it gently, hopefully, letting her fingers drape over her mother's, grabbing at the shape of her arm, its texture and warmth.

"You are here!" she nearly yelled, sitting up straight, holding her mother tight.

★ 4 ★

When Sharon took Katelyn to see Dr. Soud the next day, Katelyn could not stand up straight and could hardly walk. He verified Sharon's concern that there was more going on than some kind of infection—possibly a pinched nerve or an extended disc from lifting the heavy child. He ordered an MRI of her lower back for the following day.

The standard twenty-minute MRI took an hour and a half, with the machine scanning much higher than Katelyn's lower back, crawling up her spine to the tip of her head.

"Lord, hold me up and get me through whatever we have to face," Sharon whispered toward the sky as she leaned against the wall, watching doctors come and go from the room where her daughter was stuck in a machine that would soon reveal their future. She knew something was very, very wrong.

When Dr. Soud got the results that afternoon, he called Sharon on the phone.

"I can't get away from the office, so I'm sorry to have to tell you this over the phone, Sharon," he said. "I'd be there with you if I could."

She knew this was serious. Dr. Soud had never diagnosed Katelyn with anything more than a cold, had never treated her with a single antibiotic until the week before when he thought her symptoms indicated a bladder or kidney infection. She had always been the picture of health.

"Katelyn has cancer," he said.

Sharon needed answers.

Immediately.

She could remain calm in every storm as long as she knew exactly what was going on—as long as there was a plan. Dr. Soud's brief hesitation silently told Sharon she'd better pay attention.

He's fixin' to tell me something I need to hear, Sharon thought.

"We aren't sure what kind of cancer we're dealing with yet," Dr. Soud continued. "We need to admit her to Wolfson Children's Hospital for blood draws and scans to see how her organs are doing."

That was the plan. There was a next step.

Clarity.

Direction.

Any tears that might have threatened to fall in the midst of the word *cancer* hid behind the walls of Sharon's strength, her confidence as a mother who knew that God would prepare her for His will, no matter what it was. To the center of her being, the core of everything she believed, she knew that if His will was to take Katelyn from them, she would know.

And she did.

Katelyn isn't going anywhere, Sharon thought.

They got her admitted, and later that evening, Dr. Soud made a visit to his little patient, a girl he had known and taken care of for the past twelve years. He sat down beside her on her hospital bed and explained.

"I'm not sure what you have, but I'm confident we'll be able to figure it out and we'll get you well," he said gently. "We'll be running some tests, and right now we're just trying to figure everything out, so you have to be patient with us, okay?"

Katelyn smiled with half her heart. The other half pounded with fear. She knew that the mass they had found on her spine appeared cancerous, and, like in the minds of most twelve-year-olds, cancer meant death.

The night Ray arrived at the hospital after chasing down Crystal's bus, Katelyn was still awake. She had waited for him, just as she had done from the time she was a little girl. It was a rule in their house that Ray was always the last to tuck her in, and those moments before bedtime were meant for snuggling and talking about everything and nothing. He knew she would be awake, waiting, ready to talk.

Before he opened the door to her room, Sharon's words echoed in his mind as if they were his own.

You can't be crying, she had said. *You will scare her to death.*

So he wiped his tears once again and walked into Katelyn's room, where she lay beneath a tree of IVs dripping relief into her veins to keep the pain in her back at bay. As he approached her bed, his mother's voice joined his wife's.

Pull up your bootstraps, and pull 'em up tight.

It was the advice his mother had always given in hard times.

It was time to be strong.

"I knew you'd be up," Ray said nonchalantly with a smile before sitting down beside Katelyn and taking her hand. She looked every bit as healthy as she had a few days before, when he had tucked her into her own bed at home.

"Don't worry about this," he said to his daughter, hoping to give her the confidence he knew she and Crystal had always depended on. "Whatever we're dealing with, everything will be fine."

Katelyn nodded gently. He kissed her goodnight and stepped into the hallway, where he found Sharon and wrapped her in his arms.

"We're gonna get through this together," he whispered in her ear.

They had witnessed the ending of a marriage between two of their closest friends after the loss of their daughter, and that was not going to happen to them.

"We are going to do this together, talk about it together, feel it together," Sharon said, her head buried in Ray's shoulder, and all he could do was nod. They needed each other more now than ever.

The next day, they knew exactly what they were dealing with.

"Katelyn has leukemia," said Dr. Michael Joyce, an oncologist from Wolfson Children's Hospital in Jacksonville, where Dr. Soud had referred Katelyn and her family.

"She has Acute Lymphoblastic Leukemia, or ALL, one of the most curable types of cancer," he said, giving them some hope. "We can treat her here, but I think you should get her to St. Jude in Memphis. They are known for their work with cancer and they are up-to-date on all the latest and greatest treatments. We consult with St. Jude and we follow their protocol. It's an option for you, but the decision is yours."

They had called Memphis "home" for the past year, so the decision was easy. The next day, they were on a plane and admitted to St. Jude Children's Research Hospital, where they learned Katelyn's protocol—two weeks of intense chemotherapy to get the cancer into remission and then two-and-a-half years of daily, weekly, and monthly drugs to keep it there. After blood work and DNA testing to see how well Katelyn would respond to treatment, they learned that her cure rate was 98 percent.

This is gonna be a breeze, Sharon thought.

There was a clear-cut plan, a fourteen-drug protocol, a strict regimen with precise doses, deadlines, direction, and a predicted, successful outcome. They just needed to take one step at a time, and those steps would lead them to the beginning of a cancer-free road.

But less than two weeks after being admitted, Katelyn developed a high fever and doctors discovered through cultures and blood work that she had bacteria in her blood and bowels, so they started her on antibiotics.

"Mom, my back hurts really bad," Katelyn complained one

night, so Sharon went into the bathroom of her hospital room and filled the jetted Jacuzzi tub to the brim.

"Hop in," Sharon said, and Katelyn sank into the water's warm embrace. She closed her eyes and let her head rest gently on the cool porcelain—her body weightless, her mind free of cancer.

From the time Katelyn was six years old, she had spent nearly every single day of her life in a pool, swimming with her teammates, preparing for meets. The rise and fall of the breast stroke, the feeling of her body's movement through water, its calming sensation, were all as natural as breathing, and, to her, just as important.

She lay in that tub as still as the water until her goose-bumped skin was as shriveled as a prune. Sharon smiled. She remembered the time Katelyn's coach blew the whistle during a swim practice in the middle of winter and shouted, "Hit the showers!"

The other kids had climbed from the pool, but Katelyn continued down its length, lap after lap, lips quivering, breath lost, determined as ever.

"Time to get out," Sharon said, helping her daughter from the tub and back into the hospital bed, her body as relaxed and free as the tide.

The next morning, Katelyn woke up with a splitting headache, worse than she had ever felt in her life.

"I can't stand it," she said with her hand pressed to her forehead, and Sharon filled the tub again. Katelyn climbed inside, and as she had the night before, she let her body sink to the bottom, become one with the water as her head rested peacefully and her eyes closed. Gentle water lapped against her body almost invisibly with every drip from the faucet. Sharon watched as water did its magic on Katelyn, soothing her from the inside out, before it turned on her and crashed violently, suddenly, against her.

Katelyn's body jolted and stiffened, thrashed the water's calm, sending tiny tidal waves onto the hospital floor.

"Help!" Sharon screamed, pulling the emergency cord with frantic, shaking hands as a nurse ran into the room and jumped, fully clothed, into the storm, lifting Katelyn from the tub into her arms until other nurses arrived to help drag her out.

Words and screams stuck in the back of Sharon's throat as she watched the nurses and her shaking daughter with frightened eyes. She needed to know what was going on. This was not part of the plan. She stood, frozen, chaos circling, as Dr. Bob Timbarrough came into the room and took her hands.

He looked straight into her eyes and said, "Mom, you've got a very sick little girl here. You're going to see a lot of people coming and going. I need you out of this room right now. As soon as I know something, you'll know something. Give me a little time and we'll get this thing figured out."

He was polite but forceful, kind but stern. He gave her the direction she needed, and all Sharon could do was wait. She paced the halls and prayed to God.

After several tests and a spinal tap, doctors determined that the bacteria in Katelyn's blood and bowels had migrated to her brain.

"We've never had anyone with these bacteria in the brain live for more than forty-eight hours," a neurosurgeon said to Sharon as he discussed test results with her, viewing scans of Katelyn's brain. "And we're in hour twenty-three."

Sharon sat as still as the room, stared through the scans, waiting for her words and thoughts to come together, to make any kind of sense. It was 6:00 a.m. and Ray hadn't made it to the hospital yet. This doctor was giving their daughter a day and an hour to live, and that was his plan. There was no other.

"Thank you very much," said Dr. Timbarrough, almost

sarcastically. He looked at the other neurosurgeon and then at Sharon. "Let's take a little walk."

Does he have another plan? Sharon wondered.

"What he's saying is true," Dr. Timbarrough nearly whispered in the quiet hall. "We've never seen anyone live longer than forty-eight hours once these bacteria reach the brain. But there's always got to be a first. I'm ready to call somebody else. Is that okay?"

"So you're not ready to give up on her?"

His expression, the hope in his eyes, was her answer. He called in Dr. Stephanie Einhouse, a neurosurgeon he knew would help attempt to save Katelyn, and Sharon called Ray, who headed straight to the hospital.

The first step in Dr. Einhouse's plan was to drain fluids running like rivers through Katelyn's brain. After a successful surgery, however, the external drain wasn't enough and fluids pooled and rushed in again like an undammed lake.

"She's not strong enough," said one doctor when Dr. Einhouse's next proposed step was to insert two internal brain shunts to relieve the pressure.

A ventilator was breathing for Katelyn, who was officially comatose. A tube was feeding her, and her immune system had nearly disappeared beneath the weight of chemotherapy. "She's been too compromised already, and we don't think she can handle the surgery."

"So she'll *for sure* die if we don't do anything, and she *might* die if we do the surgery," Sharon confirmed, her plan forming.

The doctors nodded.

"I'd rather her die trying," she said, and Ray agreed.

After another successful surgery, the fluids continued to rise and fall like tides, and though Katelyn remained asleep, she was alive. Her parents manually kept her that way with the push of a button beneath Katelyn's scalp, which activated a pump to drain the fluids and keep them temporarily at bay. Nurses had explained to Ray and Sharon how the soft button worked—any amount of resistance indicated too much fluid, meaning more pumps of the button were needed. The resistance behind every push, the bacteria's determined stance, made Sharon and Ray fight even harder, believe even deeper.

Sharon knew in her heart of hearts that nothing was going to happen to Katelyn until God prepared her for it, but day after day, hour after hour of staring at her daughter's face, wanting so desperately to look into her eyes, began to wear on Sharon's spirit and she started to question her daughter's destiny.

★ 6 ★

After three months of Katelyn's silence, Sharon left her daughter's side to stand in front of a large prayer map that she had hung in her hospital room. She stared at the hundreds of colored tacks pushed into towns, cities, and states across the country praying for Katelyn. Ray and Sharon's family and friends, as well as their six thousand-member church congregation, had started a prayer chain that eventually left the country and reached people in China and Australia.

"Lord, don't leave her like this," Sharon pleaded, eyes on the pushpins, reminders that she wasn't alone. "Lead her home or wake her up."

Later that evening, as Ray wrapped Sharon in his arms and kissed her good-night, the door to Katelyn's hospital room slowly opened and a nurse poked her head inside.

"Excuse me, there are two gentlemen here to see you," she said.

It was nearly 10:00 p.m. Sharon looked at Ray and he shrugged.

Two men with dark, kind eyes walked into the room and introduced themselves—one as the pastor of a Baptist church in Holly
Springs, Mississippi, the other a deacon. They had never seen these
men before, never heard of their church, never been to their town.

"A member of our congregation requested a prayer for you and
your daughter, Katelyn," the pastor said, "and we felt like we needed
to come pray over her."

They had driven from Mississippi—from a town more than an
hour and a half away—late in the evening to pray over their daughter, a stranger to them. Ray and Sharon stood speechless. The men
studied their faces, their eyes, and their expressions with the concern and compassion of long-lost friends. They were born to love
others, to feel their pain, to care deeply, and to heal with words.
Sharon invited them further into Katelyn's room and granted them
permission to pray.

Before placing their hands over their daughter, the pastor said,
"I can see now why we came to pray for you."

He stared intently at Sharon, who could not hide her worries or
fears in the presence of this man, this perfect stranger. "I'm here to
tell you to stay strong in your faith in what God is telling you, not
in what man is telling you."

How did he know about the death talks they'd had with Katelyn's
doctors?

He didn't.

And when the pastor added, "You go with what God tells you,"
Ray's faith, which had started to sink beneath the weight and into
the darkness of their nightmare, was restored. God had been telling
Sharon all along that He would prepare her, and since He hadn't,
Ray knew, once again, that nothing was going to happen to their
daughter.

Over the next couple of months, Katelyn slept peacefully

through countless brain surgeries and chemotherapy treatments until the bacteria crawled slowly, greedily, and victoriously into her brain stem.

"I'm not sure what's going on with her," said a nurse who saw on Katelyn's monitor that her heart was beating 160 beats per minute. "I need to check the machine. There's no way her heart is beating this fast. . . . "

The nurse fumbled with the wires, convinced of a malfunction, but found nothing. She took Katelyn's temperature, and when the thermometer read 107°F, she quickly called for help and Katelyn's hospital room, once again, became a ballroom of frenzied doctors and nurses dancing to the beat of chaos. The music—frantic shouts, relentless beeps, slamming doors, voices of panic—spun through Sharon's head, its chorus familiar and heartbreaking.

She closed her eyes and an unexpected calm, a sense of hope and knowing, warmed her, filled her mind and spirit.

It's going to get worse before it gets better. It's going to get worse before it gets better.

She repeated the words over and over in her mind.

This had to be the worst of it.

Sharon felt the heat from Katelyn's skin, like rays from a small sun, inches before her fingertips touched the fire. She watched the monitor, listened to the flutter, the vibration of her daughter's heart.

Things will get worse before they get better.

Three hours earlier, when these words had poured from the lips of a visitor, another stranger, Sharon knew that God was holding the strings. They were His words, His message. Just like the men who had visited a few months before, the visitor who came to see Sharon the day Katelyn first "stormed", as doctors called it, with dangerously high fevers and racing heartbeats, had never met her. She had only heard her name but knew nothing of her story.

That visitor was a nurse from Le Bonheur Children's Hospital in Memphis, where Katelyn had been transported to undergo all of her brain surgeries. One late, quiet night, as the nurse manned the hospital's suicide hotline, the glow of the small TV in her office flickered.

At 2:00 a.m., the Sunday service at Ray and Sharon's church was aired, as it was every week. The nurse watched as Pastor Sam Shaw talked about Katelyn, asked the congregation for their support, their prayers, and the nurse decided to make a visit to this girl—no face, only a name.

Something told the nurse she was the same Katelyn who had been admitted to Le Bonheur numerous times, the same girl she had tried to visit during one of her recent shifts. But Katelyn had already been transferred back to St. Jude.

After calling the church to find out where Katelyn was—to find out if she was still alive—the nurse showed up in her hospital room with a blanket that she and twenty other nurses had prayed over.

After a short visit with Ray and Sharon, she walked out of Katelyn's room and into the hall, and Sharon followed.

"I appreciate you comin'," Sharon said, and the nurse stopped and slowly turned to face her.

"This might sound crazy," she said, "but this is what I'm supposed to tell you."

What does she mean, "supposed to?" Sharon wondered, and then she knew.

"Things will get worse before they get better," the nurse said, and it was clear that the message was not from her. It was sent through her.

The nurse's words, God's message, stayed with Sharon for the next nine hours as her daughter's temperature increased to 109°F, her heart trembling at 240 beats per minute, her blood pressure at

185/135. Sharon reminded herself of the pastor's message—*Stay strong in your faith in what God is telling you.*

God had spoken through the nurse, and Sharon needed to listen, to obey.

She needed to keep her faith, realizing that these autonomic "storms" needed to happen before things could get better.

After every twelve-hour storm—where bags of ice were defeated instantly by the heat of Katelyn's skin, where her heart raced, she panted with stubborn breath, and her body lifted in agony—her body would rest, lie calm and cool for three hours, before storming again.

Things are going to get better, Sharon reminded herself daily, hourly, with each rise and fall of Katelyn's temperature, every fast and slowed beat of her heart. No cooling blanket or amount of ice could put out Katelyn's fire; no medicine could bring down her temperature or slow her heart. Certain that the fevers were killing her brain, doctors also believed that a stroke would take her life long before the cancer did.

But Sharon's mind wasn't on death or stroke or heart failure. She knew that somewhere, deep inside Katelyn's mind, she was still there, a part of her was still living. She believed that somehow, despite the storms, despite the doctors' words and doubts and numerous talks of death, Katelyn existed.

Every time they discussed calling family or "making arrangements," every cell of Sharon's body, every ounce of her being, knew it was wrong. She forced every negative word, every bit of bad news, out of Katelyn's room and into the halls—away from her daughter, whom she believed might be able to hear and understand everything.

She couldn't risk the word *death* seeping into Katelyn's mind, crawling viciously through the part of her brain, her soul, that might, on some level, remain hopeful. She had heard stories of people whose bodies had shut down while their minds remained wide awake. Sharon clutched onto that possible sliver of hope with both arms, trying to fill Katelyn's silent life with as much normalcy as possible.

Every morning, Sharon dressed her in shirts from her closet at home and painted her nails to match, as Katelyn would have done. Red, blue, orange, green, purple: the colors changed daily, everything coordinated. From the time Katelyn could dress herself as a little girl, she had put together outfits with every article—clothes, purses, shoes, accessories—matching, every detail a well thought out artistic plan. She wore gloves and hats to school, paid no attention to trends or labels, and often left the house dressed like she was going to church, strutting like a star.

Under Katelyn's direction, guests had come to her sixth birthday tea party wearing fancy dresses, gloves, hats, and shoes. Sharon had always respected her daughter's style, admired her flare, and honored it through sickness—just in case it somehow connected Katelyn with her old self, her well self; just in case part of her was still there.

⋆ 7 ⋆

After six months in the hospital—Katelyn in a coma for five and a half of them—every doctor had given up hope for her survival. They were waiting for her to die.

But Ray and Sharon were waiting for her to wake up. When doctors said there was nothing left to do but keep her alive, maintain her condition, Ray and Sharon had to make the toughest decision of their lives.

"We'll take her home," Sharon said after discussing their situation with Ray and Crystal.

Crystal confirmed Sharon's instinct, saying, "Let's bring her home and see what God can do."

With Katelyn hooked to an IV tree of medicine, breathing and eating from machines, battling cancer and a rare brain infection, Sharon knew she might be getting in over her head, but she believed she could do it. Ray went to work, Crystal continued tenth grade, and Sharon became a full-time nurse, administering thirty-two different drugs at precise times day and night.

The hospital set her up with monitors and a bed at home, and after a day and a half of collaboration among doctors, nurses, and pharmacists, Sharon had a plan—very specific guidelines of times and dosages. She created a spreadsheet and determined the hours every day that she could sleep, the only hours not filled with administering drugs—between 2:00 a.m. and 6:00 a.m.

They brought Katelyn home on Christmas Eve. It was the first time Sharon saw the home Ray had purchased while she and Katelyn were in the hospital. When Katelyn's doctors said the small, two-story condo they were renting was not adequate for Katelyn's condition, Ray searched for a house, bought one, moved all of their stuff with the help of Sharon's mom, and placed a Christmas tree with twinkling lights in the front room to welcome them home with holiday cheer.

Sharon made a traditional Christmas meal that year, wrapped presents, and the family opened them together as they had every year since the girls were born. They said a prayer that evening, as they would on every holiday, that Katelyn would make it to the next. Celebrating Valentine's Day as a family was the plan, the focus.

On Valentine's Day, Ray brought chocolates home to his daughters, and as he, Crystal, and Sharon indulged, Sharon teased, "C'mon girl, wake up so you can eat some."

They treated Katelyn the same as they always had—took her to see movies, ice shows, shopping, restaurants, baseball games. People stared, kids asked questions, but Sharon and Ray were determined to live life, to give Katelyn a life, as long as she was breathing. Their outings—as difficult as they were to transport Katelyn, her meds, her pole, her machines—became their sanity.

Months passed and they dressed Katelyn in green on St. Patrick's Day, dyed eggs and made cookies on Easter, took her to see fireworks on the Fourth of July, and shopped for Crystal's prom dress the following April.

"Do you like this one?" Crystal asked, twirling in the dressing room.

Katelyn, big, green eyes closed peacefully, pretty face resting against the side of her wheelchair, machines and IVs at her side, looked almost thoughtful as Crystal stepped out of her dressing room and modeled the floor-length, black and blue, iridescent gown.

"See, she likes this one, too," Crystal said, and the decision was made.

———✴

They went to church every Sunday and on some Wednesdays. After one Wednesday night service, Sharon and Ray took Katelyn to a Wendy's restaurant as they often did. When they sat down, Ray noticed a woman staring at them from across the dining room, and he wondered if she was someone they knew. With the mystery of a stranger and the eyes of a loving friend, the woman finally got up, walked across the dining area, bent down, and cupped her hands around Sharon's, placing a napkin in her palm. She walked away as quietly as she had come, and Sharon looked at her husband.

"That was kind of strange," she said.

Sharon shrugged and opened the napkin, her heart folding with every written word.

Don't worry, He is in control, it said.

Every moment of question or doubt, every emotional dip on this roller coaster, God sent Sharon a sign to stay strong, stay focused, and pray for Katelyn to open her eyes—a clear message to Sharon and Ray that someday she would.

As the woman walked through the swinging door and into the night, Sharon reminded herself that they just had to keep doing what they were doing—keep praying through every twelve-hour storm, monitoring her around the clock, administering every med, checking every vital sign. No amount of tears could wash away their reality, and no amount of worry would make their situation better or worse. They just needed to have faith and keep living—and that meant exploring the world beyond the walls of their home, beyond the walls of the hospital, where they still went every single day.

⋆ 8 ⋆

A week after Katelyn fell into the coma, her body had listened to her brain and started curling inward, inch by inch, like that of a baby. Her muscles weakened and gave up, pulling in, shutting down. Intense physical therapy slowly tugged back, one limb at a time, stretching and strengthening with boots and braces and creative therapy techniques.

A month after bringing her home, when Sharon called Katelyn's oncologist, Dr. Jeff Rubintz, for prescription refills, he asked how Katelyn was doing.

"She's still storming every day," Sharon said, "but she's still here."

Amazed to hear those words, shocked that Katelyn was still alive, Dr. Rubintz said, "Let's bring her in and see how she's doing."

Having never seen anyone in Katelyn's condition live longer than forty-eight hours, Dr. Rubintz was still unsure whether or not she would pull through, but just in case, he recommended that she continue physical therapy.

"If she does wake up, we want to make sure she can walk," he said, and though the doctor still looked uncertain, still had doubts, Sharon found hope in the fact that even *he* was talking about the possibility of Katelyn's waking up. Never imagining she would find comfort from the hospital, Sharon was glad to have somewhere to go every day, a place where a team of people, of doctors and nurses, were rooting for them, if quietly.

In addition to outings that allowed Sharon to feel somewhat "normal," she took Katelyn to physical therapy at St. Jude hospital every day for two hours. With the help of tools and therapists, Katelyn's body would uncurl during the day, and every night, Ray and Sharon would watch it fold back into itself.

A few months after bringing Katelyn home, the weather warmed and Sharon decided, after watching her daughter's body resort to the fetal position every night, to try something that had always worked to heal Katelyn.

Water.

Crystal's friend from church, Jonathan, had a pool in his backyard, and his family opened it up to Ray, Sharon, and Katelyn every day when Ray got off work. They spent hours transporting Katelyn, her wheelchair, and all of her IVs to Jonathan's house to dip her in the water, inch by inch, careful not to let a drop into her tracheal tube.

Holding her from behind, swaying her gently through the water, Sharon and Ray watched as Katelyn's weightless body immediately unfolded, succumbed to the water's peace. Curled, white-knuckled fists loosened, feet, legs, and arms relaxed, and within moments, her entire body, long and straight, moved fluidly with the water.

"What are you guys doing to get her so relaxed?" asked Katelyn's physical therapist, Swathi Salin, a week after they started putting Katelyn into the water.

Sharon smiled. She knew how well Swathi and Katelyn's doctors would receive the news that they were placing Katelyn, comatose with a tracheal tube, in water.

"Do you really want to know?" she asked.

Swathi, who had been working with Katelyn for more than a year, studied Sharon's face, lowered her brows with suspicion.

"I'm not sure ... " she said slowly.

"A friend of ours has a pool . . . " Sharon started, and Swathi covered her ears.

"Don't tell me," Swathi said, laughing. "I don't want to know. Just keep doing whatever you're doing because it's working. Just don't tell me about it."

Day after day, week after week, month after month, Sharon and Ray continued what they were doing—administering meds around the clock, daily physical therapy, monitoring storms, placing Katelyn in the pool, praying hard, and waiting for a miracle.

One morning, after a year of watching her daughter sleep, never knowing if she would wake up, focusing on the plan, staying strong for herself and her family, Sharon stepped into the shower and lost it. The water and her tears poured down her face, her sobs filling the bathroom, echoing against the tile. Ray was working, Crystal was at school, and her cries, her pleas, filled the quiet house.

"Lord, if you're not going to heal her, then take her with you," she cried. "Do not leave her lying here forever, trapped in this body."

Up against the shower wall, she slid slowly to her knees and closed her eyes as water crept down her body. Katelyn's voice became loud in Sharon's head, her smile the only thing her mind's eye could see. Thoughts that this life could be Katelyn's destiny were too much for her to bear. The pain of remembering Katelyn before she became ill, the desperation she felt to get her back, poured from her that morning and continued throughout the day.

She managed to pull herself together long enough to take Katelyn to physical therapy, but as Swathi started to stretch her and put her braces in place, Sharon had to leave the room.

"I'm just gonna go grab something to eat," she lied and walked with weak legs and a weaker heart to the hospital chapel.

"I don't want to be selfish anymore," she cried with long, breathless sobs, on her knees, alone in the chapel. A few months before, during a routine checkup, doctors found no trace of cancer in Katelyn's blood. She was officially in remission. Why would He heal her from cancer but not wake her up? "If you've been holding on to her long enough for me to realize that I need to let go, then I let go. I'll survive. I won't survive well, but I'll survive."

Just those words, those thoughts, made her cry harder than she had ever cried before, feel pain deeper than she had ever felt in her life.

Sharon had stayed strong, focusing on the next step, on the plan, for so long, but on this day, a day no different from any other, something inside of her broke. She needed her daughter back or she needed her to be at peace.

When Ray got home from work that evening, he asked, "What's wrong, sweetie?"

"It's just been a rough day," Sharon said with a forced smile.

He looked at her with concerned, loving eyes, but she found no reason to drag Ray into her black hole. He needed her to stay strong. If she lost hope, so did he. All of her tears had fallen, and after all her pleas and prayers with God, her heart had spoken.

She woke up the next morning and said to herself, "Today's another day," before crawling out of bed. She was back on track, back to the task at hand—getting Katelyn to physical therapy, preparing her for the day she would wake up.

★ 9 ★

A few months later, after a trip to the mall and an afternoon in therapy, Sharon brought Katelyn home, cooked dinner, and talked about her day with Ray and Crystal before getting Katelyn ready for bed.

She dressed her in pajamas and carefully tucked her in, leaning down to kiss Katelyn's cheek. Sharon studied her face, a lifetime of memories behind her daughter's closed eyes, a million more to make if they ever opened, and whispered, "I love you, Katelyn."

Sharon stood up and looked down at Katelyn as her lips parted and mouthed slowly, "I love you, too, Mom."

"Oh my …!"

Sharon cupped her hands over her heart and let out a scream that sent Ray and Crystal running to Katelyn's room. Had she wanted Katelyn to wake up so badly that she imagined it?

"She just … "

Sharon couldn't speak. She closed her eyes, gathered her thoughts, and pointed at Katelyn.

"She just mouthed words to me!" she managed.

"Kate?" Ray asked.

"Dad," Katelyn mouthed.

Her eyes had opened and her head turned slowly from one side of the bed, to the foot, to the other, as her parents and sister, surrounding the bed, excitedly threw questions at her.

"How do you feel?"

"Did you know you were asleep?"

"Are you in any pain?"

"Do you remember being diagnosed with cancer?"

There were no answers, just slow head turns as Sharon, Ray, and Crystal, wrapped in one another's arms, jumped around, tears pouring endlessly. They hugged Katelyn, kissed her face, held onto one another, as Katelyn's eyes slowly closed, back to peace. The same, silent question entered all of their minds.

Will she wake again?

They studied her sleeping face, the same they had seen for the past year and a half, before leaving the room quietly. Crystal went to bed while Sharon and Ray stayed up, reliving the moment, praying together, questioning if Katelyn would open her eyes in the morning.

"Thank you for this precious moment, for allowing us to see a glimpse of her again," Sharon said to God that night, then begged, "Please wake her again in the morning."

After several hours, Ray and Sharon finally managed to fall asleep, and the next morning, they stood over Katelyn's bed and held their breath as Sharon jiggled her arm.

"Hey, Katelyn, it's us," Sharon said.

After Katelyn opened her eyes, she mouthed, "Hi, Mom."

Their daughter was back. Ray and Sharon hugged each other, happy tears falling, and after wrapping their arms around Katelyn, they looked at her and watched as her head moved back and forth with their voices, but her eyes did not.

When Sharon took her to therapy that morning, Swathi said, "C'mon, Katelyn, let's get you over to the mat." Katelyn, who had just met Swathi for the first time since waking, mouthed, "Okay, Miss Swathi."

"She knew your name!" Sharon said excitedly with realization.

Katelyn, on some level, had heard and remembered Swathi's name when she was in the coma. Sharon smiled at the thought that

Katelyn's mind, after all those storms, all those 109°F temperatures, was still there. Her smile crawled into a proud grin when she realized that, along with Katelyn's memory, her mind remembered its good Southern manners—she had added "Miss" to Swathi's name.

Once Swathi saw Katelyn, it didn't take long for every doctor and nurse at St. Jude to hear the news that Katelyn had woken up, and her oncologist, Dr. Rubintz, was the first to visit. His face, his eyes, beamed when he saw Katelyn, and after hugging her, he said, "Kate, you made my day, my week, my year!"

*   10   *

Katelyn awoke from her coma with no vision, no voice to speak the words trapped in her mind, no ability to walk or eat, so she continued intense physical, speech, and occupational therapy. It took four months for her vocal chords to heal and allow a whisper to form, and eventually a soft voice, just in time.

"I would like to swim with dolphins," Katelyn whispered to a Wish granter who came to visit her home one afternoon, repeating the words she had spoken more than a year before.

When Katelyn was first admitted to the hospital a year and a half before, Sharon's best friend, Lyn, had told Sharon about the Make-A-Wish Foundation. A day or two before the seizure that sent Katelyn into a coma, Sharon spent hours filling out paperwork and getting ready to meet with Wish granters, and without thinking twice, Katelyn had said "swim with dolphins" when Sharon asked what she would wish for if she could wish for anything in the world.

Katelyn had a fascination with dolphins from the time she was a little girl and a passion for water. The wish made perfect sense. And now that Katelyn was well enough to officially make a wish, Sharon wasn't surprised that it hadn't changed.

"You've gotta get strong to hold onto that dolphin," she told Katelyn almost daily after Katelyn had made her wish. She pushed and struggled through therapy, and with every reminder came a boost of energy, a drive to push harder, grow stronger. The look in Katelyn's eyes, the grimace on her face through every demanding challenge, her determination to get better, came from the same place from which it had always come when competing for first place in swim meets.

Her competitive spirit was back, but there were no swimmers in lanes beside her. Nobody to race, nobody to beat. Only herself—her illness. The dolphin was waiting at the finish line. But first, she had to get well.

"I've gotta get strong enough to swim with the dolphins," she told her doctors and nurses as she struggled through months of working to sit up on her own, to stand up, and eventually, after a year of therapy, walk slowly with a walker.

During that year, Katelyn also relearned to eat, and the family's first meal out was to CiCi's Pizza, where Sharon and Ray sat patiently for six hours, watching Katelyn eat four slices. Under the cruel demands of chemotherapy, her young swimmer's body, with solid muscle tone, heart-shaped calves, strong abs and shoulders, had dwindled to flesh and bones—fifty-eight pounds—skin stretched over skeleton. After a slow-dripping tube had kept her alive, kept her nutrition just where it needed to be, watching Katelyn eat each slice of pizza was like watching her get her life back, one bite at a time.

It was a year after waking from the coma that Katelyn's eyesight returned, first by light, then shadows, then pinhole vision.

"They're going to test your eyes and brain to see where the problem is," Sharon explained as she drove Katelyn to an appointment one morning.

"Mom, I can see light," Katelyn said as though it was something Sharon should already know.

"What do you mean you can see light?" she asked, looking at her daughter, trying to keep her car in its lane.

"It's not just darkness anymore," she said. "I can see some light."

Sharon smiled at the thought that Katelyn's world was slowly coming back to her. Her body, her mind, her spirit were waking up, slowly remembering how to live.

"Well, that ought to help them figure out what's going on," Sharon said, and within a week, objects became figures, figures turned into shadows, and those shadows eventually stepped into the light, creating sight that let Katelyn see the world through a piece of Swiss cheese. But at least she could see.

The other abilities Katelyn had lost and started to gain back—the ability to eat and walk and talk—worked with her body's determination to exist, and every day grew stronger and stronger.

* 11 *

It was more than a year after waking from the coma that Katelyn's relearned abilities gave her confidence and hope for a normal life.

"Let's surprise Miss Penny!" she said excitedly to Sharon one afternoon.

Penny was the hospital receptionist, an older, grandmotherly type of woman with big smiles and even bigger hugs.

"There's my girl," she said every time she saw Katelyn. "Where's my bear hug?"

Katelyn's goal was to walk from the therapy ward to Penny's desk.

"You got it," Sharon said, then walked ahead of Katelyn to stand at Penny's desk and watch.

As Katelyn pushed her walker slowly around the corner of the hall and started walking toward them, Sharon's eyes welled up with tears. She pursed her lips, hoping they wouldn't fall, but as they did, Penny wrapped her arms around Sharon.

"What's the matter, sweetie?" Penny asked, squeezing Sharon tight. She hadn't seen Katelyn yet.

With her head on Penny's shoulder, Sharon smiled, wiped her tears, and turned her around slowly to face Katelyn.

"Oh my goodness!" Penny hollered, covering her mouth, clapping her hands. She quickly picked up the hospital's paging system phone and shouted, "Attention St. Jude! Katelyn Atwell is walking!"

Katelyn, maintaining a turtle's pace, had not yet made it halfway down the hall before it was filled with doctors and nurses who, nearly a year and a half before, believed she would not live longer than forty-eight hours, believed she would never wake up. They cheered, clapped, and cried as she made her way toward them, her bright, proud smile leading the way.

The same support continued for the next few months until Sharon got the phone call that would soon change their lives. She kept the call a secret from Katelyn and simply told her one morning that some people from the Make-A-Wish Foundation wanted to speak with her.

"Wow, Mom, look at this!" Katelyn said when a limo pulled up in front of their home.

She slid onto the car's long, black, leather seat and pulled out her cell phone.

"I'm fixin' to go talk with some people from Make-A-Wish!" Katelyn said excitedly to her mom's best friend, "Aunt" Lyn. "I'm going to read them my poem!"

That's all Katelyn knew, that she would read a poem she had written for her parents. She didn't know that the local FedEx had chosen Make-A-Wish as their charity to support that year or that hundreds of golfers would be waiting to meet her, to hear her speak, at a golf tournament that would raise the funds for her wish. When she arrived at the tournament, event spokesperson Flynn Wallace introduced Katelyn to the crowd and asked her to read her poem.

"We want to give you an idea of why we're out here raising money for this little girl," he announced.

Katelyn had always been an honor roll student, a well-behaved child, but every one of her elementary school report cards stated the same thing: "excessive talking in class." She wasn't a wallflower or the pretty girl in the back of the class with opinions but no confidence to express them. She was a hand raiser, a voice. She didn't mind crowds or strangers, and though her strong voice was now weak, her message was just as clear and just as strong.

She walked slowly onto the stage, took the microphone from Flynn, and began to recite her poem:

For the past two years, God has been closely monitoring me.
For the past two years, he has used you to fulfill my destiny.
For the past two years, your looks of grave concern have changed to
   astonished delight.
For the past two years, my eyes have gone from complete darkness to
   blessed sight.
For the past two years, tube feedings gave way to "real food" eating.
For the past two years, you have watched me go from lying to sitting,
   sitting to standing,
Standing to now taking steps.
For the next one hundred years, I could never find the words to say
   "Thank You" for getting me through the past two years.

Flynn kneeled beside Katelyn on the stage, head in hand. After she finished her poem and shared her story, he stood before the crowd, hundreds of teary-eyed golfers, and gathered himself.

"Katelyn, we know you'd like to go swim with the dolphins," he said, pausing, forcing her to look with anticipation in his direction. When she did, he shouted, "And baby, you're goin'!"

The crowd erupted and Katelyn shouted her best, "Woo-hoo!"

✳ 12 ✳

Two weeks later, Katelyn, Ray, Sharon, and Crystal were on a plane to Orlando, Florida, to spend a week at Discovery Cove. Thick, damp, hot air hit them in the face the moment they stepped outside, and in all its sticky misery, that humidity was familiar—it was home. They had moved from Jacksonville, Florida, to Memphis three years before, a lifetime ago, before sickness, hospitals, medicine, and surgery had defined them as a family.

While living in Jacksonville, Ray and Sharon had made the three-hour drive to Walt Disney World Resort and SeaWorld every year, when those places meant everything to a young child. And here they were again, as a whole family, which, for so long, they didn't know if they would ever be again.

Before visiting SeaWorld, sitting in the splash zone of a Shamu show as they did when they were little girls, before riding Space Mountain at Walt Disney World, Katelyn's wish came true. At Discovery Cove, Ray parked her wheelchair in the white sand and, because of the distance, carried her to the bright, blue water lagoon, where Dixie, Katelyn's dolphin, was waiting.

A trainer by her side, Katelyn learned to send Dixie swimming backward and get the dolphin to wave her fins and jump toward the sky, all with a few motions of her hand. Ray and Sharon stood behind, supporting Katelyn's body in the warm water as she played with the dolphin, free from everything.

Then, supported by a jacket, Katelyn sank into the water's gentle grip, pushed and pulled her arms through it effortlessly. She closed her eyes, face pointed toward the hot sun, and felt her body relax, the weight of her illness, its burden, washing away. Ray, Sharon, and Crystal bobbed beside her, laughing as the dolphin danced through the salty water, brushing them with her fin, teasing.

They had spent countless hours, handfuls of summers, floating together as a family in the waters of Lake Broward in the small town of Pomona Park, Florida, where Ray grew up and where he and Sharon lived when their daughters were little. With the dolphin, they shared the same laughter, the same joy they had always found as a family, something Ray thought was gone until that moment.

"Grab on!" the trainer yelled, and Katelyn watched as Dixie, bottlenose smile leading the way, swam toward her. Katelyn waited patiently, her smile reflecting the dolphin's, and threw her arms around Dixie's dorsal fin as she swam quickly by. The force pulled against Katelyn's fragile body, but her mind was stronger.

She held on with every ounce of determination inside of her, engaging every muscle she had worked so hard to strengthen for this very moment. The dolphin became her force, her power, as her own body had once been when she competed as a swimmer. Once again, Katelyn was plowing through water, the spray of it on her face, family in her wake watching through happy tears.

Katelyn would never become a competitive swimmer, her body and mind would never work quite the same, but she was not going to sleep through the rest of her life. That gift, that miracle alone, was something she and her family would never take for granted. As they had from the time Katelyn became ill, they would focus on what they had, not on what they did not have. And one thing they had was this day, this very special day of renewal and hope.

As Katelyn and Dixie circled the lagoon, Sharon and Ray knew it was a moment that would change them forever. They were no longer a family with a dying child, the hospital was no longer their second home, doctors were no longer their extended family. Their lives would no longer revolve around tests, surgeries, and medicine. They learned, in that moment, what the rest of their lives could be.

They could have fun; they could travel, and laugh, and make plans for their futures. Knowing she would always be in therapy, always work toward maintaining and gaining strength, Katelyn also knew, after her Wish trip, that there were no limitations. She got home from her trip and sat down with a pen and paper. She wrote:

Katelyn's Bucket List:
- Ride a zip line
- Fly an airplane
- Sky dive
- Travel to Hawaii, Virginia, Hollywood, Washington, D.C., and New York
- Take a trip by train

Before her Wish trip, the farthest Katelyn had ever traveled from her Florida and Memphis homes were North Carolina and South Carolina to visit family. In the past thirteen years, since her original diagnosis, she has been to the White House in Washington, D.C., ridden on a subway in New York City, placed her palms in the hands of celebrities on Hollywood's Walk of Fame, visited Thomas Jefferson's house in Virginia, and walked the sandy beaches of Hawaii. She has flown an airplane over Deland, Florida, zip-lined at Mammoth Cave, Kentucky, and jumped from the belly of a plane.

All it took was one day, one moment, for Katelyn and her family to learn to live again.

* 13 *

"I thought you might like to know what it took to have me standing here tonight," Katelyn said to a group of employees at the New York Stock Exchange a few months after returning from her Wish trip to Orlando. Inspired by what hope she had found on her trip—not only in her miraculous abilities but also in the reconnection she experienced with her family—Katelyn had made two commitments: to help grant five wishes by raising money for the Make-A-Wish Foundation and to pay St. Jude back every penny it took for them to save her life—$3 million.

She started by sharing her story with the world, one group at a time. She spoke to schools, hospitals, universities—any platform she could find—and sat down with individual investors and potential donors, gearing every speech, every point, to her audience.

"You're number people, right?" she teased in New York. "For me to be here tonight, it took 203 days in the hospital—109 in the ICU—645 outpatient visits, 1,262 hours of rehabilitation, 81.5 hours with the psychology department, twenty brain surgeries, sixteen EEGs, twelve types of braces, two different wheelchairs, a walker, crutches, and a cane. "

As if they needed to hear more, she continued.

"I have no memory of 812 days. I missed my thirteenth and fourteenth birthdays. I had forty-three CAT scans, eighty-seven X-rays, and thirty-two MRIs. And $3 million of St. Jude's money was spent on me. I plan to make a difference with my life. I also plan to personally raise back that $3 million for St. Jude so that, one day, every patient will be a miracle. None of my friends will have to die."

In the past thirteen years, Katelyn, now twenty-six years old, has traveled roughly ten times a year for speaking engagements, organized twelve golf tournaments that, combined, have raised nearly

$180,000, and has been sponsored for 5K runs, earning between $5,000 and $10,000 for each.

To date, she has raised $200,000 for St. Jude.

"Your life becomes nothing but the hospital," Katelyn has explained to crowds of potential Make-A-Wish donors. "While most parents are taking their kids to soccer or football practice, mine were taking me to physical therapy. Other kids were doing all these things while I was just trying to learn to live again."

Money resulting from Katelyn's speeches, in addition to the one-hundred dollars she collected by selling handmade beaded bracelets—each with a dolphin bead to represent her wish, a shooting star bead to symbolize Wish children, and a wishbone bead to signify wishes—eventually added up to $25,000, enough to grant five wishes.

She continues to be a voice for the Make-A-Wish Foundation, and the message she sends with each speech, the message that lives on with the memories of her trip, is the same: *My wish healed my spirit.*

⋆ 14 ⋆

The moment Katelyn's flame touched Sharon's dark torch, something inside of her ignited. Shouts of her daughter's name receded to hushed whispers surrounding her, as her black torch came to life with vibrant flames.

She did it.

Doctors had told Sharon and Ray countless times to call family, to make arrangements. They said Katelyn would never wake up. Never walk again. Never talk. Never eat or see or laugh or smile. Never, never, never . . .

But there Sharon was, with those same doctors watching through their tears on the sidelines as Katelyn reached her flame toward her mother's, and Sharon knew in that moment that absolutely anything was possible and nothing would ever be taken for granted again.

Piles of unfolded laundry, aggressive drivers, a dirty house, running late—these things were once the culprits of ruined days. But laundry can be folded tomorrow, as can cleaning a house; impatient drivers must need to get somewhere quickly; running late means you have some place to go and the ability to go there.

Every day that Katelyn wakes up and crows like a rooster, happily saying, "Good morning, Mom," is another day Sharon has with her daughter—a day they would not have if they had listened to those doctors, a day that would not exist if they had lost their faith.

Katelyn had missed her seventh- and eighth-grade school years, and when she had returned to ninth, Sharon rested against her car and watched as Katelyn was wheeled through the high school campus, her future waiting. She had a future to pursue, a reason for defying all medical statistics, a reason for living. Surrounded by the sounds of noisy buses, screaming teenagers, the hustle and bustle of school, Sharon watched as Katelyn re-entered life.

It was the same feeling she got when she turned from her daughter, red fire leading the way, and jogged with the Olympic torch for the next five blocks down the streets of Memphis. Tears poured from her eyes, once again drenching the city, and a smile crawled across her face. There was so much to look forward to—so much to run toward—and Katelyn would be a part of that race, a part of that journey.

Their Wish trip had taught them to enjoy life, regardless of limitations, in spite of difficulties. It showed them how.

Their journey had made life's small problems disappear, and that walk, that experience of carrying the torch—a dream that had once been Katelyn's to carry an Olympic medal—was a reminder of how far they'd come and how far they could go.

Brittney Wolfe

"Cherish yesterday, dream tomorrow, live today."

—T'Ann Wolfe

SHE JUMPS, *I jump*, T'Ann thought, peeking over the side of the swaying boat into the dark water below. It splashed gently against hundreds of shiny fins that sliced through the tepid water, circling her daughter, who was bobbing in the waves. Brittney had fearlessly stood beside the tour boat guide just a few moments before and plunged right in. The water around her crawled with shadowy movement, and T'Ann watched nervously as Brittney poked her goggles through the surface to get a closer look at the reef sharks surrounding her. T'Ann plugged her nose, scrunched her face, and jumped, reminding herself as she hit the water, *She jumps, I jump.*

Over the past eighteen months, those mirrored words began to define everything in T'Ann's life. Brittney's battle with cancer was her battle. The time she spent in remission, cancer-free, was T'Ann's freedom. The tears Brittney cried were hers, too. They shared joys and fears, heartache and triumph. T'Ann had promised Brittney they would do everything together on Brittney's Make-A-Wish trip, even if it meant swimming with sharks. The promises they made to each other were kept, and it was Brittney who had kept the most important promise of all.

———————— ✶

"Brittney, it's over," Dr. Meltzer said quietly as he stood above her small, tired body. "Can you hear me?"

A thin sheet hugged her as the doctor's voice poked through the fog in her waking mind. Her cracked lips remained still beneath her pale cheeks as the sunlight crawled through the small window of her third-story hospital room, illuminating her dark brown, shoulder-length hair. Brittney knew before the surgery that the doctor would cut the hair she had worn past her shoulders since she was a little girl, so her mom, T'Ann, had taken her to one of those fancy salons to get a cute, short style she would enjoy after it was over.

Her hair clung to the back of her sticky neck that afternoon as the doctor's voice and others reached for her. Their words sank and resurfaced as she fought to put them together. Whispers calling her name floated by while the steady beeps of a monitor grew louder and sharper, becoming real. Big, brown eyes that had been hiding beneath their lids for the past eleven hours began twitching as jumbled voices became one.

"Brittney, it's time to wake up. Can you hear me?"

It was the voice of the man who had delivered the most painful news she had ever received in her twelve years of life, and though it was a familiar voice, she strained to remember the face to which it belonged. Her eyes stayed closed as one clear thought repeated in her mind: *You're awake, keep your promise,* she demanded of herself. *Keep your promise, Brittney.*

The doctor's voice faded as her mental strength crawled into the deepest realm of her consciousness, clinging to a little voice that had turned her into the resilient, independent young girl she was. That voice begged her to gain the strength she knew she needed to keep the promise she had made to her mother. A powerful internal force pushed through the thickness of her mind, sending signals to the tips of her toes. Her feet pushed slowly through the tucked covers at the end of the bed and her toes, painted a loud shade of green, curled.

Dr. Meltzer's eyes grew wide as he watched them bend back and forth slowly before becoming an unmistakable, intentional wiggle. He was the one who had told Brittney only days before that the odds of her becoming paralyzed from the surgery were even greater than the odds of her dying. Now she was moving all of her toes, and he watched in awe in that quiet hospital room.

Staring at his little patient, Dr. Meltzer ran a hand through his pointy black hair and covered his gaping mouth with the other as a second miracle unfolded.

Brittney, with eyes still closed, slowly lifted both arms into the air, fists leading the way, and popped her white-tipped, manicured thumbs toward the ceiling, giving the most determined thumbs up the doctor had ever seen.

Dr. Meltzer finally left Brittney's side and raced to the hospital waiting room where T'Ann sat with her family, including Brittney's father, Charlie, and T'Ann's boyfriend, Andy.

"She kept her promise," Dr. Meltzer said, surprise and delight in his voice.

The eleven hours it took T'Ann and Charlie to hear those words were the longest hours of their lives. Filling the minutes and seconds with puzzles and nail biting, crying and pacing, it felt as though eleven years had passed.

⋆ 2 ⋆

Brittney's promise was born from a nightmarish time that began one sunny Mother's Day afternoon in 2001, when T'Ann discovered that her perfectly healthy twelve-year-old daughter had an eleven-inch tumor woven around her cervical spine.

Complaints of a sore neck and numb fingers had resulted in a few visits to Dr. Meltzer, a neurosurgeon at Rady Children's Hospital San Diego, who confirmed his suspicion with an MRI and diagnosed Brittney with a tumor so rare it hadn't been given a name.

Days inevitably passed after T'Ann and Brittney received the news, but time had stopped and the world no longer looked the same. The guarantee of Brittney's growing up, going to college, getting married, and having children had been taken away. She was about to turn thirteen and complete the seventh grade, but there was no way to know if she would make it to the eighth. The last trip they had made to the desert to camp and ride dirt bikes might have been just that—her last. This was a time when T'Ann thought her daughter, who was stronger and more self-assured than T'Ann had ever been, might lose all hope and claim defeat before putting up a fight. But Brittney had decided that losing wasn't an option.

"I'd like to get fake fingernails, Mom," she said softly one night shortly after finding out about the tumor. "I've always wanted to do it, and I think I'm old enough now. I want to get them done before the surgery so they look nice and pretty for when it's all over."

Her daughter, who seemed to look at this surgery as an obstacle in her life rather than a possible end, stared up at T'Ann with a hopeful and teasing smile. It was hard to believe she was the same tomboy who loved camping and hiking. She was the girl who played Barbies in the dirt and couldn't pass a puddle, muddy or not, without jumping into it.

"Fake nails?" T'Ann said, hardly able to form the words. "You're not old enough to get those. You can get your hair cut and I'll take you to get a pedicure. If you want, you can get a manicure, too, but no fake nails."

Brittney's persistence didn't surprise her mom. It was the same persistence she had shown on her first birthday when she decided it was time to eat Mickey Mouse cake instead of open presents. When Brittney was five, T'Ann started letting her decide what clothes she would wear to school. She would put together three outfits and let Brittney pick the one she'd like to wear. When her mom left the room, Brittney would put on a top from one outfit and the bottoms from another and insist on going to school with stars and stripes and mismatched colors.

Well, I told her she could pick out her outfit, T'Ann would remind herself and laugh quietly as she dropped her colorful daughter off at school every morning.

This innate determination to get what she wanted only grew stronger with age, so T'Ann knew Brittney would need to hear the word *no* a few more times before accepting that she was not getting fake fingernails.

It was after dinner one evening that T'Ann changed her mind. During the week between finding out about Brittney's tumor and the day of the scheduled surgery, she and Brittney found endless ways to spend their days together just in case they were their last. They cuddled and watched movies, baked, played games, and did puzzles.

Brittney, T'Ann, and her boyfriend, Andy, sat one evening with a bright, spirited woman named Patty, who had changed Brittney's diapers and earned the title of "Grandma" rather than "friend of the family" during the course of Brittney's life. As the four of them put together a puzzle that, in the end, would bring to life a small dolphin jumping out of the ocean, there was a moment of silence between stories and laughter when Andy turned to T'Ann with a thoughtful look.

"You should let her do it," he said.

"Do what?"

"Get the fake nails."

T'Ann wasn't sure where it came from, but she looked into Andy's loving eyes and decided he was right. They had been dating for nearly a year, which was how long it had taken Brittney to get past the stages of hating him, resenting him, warming up to him, eventually accepting him, and finally loving him.

"All right," T'Ann said, turning to Brittney. "You can get those fake nails."

"Yes! Thanks, Mom ... "

"Hold on a second," T'Ann said with a look that told Brittney there was more to it than that. "You can get those nails if you make me a promise."

She stared with intense eyes at her beautiful daughter then leaned toward her delighted face.

"When you wake up from this surgery, promise me you will wiggle your toes and give the doctor a thumbs up," she said, choking out her words as her throat swelled.

Though she knew the odds of her daughter's waking from the surgery, and the chances of her ever walking or moving her arms again if she did, were very slim, she believed it was a promise Brittney could keep. T'Ann's eyes filled with tears, but she didn't blink—she kept them on her daughter as she squeezed her small hands and waited for an answer.

"Done," Brittney said without hesitation, turning back to the puzzle. She glanced quickly at Andy and gave a small smile.

"Thanks, Bunk," she said to Andy, a nickname she had given him that referred to a contestant from one of her favorite reality shows, *Big Brother*.

★ 3 ★

The assurance in Brittney's answer that night had put T'Ann at ease, and now, staring at Dr. Meltzer in the doorway of the hospital, she fell to her knees and sobbed as her family collapsed beside her, wrapping their arms around her shaking body. Brittney had kept her promise, and now T'Ann was breaking hers. She had promised Brittney from the beginning of all of this that she would be strong and never let her tears fall.

"You're not allowed to cry and neither is anybody else," she had told T'Ann the afternoon they came home from the hospital after hearing the MRI results. "I don't want anyone feeling sorry for me. Everything's going to be fine."

It was profound coming from a twelve-year-old, and T'Ann resorted to saving her tears for the pillow at night. But in the waiting room of the hospital, she knew the "no crying" rule did not apply; these were tears of joy and relief. So she let them fall, long and hard down her reddened face, letting them drip from the bottom of her chin onto the polished tile floor. Dr. Meltzer placed a hand on her shoulder and gave her the rest of the news.

"We were able to remove half of the tumor," he said with a serious yet compassionate voice. "During surgery, we tested several pieces, and results came back benign in some tests and malignant in others. This tumor has obviously lived a long time inside your daughter."

"Is that even possible, for a tumor to be both malignant and benign?" T'Ann asked.

"No, it isn't, so we're going to send samples of the tumor out for more testing."

He paused and took another breath. "Brittney's in the ICU right now and our next step is to get her off the breathing machine."

T'Ann didn't know what the steps after that would be or how she would find the strength to take them. She just knew Brittney had survived the surgery and was on her way to fighting a larger battle, and T'Ann was determined to make sure they won.

As Dr. Meltzer spoke, she felt dizzy and suddenly anxious. She needed to see her daughter, to hold her and make sure she was okay.

She wanted so badly to see Brittney's shining smile and bright eyes, to hear her laugh and see her run around. So when Dr. Meltzer took T'Ann to Brittney's room, where she was lying still in a hospital bed covered in white linens, IVs spilling from the creases of her arms, she stood in the doorway, covering her mouth while every ounce of sorrow and worry and sadness inside of her escaped.

She wept into her shaking hands and pushed her face hard into Andy's chest, waiting for the pain to pass. Just weeks ago, her baby girl was a healthy, active seventh grader passing notes in class, her entire life ahead of her.

But everything had changed. Now she was lying in a cold room, alone, waiting to hear whether she was going to live or die. Dying shouldn't be an option for a twelve-year-old. As T'Ann stared at Brittney through the tears in her eyes, she collected herself, somehow, for her daughter's sake.

Brittney's closed eyes twitched and she knew her mother was there. T'Ann could feel it. The bond they shared had never been tighter, and it would only get tighter from that point forward. With a gentle hand, T'Ann touched her daughter's cheek, tucked her hair behind her ears. She held her hand, careful not to bump the IVs, and Brittney squeezed it back.

She knows I'm here, T'Ann thought, forcing back threatening tears. It would take time and patience to know what to do next, and she had plenty of both. Suddenly her full-time job became a little detail, and little details meant nothing. All that mattered now was her daughter's survival.

Two hours after the surgery, Dr. Meltzer took Brittney off the breathing machine, which he had thought she would need for at least three days, confirming his belief that she was a fighter. She spent one week in the ICU, motionless, keeping her neck still in its brace, while T'Ann slept curled up in a chair behind her bed, never leaving her side. Brittney had five hundred dissolvable stitches beneath her skin and one hundred lining the back of her neck from her hairline to the middle of her shoulder blades. They itched with miserable persistence, but she remained still.

"On a scale from one to ten, how bad is the pain?" asked a friendly nurse the first day Brittney was in the ICU. There was skepticism in the nurse's voice. She obviously had not believed Brittney's answers in the past.

"I'd say, two," Brittney said with determination that did not quiver.

"I need an accurate number," the nurse said.

Brittney glanced at the ceiling. "Five."

"That's better. But I have a feeling it's a little more than that."

Brittney would have shrugged if she was able, but her eyes spoke instead. It was much more than five. Much worse than ten. But she could handle it. Nobody needed to worry about her.

"Okay, I'll be back to check on you in a little while," the nurse said before leaving the room.

"Brittney, why won't you give her an accurate number?" T'Ann asked.

"Mom, I can't be a baby about this," she said matter-of-factly.

Her mental strength outweighed her physical strength. Her hands, especially her right, were very weak, but as far as she was concerned, it was so minor compared to other possible outcomes that it wasn't worth fussing over. Still, it was worth spending some time in the physical therapy ward, which, after a week in the ICU, Dr. Meltzer announced would be their next destination.

"All right, Sunshine," he said. "You're doing too well to stay in intensive care. We're moving you to physical therapy."

At times, Brittney felt like a child whose parents had moved her into a mansion with endless rooms to explore and a different name for each. She didn't know how long she'd be there or what to expect from the physical therapy ward, but she knew a change of scenery would be nice. Dr. Meltzer explained that they would start therapy to help her gain strength in her hands and relearn to walk.

During her stay there, doctors and nurses came in and wheeled Brittney from her room to take MRIs of her back. She knew they needed to monitor the tumor, and as strong as she had been to that point, Brittney could only pretend that the pain she felt when they simply touched her gurney was not the most she had ever felt in her life.

With the weight of her head resting on her neck, Brittney let out screams that tore through the room and echoed down the hallways. Those pain-drenched screams haunted T'Ann at night and reminded her of how helpless she felt, how helpless she was.

Weeks passed slowly in physical therapy as Brittney's condition improved. She was gaining more strength in her hands, and on her thirteenth birthday she managed to sit upright for the first time since surgery. After a month in the ward, they heard the magic words.

⋆ 4 ⋆

"We're sending you home," Dr. Meltzer said to Brittney and T'Ann one afternoon. "You've made great progress since the surgery. You'll be here often for therapy, and we'll be monitoring the tumor."

He paused, then added, "You'll have to wear the hard plastic brace for a few months, and then we'll switch you to the soft collar."

T'Ann threw her arms around her daughter and cried. At this point, any little thing, good or bad, set her off, but Brittney was used to it. They held each other while Dr. Meltzer gave them specific instructions to follow once they got home.

"Keep her walking," he told T'Ann, and then said to Brittney,

"You have to keep walking. We need to build strength up in your neck and your back."

She smiled and nodded and promised Dr. Meltzer she would practice walking every day, and he knew she would keep that promise—she hadn't broken one yet.

A few nights after going home, T'Ann lit a candle and placed it in the middle of the patio table in her front yard, where she sat with Brittney and Andy for dinner. As the sun was setting behind them, T'Ann stared at her daughter with overwhelming joy that she was back at home where she belonged.

"How are your hands doing?" she asked. The only thoughts she seemed to have lately were of Brittney's recovery, and every question she asked reflected those thoughts. Brittney was right-handed, so she found it clumsy and awkward to use her left.

"I still can't move them very well," she said, "but I can move the left one better than the right."

She perked up with a mischievous smirk and offered a challenge to Andy and her mom. "Since I have to eat with my opposite hand, why don't you?"

They smiled and told her "no problem", and the three spent the rest of the meal laughing as food fell from their forks and their mouths.

"See, it's not as easy as it looks," Brittney said, satisfied.

After dinner, she offered another challenge to her mom.

"Here, wear this and walk with me down the street," she said, handing T'Ann the soft collar Brittney would wear once she was out of the hard brace.

Each in a white neck collar, they linked arms and walked clumsily, side by side, down the sidewalk with the glow of overhead street lamps lighting the way. The brace perched their chins high in the air and forced them to walk without looking down, an unnatural way of walking to which Brittney had become accustomed.

T'Ann, however, stumbled awkwardly over her own feet and threw her arms out to the side when she tripped and nearly fell to the ground. Brittney laughed hysterically and tossed her a smug look that announced her satisfaction.

"See, Mom," she giggled. "It's not that easy."

Over the next few weeks, life for Brittney and T'Ann was starting to get back to normal. They took each day as it came, one at a time. That's all they could do. They spent time relaxing and playing together, walking, and staying as active as possible. They shared mother-daughter talks at night, and T'Ann held her as she fell asleep.

Nothing bad is ever going to happen to my beautiful girl again, T'Ann thought.

Brittney's father, Charlie, from whom T'Ann had been divorced for a year and a half, lived only minutes away and spent the weekends with Brittney.

"Let's go fishing at the lake," she'd suggest to her dad, and they would spend all afternoon cruising from one perfectly good fishing spot to the next.

She loved that her dad let her drive the boat, and cruising was more exciting to her than actually fishing.

"I don't want to stop," Brittney would say with a smile from behind the wheel.

"We can cruise all day if you'd like," he'd reply.

One afternoon toward the end of June, Brittney and T'Ann were wrapped in blankets on the couch together watching a movie when the phone rang. T'Ann jumped and ran to the kitchen to answer it, and Brittney stared from the living room couch with big eyes as her mother's face whitened and dropped slowly toward the floor. She closed her eyes and turned her back to Brittney and asked, "What is this all about? Can you just tell me what's going on?"

She hung up the phone and explained that they needed to go see Dr. Kadota later that afternoon.

"Who's Dr. Kadota?" Brittney asked softly.

"I don't know, sweetie," she said, feeling the world around her fall apart again. Panic and uncertainty tore at her. T'Ann wasn't cut out for this and she knew it. She needed this nightmare to end. No more doctors. No more phone calls. This all needed to go away, to disappear.

But as she stood there, staring at her daughter, she knew she had to face the reality of it all. It hadn't gone away, and there was no guarantee that it ever would.

Brittney and T'Ann somehow made it through the rest of the afternoon, and when they got to Dr. Kadota's office, T'Ann went in alone to face the news.

Inside, she met a short Asian man.

"I'm Dr. Kadota, pediatric oncologist," he said to T'Ann.

He shook her hand as she said, "I'm T'Ann. Nice to meet you."

"It's nice to meet you as well," he said. "Please, take a seat."

T'Ann sat down and studied him: his hair was black and speckled with gray, and he looked at her with dark, friendly eyes. With her legs crossed, ankle dancing impatiently, she wished they could skip the formalities.

"I was notified by Dr. Meltzer of your daughter's case, and as you know, we've been researching her tumor."

T'Ann was aware that they had sent pieces of it to oncologists in Boston and New York for a diagnosis, and the only one they had given so far was a Primitive Neuroectodermal brain tumor (PNET) because "it's the closest we can diagnose," as one doctor put it.

She nodded and waited for the doctor's announcement. He paused for a long moment and sighed. "The tumor is malignant."

His words fell in slow motion, and T'Ann knew what that meant. The demon was alive, and the portion left inside her daughter would not let her go. It was determined to take her life.

"Noooo!" T'Ann sobbed into her hands as violent waves of pain crashed through her. The world around her turned white, and the words dripping from the doctor's tongue became nothing but deep, subtle noise—a useless rumble in the background of her cries that blotted out answers she didn't want to hear anymore.

"The other half is too entwined to remove surgically, so we're going to start Brittney on seven types of chemotherapy and six to seven weeks of radiation," he said, taking T'Ann's trembling hands into his own. She didn't want them, but she needed his answers.

"What are the chances we will beat this?" she asked, sitting up straight, hanging on to the strength her daughter had instilled in her during the past few months.

"Forty percent, and that's generous," Dr. Kadota said sadly.

"Well, she's going to beat it," T'Ann said, growing angry. Defeat was not an option. She gathered herself in that small room while the doctor left for a moment and came back with a stack of pamphlets and brochures. He handed them to her, and as she dried her tears, she read headlines such as "Coping with Cancer" and "Childhood Cancers: How to Communicate with Your Child."

She saw a brochure for the Make-A-Wish Foundation and tossed it to the back of the pile. That foundation was for dying children, not for Brittney. She stuck the brochures into her purse, glanced at her feet, and slowly made her way out of the room.

★ 5 ★

T'Ann found Brittney in the waiting room and told her something a mother should never have to tell her child.

"Sweetheart," she said, breathing out for a long moment and back in, hoping some strength remained in her voice for the sake of her little girl. "The tumor is cancerous."

She took Brittney's hands and waited for her response. T'Ann had cried long and hard enough for them both with the doctor, and now she knew she had to stay strong for Brittney's sake.

"Yeah, Mom, I kind of knew," she said, shockingly calm and straightforward.

"You knew? How?"

"I could just feel it."

T'Ann let that sink in for a moment before asking the obvious. "Why didn't you tell me?"

"I didn't want to make you worry," Brittney said, "especially since I wasn't sure."

Brittney's grown-up response kept T'Ann calm, so she explained to her daughter what would happen next, as the doctor had just told it to her. She would go through a very structured series of treatment, including chemotherapy, radiation, endless pills and shots, and, of course, frequent trips to the hospital. In a "perfect world," the entire process would take a year and a half.

"If the treatment makes you too ill at any time, they'll have to figure out what to do, and then it could take longer than a year and a half," she said, eyes filling with tears. She snapped her head back and forth with closed eyes, took a deep breath, and hugged her daughter tighter than she ever had before.

———— ✳

They ate dinner together that night, and after tucking Brittney into bed, T'Ann sat on the couch with a cup of coffee, staring at the floor, numb with fear, broken from worry.

The phone rang, snapping her from her thoughts, from the concern consuming her mind. It was Dr. Meltzer checking on Brittney and apologizing for not letting her know that Dr. Kadota's office would be calling. T'Ann vented her shock and anger on Dr. Meltzer.

"I thought you said the tumor was benign," she demanded. "How did this happen?"

"I said I *thought* it was benign based on its size and the fact that Brittney *walked* into surgery," he explained. "It was such a large and rare tumor that I figured it was not possible for her to be as strong and healthy as she seemed before the surgery if the tumor was malignant. That's why I thought it was benign. I was as shocked as you were to find out." He paused for a moment. "Dr. Kadota is an excellent doctor and together we will do everything we can for Brittney."

Later that week, T'Ann and Brittney went to the hospital and met with the head of radiology at San Diego Children's Hospital, who explained how the process would work.

"We're going to do six-and-a-half weeks of chemotherapy and radiation, five days a week, on your entire spinal cord," he said. "And we'll do extra radiation on the neck. Your hair is going to fall out, and you'll be sick and fatigued."

He was delivering the news rapidly, but T'Ann figured there was no other way. Anything he said that might have scared Brittney seemed to be a witty challenge to her.

"This treatment might stunt your growth," he said, explaining that because they would be radiating only her spine and not the rest of her body, her limbs would continue to grow normally while the length of her core, stunted by the radiation, would remain the same.

"Cool, that means I'll have really long legs," Brittney replied.

He instantly loved her spirit.

"And you will become sterile," he added gently.

"Who wants a period anyway?" she pondered, then solved the rest of the problem with a quick and logical solution. "I'll adopt."

"Looks like she's got it all figured out," the radiologist said, smiling.

When they left the hospital, T'Ann was filled with a hope she prayed was not false.

This is going to be okay, she thought. *This schedule is okay. We can really, really do this.*

During the first week of chemo and radiation, the "perfect world" was instantly shattered when Brittney became so ill and weak that they had to stop chemotherapy, blowing the plan in its earliest stage. They continued radiation, and though it made her frail and sick to her stomach, her body was taking to it and the tumor was starting to shrink.

As the end of those six-and-a-half weeks approached, T'Ann spent every waking minute worrying and wondering if Brittney was going to make it through. Her daughter's once rosy cheeks were pale, her hair was falling out in large clumps, and the little bit of extra weight she had carried that made her a perfectly darling thirteen-year-old girl was dropping dramatically. During that time, T'Ann took Brittney to the movies every Wednesday afternoon that she felt up to it, getting them over the hump of the week.

To get through the rest of each week, Brittney brought her boom box to the hospital and blared Madonna and Christina Aguilera during radiation, demonstrating that, as she told her mom, "If I'm gonna do this, I'm gonna do it my way."

During radiation, Brittney made such an impact on the hospital staff that they threw a party for her on her last day of treatment. Brittney and T'Ann walked hand in hand for the last time through a white maze of hallways leading to the large radiology room. Their usual tear-stained faces were bright and smiling with the knowledge that this was their last time down those halls. As they approached the double doors, the pulse of loud but muffled music beat with every step. They looked at each other, puzzled, before the doors swung open, and every doctor and intern that had administered her radiation over the past six weeks was dancing to Christina Aguilera's "Genie in a Bottle."

They laughed at Brittney's shocked expression and continued their choreographed routine. Dressed in scrubs, they jumped and twirled, swung their arms, and shook their hips, completely in sync. Her radiologist, a kind, reserved woman whose long, dark hair was always wound tightly in a braided bun, spun and lip-synched the lyrics as she yanked out the bun, whipped her head back and forth wildly, and continued the performance.

Brittney and T'Ann stood in the doorway with dropped jaws.

"What's going … " Brittney started.

A break dance spin from one of the interns cut her question in half, and Brittney started to laugh as he impressively stood on his head.

"Don't quit your day jobs!" she teased as everyone in the group snapped into final poses.

Brittney's radiologist caught her breath, walked over to her, and put an arm around her shoulder.

"You have affected us more than any other patient with your charisma, your wit, and your inner strength. We wanted to do this for you," she said with tears in her eyes.

"You always have a smile on your face … " she continued before her voice cracked and trailed off. She didn't need to say any more.

Brittney hugged her tightly and thanked the rest for a performance she would always remember.

★ 6 ★

The tumor was shrinking, Brittney was out of the hospital, and things were finally looking up—but the battle was not over. It was time to start chemotherapy again, and all they could do was pray that this time, it would work.

At home, Brittney took one pill a week and went in just as often to have her blood drawn. T'Ann continued living by the rules that could save Brittney's life—watch her weight, rush her to the emergency room if her temperature rises above 101°F, make sure she gets all of her meds, including pills for sleeping and nausea. Her cupboards were overflowing with the shots and pills it was taking to shrink the spiteful tumor.

Brittney continued physical therapy to heal her hands, and she took advantage of every moment she felt well enough to do the things she enjoyed doing—spending time with her mom and Andy, hanging out with her dad, cooking, watching movies, reading, playing with her dogs. She loved shopping and going to the drive-in movie theater with Charlie to watch double features, but she was always a little apprehensive to leave the house.

"Dad, you don't know what it's like to be bald," she said one day as they were leaving to go shopping for wigs.

You're right, I don't, he thought as he scooped her into his arms, kissing the top of her head. "But you're still as beautiful as ever."

After dropping Brittney off at T'Ann's house that evening, Charlie drove home and stared at his reflection in the mirror. He knew that the inevitable brown, leathery skin he'd developed after many years of working construction would look ridiculous with a bald head that had never seen an ounce of sun, but he pulled out his razor and did not hesitate.

With one solid motion after another, piles of blonde hair fell to the ground around him until bright bathroom light bounced from his head with a subtle white glow. He smiled, pleased, and the next time he went to pick Brittney up, her jaw dropped and her eyes bulged.

"Dad! What did you do?!"

"You said I didn't understand, and I wanted to."

She hugged him tightly and never wore a wig again.

Brittney had spent the summer before her eighth-grade year in and out of the hospital, and all she talked about as she grew stronger was going back to school to see her friends, especially Andrea, her best friend in the world. They met in the fourth grade and were instantly connected like sisters. They played in the dirt as little girls, went swimming in the summer, joined student council together in elementary school, and shared their dreams with each other.

As Brittney grew sicker and started losing her hair, Andrea was the only friend she would proudly show her bald head to. It made them laugh and smile, and though Brittney knew she wouldn't be joining Andrea when their eighth-grade year began, she would study at home and stay caught up. Their school years together would continue in high school.

In the meantime, the girl who knew she was going to grow up to become a doctor or lawyer focused diligently on her school work and, over time, decided on a new career path.

"When I beat this, I want to help kids who have cancer," Brittney told T'Ann one day. "I'll give talks and do seminars on what I went through so they'll know they're not alone."

"That's a wonderful idea," T'Ann said, knowing her daughter could change the world if that's what she set out to do.

In elementary school, Brittney had become a teacher's aide for her favorite teacher. In first grade, she was a peer helper for the kindergartners and joined the safety patrol.

She was on the student council in fourth grade, and during the summer between then and fifth, she voluntarily went to summer camp to learn Spanish. This was a girl who knew what she wanted, and T'Ann had no doubt in her mind that Brittney could inspire children with her story ... if she lived to tell it.

After three months of chemotherapy at home, Brittney's doctors changed her treatment from pill to liquid form and surgically inserted a Port-A-Cath, an implanted device used to administer the liquid chemo, in order to avoid invading her weakened veins. She went to the hospital monthly for treatment, and at home, T'Ann filled her IVs with fats and lipids and administered eight-hour drips once a day for the next six weeks so Brittney would gain some weight. During that time, she became more ill and fragile than she had ever been. Since her next round of chemo included twenty-four-hour drips followed by forty-eight-hour flushes, doctors admitted her back into the hospital.

She had more bad days than good, but when Brittney was feeling up to it, T'Ann would sneak a phone call to Andy and whisper, "Today's a good day."

He would show up a few hours later and cross the grassy courtyard area to a door leading right to Brittney's hallway. He'd walk at a swift, practiced pace while looking over his shoulder for anyone who might see him and wonder what he was hiding beneath the pile of jackets in his arms.

He'd walk quietly down the hallway and poke his head through the door of Brittney's room and present the jackets. She would sit up as much as she could and smile with big, waiting eyes until Casey made her appearance. Brown snout leading the way, their chocolate Labrador puppy would poke her head through the pile, spot Brittney and, with all four legs in gear, scramble frantically from the jackets to lick her face until it was wet.

"Hey, baby girl!" Brittney would say in the loudest whisper she could find. She giggled uncontrollably as Casey pounced across the bed, played under the covers, and licked her hands.

They were able to let Casey stay only a few hours at a time for fear that a nurse or doctor would catch her in there. Brittney became good at calming her down and hiding her at the right moments. She was thrilled every time Andy snuck her in, but those times became fewer as her good days dwindled.

As Brittney's treatment continued, her skin's girlish glow turned pasty, with charcoal rings forming around her big, brown eyes, bones straining against thin skin. Her body wasn't fighting back as it always had and she felt it giving up, shutting down. It took weeks to recuperate from her second-to-last round of chemo, and with one treatment left, the overwhelming gut feeling Brittney had learned to trust was telling her not to do it.

"Mom, will you ask Dr. Kadota if I can skip the last treatment and have my MRI early?" Brittney pleaded with a quiet voice. "I don't think I'll live through another round of chemo."

She took deep, hard breaths in between sentences and stared at her mother through hollow eyes.

Tears ran down her face when she added, "The tumor is gone, Mom. I can feel it."

Through her own tears, T'Ann nodded and whispered, "I'll ask him."

★ 7 ★

T'Ann prayed with all her soul that she had made the right decision, and when Dr. Kadota scheduled an early MRI and gave her the results, she knew she had.

"You did it," he said with a pleased grin in a tone that revealed as much surprise as excitement. "The tumor is gone."

"It's gone?" T'Ann cried. "Gone?" The word had an entirely different meaning than it ever had before.

She turned to Brittney and screamed, "It's gone!"

T'Ann fell to the floor beside her daughter and cried unabashedly.

Every fear, every worry, every ounce of desperation inside that had consumed her for the past sixteen months shed through those tears. Her daughter was free. And so was T'Ann. Together, they had won the battle.

T'Ann grabbed the handles of Brittney's wheelchair and hurried down the halls of the hospital wing, announcing to everyone that her daughter's cancer was gone. The sound of rejoice did not often fill those halls, but when it did, it was received with smiles, hugs, and tears of hope. Every victory was a reminder to the rest, to the parents poking their heads from their child's room to witness the patient's newfound freedom and happiness, to those whose lives were still fully consumed by cancer, that it could be beat. It made every parent and child in that hospital wing believe that their moment was next. They needed to believe because hope was all they had left, and watching Brittney that day filled them with that hope.

The greatest fear of someone living in remission is that the cancer will one day make its selfish return, but on this day, this very special day, it was gone.

The celebration did not end that day. Over the next couple of weeks, as Brittney regained some of her strength, she planned a "Celebrating Life" party to reunite with the friends and family she had stayed away from during her illness. From the beginning, she had found comfort in protecting them from the worst of her cancer. It somehow made her stronger to save them the heartache of seeing her that way.

Their absence gave her a reason to fight stronger, knowing she would see them when she was better. More than fifty guests—including friends from school, family from far away, and all those who had been by her side through the illness—came to the party to celebrate Brittney's life. And it was quite a celebration.

T'Ann's dad, "Papa Chuck," hosted the party at his home, which was flooded with flowers, food, streamers, balloons, guests, and gifts as Brittney arrived in a stretch limousine with seven of her closest friends, including Andrea. The nose of the long, white car plunged through a line of streamers T'Ann had hung across the driveway, and standing in the distance was a crowd of people that put an instant smile on Brittney's face and tears of joy in her eyes. It wasn't long ago she had questioned whether or not she would see some of these people ever again, and here they all were, waiting for her.

The girls jumped out of the car as people cheered and took turns hugging Brittney as tightly as they could without harming her. She weighed only seventy-nine pounds, and though fragile and pale, her eyes still twinkled with her unmistakable spirit.

As things started to settle, T'Ann cleared her throat, took a deep breath, and prayed she could get through the speech she had prepared for that afternoon. She took Brittney's hand for support, looked down at her bald little head and ear-to-ear smile and lost it before she even started. Through tears and sobs, T'Ann talked about Brittney's remarkable journey and managed to thank everyone who had helped during her illness—from her brother Troy and his wife, Michelle, for their endless toys and visits, to Patty for delighting Brittney with homemade beef jerky, to her younger brother Todd for bringing in an abundance of food from his restaurant.

She looked down to let her tears fall and looked up, peered through the crowd, and locked eyes with Andy.

"You are my knight in shining armor," she nearly whispered, then gasped for another breath as more tears poured from her eyes.

Standing before every person she cared about and loved, she closed her eyes and recalled the hundreds of hugs Andy had given, the thousands of tears he had wiped, the endless love he had shown to her and to Brittney, and his unfaltering strength.

T'Ann opened her eyes, smiled at Andy, and used Brittney's words to finish her speech. "Thank you for standing behind me and keeping me standing."

With that, there was not a dry eye at the party.

Later that evening, sitting in Brittney's bedroom, T'Ann held her daughter and pondered a thought that had been lingering in her mind for the past few weeks.

"You know, you could still have that wish if you wanted it," she said, sitting up.

"From the Make-A-Wish Foundation?" Brittney asked, and her mother smiled. "I thought that was just for kids who were dying."

"Well, I read the brochure that Dr. Kadota gave me, and it said it's for children with life-threatening illnesses," she explained.

"Let's do it!" Brittney said with excitement.

"Start thinking about the wish you'd like, and make sure it's a wish I wouldn't be able to give to you," T'Ann said.

They waited a few months to let Brittney regain even more strength before contacting the foundation, and during that time, it didn't take long for her to decide what she wanted. As excited as T'Ann was to hear her daughter's wish, Brittney made her wait until volunteers from the foundation came to visit.

"Why can't you just tell me?" T'Ann asked.

"I'll tell you when they get here," Brittney said, determined to keep her mom in suspense.

The volunteers came a few days later, and sitting on the couch in their living room, one of the volunteers said, "We're here to grant you any wish, so what will it be?"

She didn't even need to think about her response. Once Brittney had chosen her wish, she had spent hours and days dreaming about what it would be like to go there. In her mind, Tahiti was a place with no surgeries, no chemo, no pills, no doctors. It was a safe place far away from home where she could do anything she wanted without worrying that it might send her to the hospital. To her, it was heaven, and when she told the volunteers her wish, her brown eyes gleamed with anticipation.

"That sounds like a wonderful wish," they said happily, and they called a few days later with available dates in December and January.

Finally, Brittney heard the word *yes*. After months of pain and uncertainty, sickness and defeat, somebody gave her an answer she wanted and deserved to hear.

They were going on a ten-day trip to stay in a little bungalow on the beach of Moorea, Tahiti, and it would be just the two of them. T'Ann had her healthy little girl back, and at the end of their dark journey together, Tahiti was their light. And so was the Make-A-Wish Foundation, which was offering much more than just a free trip to a place in paradise. They were giving hope at the end of a young girl's worst nightmare. It was reassurance that she was indeed strong enough to board that plane and take the flight, and after being in remission for four months, Brittney knew she was ready.

She packed the perfect outfits to wear—twice as many as she needed, just in case—made sure her camera was ready to go, and literally counted the days until they left. T'Ann took her shopping for new swimsuits and clothes, and Brittney beamed when she popped repeatedly from behind her dressing room door, modeling one swimsuit after another for her mom and a group of excited sales ladies.

Brittney's bald head had given away the fact that she was a cancer survivor, but she proudly and excitedly told the women that she was in remission and was shopping for her upcoming Wish trip to Tahiti. They brought handfuls of suits for her to try on, and Brittney left the store with a few more than she needed.

When they got home, she pranced up and down the hallways wearing her new swimsuits, imagining her toes in the sand, playing in the blue waters of Tahiti.

Brittney spent all of her spare time at home researching Tahiti, figuring out how to squeeze everything in that she wanted to do while they were there. She daydreamed about swimming in the warm waters, riding horses on the beach, taking jeep tours, swimming with sharks and stingrays, riding in a helicopter, hiking, shopping, and at the top of her list, swimming with the dolphins.

Even during the sickest moments of Brittney's illness she would walk around the house in her swimsuit, just for the sake of wearing it, just to feel somewhat normal. Chemotherapy had forced her to stay out of the sun, but she refused to let it win. A lover of swimming and sunshine, Brittney did not succumb to the sadness she felt when she could no longer do those things. Instead, she remained hopeful that she would be able to frolic in the sun again one day. Wearing her swimsuit in the house had kept that hope alive.

The time finally arrived when she was well enough to wear it outside in the bright sunshine. Brittney counted down the days until they left for Tahiti, but she had one last thing left to do. Having never left the country, she needed a passport. Knowing the process could take months made her and T'Ann nervous as they headed down to their local city hall, where the paperwork would be sent off.

"I need to get my passport because I'm going to Tahiti!" she excitedly said to every person they passed in the hall. "It's my wish from the Make-A-Wish Foundation!"

By the time they found the correct office, there were people lining the room who were all rooting for her. "This girl needs a passport … put a rush order on it!" they heard from strangers standing behind them.

The woman guiding them through the paperwork smiled and sent them to Kinkos to get a passport photo taken. Brittney stood against a blank wall at Kinkos and smiled radiantly. T'Ann had never seen her so happy. When they handed the photo to Brittney, she held it up like a badge of honor. It was proof she was going to take the trip.

"You know, that's the picture you're stuck with until you're twenty-one," T'Ann teased, rubbing Brittney's bald head as they left the store. "You can't renew your passport for seven years."

"I'm keeping this passport forever," Brittney said, playfully pushing her mom's hand from her head before looking down at the picture. "It'll always remind me that I survived cancer."

She was ready to go.

* 8 *

During the ten days she spent with her mom in Tahiti, Brittney was a little weak but did everything on her list and more.

Her head was still bald, but she was beautiful and playful, and T'Ann felt so blessed to be there with her, watching her walk and laugh, eat and explore.

The day after they arrived, Brittney and T'Ann took an all-day Jeep tour that circled the island. Bumpy, dirt trails guided them to lagoons, through endless, plush, green trees, and past the most beautiful waterfalls they had ever seen. Their guide made frequent stops during the tour to share interesting island tidbits and to collect random items that he would later use to create a feast for Brittney, T'Ann, and the four other passengers on the tour.

"That's pretty cool," Brittney said to T'Ann as she watched him tear giant banana leaves from a nearby tree to use as tablecloths.

After lunch, they continued the tour and made several stops so everyone could absorb the sights and views along the way. When the Jeep stopped at the foot of a steep, rugged trail, the tour guide told the passengers that if they made the short hike to the top, they would experience the most beautiful view they had probably ever seen or would ever see again.

She can't make that hike, T'Ann thought, and when she looked over to Brittney to tell her that it was okay for them to just stay behind, Brittney was already halfway out of the Jeep.

"C'mon, Mom, let's go!" she said.

Hiding her doubts, T'Ann smiled and said, "All right, let's do it."

Holding hands, they made their way up the narrow, rocky trail that was bordered by a mountain on one side and a cliff on the other. They climbed slowly, and there was no more doubt in T'Ann's mind that they would make it. When Brittney set her mind on something, she did it.

Period.

No complaining, no doubting, no giving up.

When they reached the top, the view was indeed breathtaking. Endless bright ocean water with pockets of deeper blue swelled and peaked below. They stared in silence, hand in hand, each reading the other's thought: *We made it.*

T'Ann took a photo of Brittney at the top of the hill holding up a Make-A-Wish Foundation button.

That trail signified everything to T'Ann—Brittney's battle, her strong will, and most of all, her survival. It was a turning point in her life and the start of the most special trip they would ever share together.

A few days later, Brittney continued activities that would allow her to check off more items from her mental to-do list as she plunged from the back of a tour boat, a guide at her side, into water dark with sharks.

She jumps, I jump, T'Ann thought and sprung with sealed eyes and a scrunched face.

The tepid water beneath crawled with black, and T'Ann nervously floated while Brittney fearlessly swam around, poking her goggles through the surface to get a closer look at the sharks eating their lunches. Later in the trip, Brittney swam with stingrays twice her size.

Again, T'Ann bobbed in the water a few feet away while Brittney rode piggyback on the guide as he held handfuls of chum above his head, inviting the slimy rays to swim over the back of Brittney's shoulders for some nibbles. T'Ann watched in terrified awe, realizing that Brittney's fearlessness is what helped her beat cancer. T'Ann gave her the freedom she deserved on that trip because that's what Brittney finally was—free.

The rest of their trip was spent with morning swims in the pool, luaus on the beach, shopping, eating, and laughing, but the highlight of Brittney's trip, and probably of her life, was swimming with dolphins.

In a shallow ocean lagoon, she and T'Ann spent an hour playing with dolphins, kissing their long noses, pulling them backward by their fins, and feeding them treats. Brittney's smile never left. She laughed so hard that day that all the time she spent lying almost lifeless in hospitals, waiting for MRI results, and surviving treatments and surgeries, seemed forgotten. She pulled through everything, and it was her turn to live, her turn to play.

Brittney's Wish trip was finally complete, and when they got home, T'Ann knew their lives would be drastically different. Brittney would go to high school, chase after boys, and eventually head off to Harvard, the university of her dreams.

She would volunteer at children's hospitals, completing her goal of helping other kids who were going through what she had survived. To make sure she was still on the right track, Brittney went in for an MRI every other month to check that the tumor was still gone. Each time, the results came back clean, so her checkups changed to once every three months. After seven months, she went in for her routine MRI, crawled into the machine with the ease of an expert, and waited.

She was tense and her palms were sweaty and still. Deep down, she knew what the MRI would find but prayed she was wrong. She prayed that the strange feelings she had inside of her for the past few weeks were normal. As she lay there, T'Ann could see the doctor through a glass window monitoring the scan.

She stared as a doctor she didn't recognize entered the small room, hunched down next to the other doctor, and pointed curiously at the screen. When a third doctor entered, took a step back as he looked at the monitor, and exchanged concerned glances with the other two, T'Ann squeezed Brittney's hand gently, and she knew the answer.

The tumor was back. It had to be. Why else would they look so concerned?

"We'll have the results in a few days and we'll call you as soon as they come in," said one of the doctors to T'Ann. She stared into his eyes with patient fury and said, "C'mon, sweetie, let's go home."

Their walk to the car was silent until T'Ann could no longer hold back her tears. She cried and Brittney calmly took her hand.

"It's gonna be okay," she said, playing the role T'Ann knew she should be playing.

"I think it's back, Britt," she sobbed, and her daughter squeezed her hand.

"Mom, I'm sure everything will be fine," Brittney said, the words flowing from her mouth going completely against the grain of her gut.

9

Over the next few days, life continued as normal except for the thoughts that silently consumed them both.

Maybe the doctors thought they saw something that wasn't really there. Maybe it's because it was a new machine.

While her mother dwelled over these thoughts, Brittney comforted herself with similar "maybes."

Maybe I'm wrong and everything's fine. Maybe the strange feelings I've been having are nothing more than my imagination.

When T'Ann received a phone call at work a few days later, every *maybe* was proven wrong. The tumor was back, just as they both knew deep down that it was. T'Ann left immediately and sped home, tears dripping into her lap.

How am I ever going to tell Brittney? Why her? What did we do to deserve this?

Her thoughts turned to screams, and her fists pounded furiously into the steering wheel until she plowed into their driveway. She opened the front door of the house, looked at Brittney, and didn't even need to say a word.

"It's back, isn't it?" Brittney said, before bawling until she had no more tears left to cry.

"You know, baby, it's three inches this time, not eleven. We can beat it again," T'Ann said with her hands on Brittney's cheeks.

They were hoping that the doctors would be just as optimistic, and they were.

"I think I'll be able to get the rest of the tumor," Dr. Meltzer said when they met with him after hearing the MRI results from Dr. Kadota. "This surgery will be easier than the last, and I think I can get it all."

It may have been easier physically, but for Brittney, news of another surgery was her breaking point. She kept herself together during the days leading up to the surgery, but when the day came, she lost it. As Brittney and T'Ann followed Dr. Meltzer into a cold, bright pre-operating room, she broke down and begged her mom to take her home.

"Please, Mom, don't make me do this!" she cried hysterically, breaking her mom's heart. She grabbed T'Ann's hands with hers and pulled with all her strength. "I don't want another surgery! I want to go home!"

Her face was red with panic and her cheeks, stained with tears.

"I know, baby, but I can't take you home. You're so strong and this will save you," T'Ann managed between cries. And then she spoke words that she knew existed only because of her daughter's strength and undying optimism. "You're going to be just fine."

Channeling Brittney's voice, mirroring her fearless spirit, the words poured from T'Ann's mouth so smoothly, with such confidence. Somewhere buried deep inside of her were strength and hope she could not let go of. Brittney had made it this far, and she was going to survive this, too.

When hiccups separated her cries and her arms frantically grabbed at anything they could reach, a nurse quickly poked Brittney with a needle and within twenty minutes, she was out.

T'Ann's head pounded and her face hurt from crying, but her tears didn't stop for the next eight hours. When Dr. Meltzer walked into the waiting room after what seemed like days, T'Ann jumped from her chair and raced toward him, stopping inches from where he stood with a pleading look.

"Is she okay?" she asked quickly, hoping for an immediate answer.

"The surgery was a success," he said, then paused. "However, I wasn't able to get the whole thing. The tumor was so entwined that I could remove only half of it."

"So, what do we do next?" T'Ann demanded, knowing that the inch-and-a-half-long tumor left inside her daughter was still cancerous.

"You'll have to meet with Dr. Kadota. I can tell you, though, that Brittney's recovery will be much easier this time than last."

Brittney had already received the strongest amount of chemo and the highest dosage of radiation one person can withstand in a lifetime, so the way Dr. Kadota explained it was that they had two options.

"Take her home and give her the best life you can, or put her on an experimental medication that will not shrink the tumor but hinder its growth."

After finding out that side effects of the medication were very minimal, that Brittney wouldn't feel sick, and that she could live a normal life if it worked, she began taking it right away.

Follow-up MRI's showed that the tumor was indeed maintaining its size but not growing, and Brittney, once again, had her life ahead of her. She knew she would have to take the medicine forever, but the tumor was finally at bay.

At the age of sixteen, T'Ann knew that returning to school after more than three years would be tough for Brittney, but she had studied hard and stayed caught up with her classmates, and T'Ann knew she would be just fine. They had signed her up for the eleventh grade, and Brittney got her driver's license and a job working as a receptionist in a real estate office. Her hair was getting longer, and every checkup still showed that the tumor had not grown. A year of normal life passed before the day Brittney told T'Ann that her arm felt funny.

Felt funny.

What does that mean? was T'Ann's only thought before calling Dr. Kadota to schedule an appointment.

"We can't get you in until … "

"You'll get me in today," T'Ann said, and the receptionist knew she was bringing her daughter in, appointment or not, so she found a time slot to squeeze them in.

"We'll need to do an MRI to see what's going on, so why don't you come back in two days," Dr. Kadota said.

Knowing there were no answers he could give until he had the results, T'Ann and Brittney waited two days, came back for the MRI, and waited another couple of days for the answer.

⋆ 10 ⋆

"Oh, God, no!" T'Ann screamed in her head after hanging up the phone call with Dr. Kadota a couple of days later. The tumor had grown and was continuing at a rapid rate. T'Ann's heart raced and ideas thundered through her mind. *If I don't find somebody to help my little girl, she's going to die.*

Until that point, there was always something else to try. Always a plan B. But the experimental medication was their last hope, and T'Ann was desperate.

"Let's do surgery again and cut it out," she pleaded with Dr. Kadota.

"We can't do that," he responded, looking scared and hopeless. "We would run into too much scar tissue. In addition to that, the tumor is too close to the brain stem. I've already spoken to Dr. Meltzer and he agrees. The tumor is inoperable."

He told her, in so many words, that her options were watching her daughter slowly turn into a vegetable or die a painful death. Neither was acceptable, so T'Ann made an appointment with Dr. Meltzer to hear the words from him.

"I'm sorry, T'Ann," he said. "If I do surgery to remove the tumor, I'm taking it all out."

He knew as well as she did that doing so would either kill or paralyze Brittney, and T'Ann was not going to let either happen. If it was time for her daughter to go, she would be as comfortable and safe as possible until her last breath.

"The only other option is to put her on another experimental drug, but Brittney has been on the most powerful drug possible for her tumor, and in my opinion, nothing else will work," he said with a kind but matter-of-fact tone. "The risk is not knowing the side effects of other drugs, and they could make her even more ill than she already is."

T'Ann couldn't stand to hear another word. He was offering nothing, and her mind was frantically racing. She felt dizzy and weak but determined, so she grabbed the MRI results, plunged through the front door of his office, and rushed them to another neurosurgeon at the Children's Hospital of Orange County (CHOC) for a second opinion. She met with a doctor who said four beautiful words.

"I can get it," he said. "I can save your daughter's life."

Thinking she would be fine until he returned, the doctor went on a ten-day vacation he'd had planned for months, and T'Ann took Brittney home. The doctor never imagined how rapidly her health would deteriorate in the short time that he was gone—within days, Brittney lost all feeling in her arms and legs until they were so weak they could no longer carry her—and by the time he returned, it was too late to help her. She had quickly become too weak, too sick, for medicines, for surgeries, for anything else.

T'Ann's extended family was on vacation and Andy was in Phoenix on business, so it was just the two of them. In desperation, they anxiously searched for any other option that would save Brittney's life. The only doctor who had any confidence of her survival was gone, and the other doctors they had seen said the same thing. There was nothing left to do.

Andy's brother, Donnie, lived in Massachusetts and suggested they contact the Dana-Farber Cancer Institute in Boston. With nothing to lose, Andy made a phone call that resulted in a round-table discussion with some of Boston's top doctors.

They reviewed Brittney's MRIs, analyzed her situation, and, in agreement with the doctors in San Diego, determined there was nothing they could do to save her. The only thing left for T'Ann to do was make sure that the rest of Brittney's life was the best it could be. They played endless games, swam in the pool on "good days", snuggled on the couch, and watched movies. Every second was spent together, and Brittney was in T'Ann's arms every possible moment.

———— ✦

One afternoon, they sat on the couch together and watched *Gilmore Girls*, a show they had grown to love as the mother-daughter relationship in the show reminded them of their own. With her head on T'Ann's lap, Brittney suddenly jolted forward and threw up before gasping for another breath of air.

Her body slowly jerked and twitched before T'Ann jumped from the couch, panicked eyes searching frantically for the phone, and dialed 911. She held her baby girl's hands in the back of the ambulance and let millions of tears drip from her face to her daughter's.

This can't be it, T'Ann thought. *Not now. Not today.*

The gurney holding Brittney shook with every turn of the ambulance, and T'Ann stared at her precious girl—the last person in the world who deserved any of this. It was a year ago that her daughter was in remission, splashing in the ocean waves of Tahiti, enjoying a vacation that had become a turning point in her life.

It seemed like only yesterday that Brittney had popped her tiny body from behind the big door of a department store dressing room and, with a giant grin, modeled a bright bathing suit.

Brittney was supposed to be safe now, and free. But she was neither.

God, not now! T'Ann wanted to scream to the sky.

Instead, she pressed her cheek against Brittney's and whispered that everything would be okay. It had to be. T'Ann didn't know how to say good-bye. She would never know how and she would never be ready. She just knew it couldn't be today.

The paramedics tore through the doors of the emergency room and sent Brittney to the doctors T'Ann prayed would have the answers. And they did.

"Take her home," said a neurosurgeon who worked as Dr. Meltzer's partner. That wasn't the right answer. "She stopped breathing because the tumor is growing at such a rapid rate, and her blood oxygen level is low as well."

Andy, who had just flown in to San Diego from his business trip, stood by T'Ann's side as she weakly covered her mouth with a trembling hand and muttered the words, "Okay, I'll take her home."

That was it. It was time to say good-bye.

"No," Andy nearly shouted. "I'm not taking this girl home tonight."

Through reddened, puffy eyes, T'Ann looked up at him. She was weaker than she had ever been in her life, and Andy was staying strong for them both.

"Get us an ambulance," he demanded. "We're taking her back to Orange County."

An ambulance transported Brittney to CHOC, though T'Ann and Andy knew that the doctor was still on vacation. His assistant, who had never met Brittney, sadly delivered the news.

"I've been doing this for more than twenty-five years, and surgery alone is not an option," he said. "If she survived surgery, she would need two bone marrow transplants afterward and chemotherapy."

"I can't do it, Mom," Brittney said weakly. Her voice was so small, so defeated. "If it was just surgery and there was a guarantee I would make it, I would do it. I'm just so tired, and I want this all to be over. I can't go through chemo again."

Tears welled up in her eyes. "I don't want to be sick anymore, Mom. I just want to go home."

Brittney had made her decision, and in the deepest part of T'Ann's soul, she knew it was the right one. Brittney chose to live out the last days of her life quietly and peacefully at home, and before T'Ann could tell the doctor their decision, he confirmed it after a long, deep breath.

"I have four daughters, and if I were in your shoes, I would take Brittney home and make her as comfortable as possible for the rest of the time you have with her."

Empty and dead inside, T'Ann sat beside Andy in the chilly hospital room and felt like throwing up. The pain was suffocating, nearly intolerable, and her body shook uncontrollably. She stared down at Brittney. Resting by her side were small, gray hands that couldn't possibly belong to a teenager. Brittney's chest slowly crawled up and down, and with a tilted head and mature eyes, she looked at Andy.

"Can I see Mom alone for a minute?" she asked, and Andy smiled, squeezed her little hand, and gently closed the door behind him.

"I've asked everyone in the family to make a promise to keep after I'm gone," Brittney said weakly.

She was still so strong. At sixteen, she could say the words *after I'm gone* without one tear, without one hint of anger or bit of curiosity as to why she had to die at such a young age.

Just a few days before, she asked Charlie for his promise.

"I'll be okay," she had reassured him. "I'm going to Heaven to stay with mama and papa."

Tears drowned Charlie's eyes, and he squeezed her hand gently.

"Promise me you won't worry about me," she added. "You have to keep going. Don't let this stop you or bring you down."

Charlie didn't know how he would keep that promise, but he knew he had to. He smiled slightly, nodded, and let the tears fall.

T'Ann stared down at Brittney with the same love and courage Charlie had shown.

"I'll make whatever promise you ask of me, sweetie," she said.

"You have to promise not to do anything stupid after I'm gone," Brittney said bluntly, and T'Ann knew exactly what she meant.

"Don't make me promise that," she said through sobs, knowing that the moment Brittney's life ended, she would want hers to end, too. "I don't know if I can keep it."

"I'm not going anywhere until you promise," she said.

"Okay, then, I *don't* promise," T'Ann said, poking her daughter's hand playfully. "There, now you can't go anywhere."

"C'mon, Mom," Brittney said, tears streaming down her face. "I need to know you're going to be okay."

"Okay," T'Ann whispered. "I promise."

Brittney cried that evening more than T'Ann had seen her cry in her life. Internally, she was dealing with something T'Ann had never had to face, and she saw in her daughter's eyes that she was terrified.

"I don't know if I can let go," Brittney whispered.

The most intense pains T'Ann had ever felt pulled at her heart, and all she could do was weep. There was nothing she could do to save her daughter's life, and an overwhelming feeling of desperation and helplessness took over her body as tears poured in streams from her eyes.

"I'm so sorry, baby," T'Ann cried in Brittney's ear as she held her to her chest. "I love you *so* much. More than life itself." The next five words flowed naturally from her lips, and she meant them with all of her heart.

"It's okay to let go."

They held each other for minutes that seemed like hours. It was the only place either of them wanted to be. Andy came back into the room and they waited for a miracle.

* 11 *

What came instead was a tap on the door. A young man who introduced himself as a pathology intern entered and closed the door gently before sitting down in a chair across from them.

"I've been up all night and something doesn't make sense here," he said. "I think your daughter is having an allergic reaction to Dapsone, which I understand she's been taking for three years now?"

"Yes, that's correct," T'Ann said with wide eyes, hoping he knew something the rest of the doctors didn't.

"I don't think the tumor is the reason her breathing is so abnormal," he said. "I think it's from a reaction she's having to her medication. Would it be okay if I gave her an antidote?"

Without hesitation, T'Ann gave him her blessing. The head nurse had asked them earlier that day to start letting family members know that Brittney wouldn't make it through the night, and here was this young intern, offering them something other than taking her home to die.

In T'Ann's eyes, they had absolutely nothing to lose. Brittney, who lay, cold and gray, on her hospital bed next to T'Ann and Andy, remained still as he poured what looked like blue ink into her IV, and within minutes, her face lost its pasty tint and her cheeks turned bright pink. She looked alive again, and for the next two weeks, she was. T'Ann and Andy brought her home and waited.

There was nothing more they could do. Hospice had set up a hospital bed in T'Ann's living room and had given them all the meds they would need to keep Brittney comfortable and, most importantly, free of pain.

T'Ann pushed her slowly through the front door of their house, carefully picked Brittney up from the wheelchair, and placed her on the bed where she would spend the rest of her days. She was paralyzed from the neck down but had full use of her mouth for talking and eating when T'Ann fed her. They took naps together, watched movies, and exchanged more than a million *I love yous*.

T'Ann's, Andy's, and Charlie's entire families came every day to visit Brittney, and when she was awake, they were by her side.

A morphine patch on Brittney's arm kept most of the pain at bay, but when it crept back with unbearable intensity, T'Ann dotted liquid morphine onto her gums, numbing it instantly.

"This is the first time in three years that I don't hurt," Brittney said to T'Ann one evening.

Her words broke any part of T'Ann's heart that wasn't already in pieces.

"I love you *so* much, Britt, and I'm *so* sorry I couldn't make you better," T'Ann said through thick tears. "I would trade places with you in a heartbeat if I could."

Brittney smiled up and whispered, "It's not your fault, Mom. You did *everything* you could. Please just remember the promise you made to me."

She must have known her time was soon. A few nights later, on a Sunday evening, Brittney slipped into a coma that let her heart beat but shut everything else down. Aside from the rise and fall of her chest, her baby girl was gone. Candlelight danced on her beautiful face and T'Ann sat with Charlie in the quiet of the room, waiting.

He had been sleeping on the floor beside Brittney's bed for the past two weeks, and he sat up that night and said quietly, "This is it. She's going."

"Her heart is still beating," T'Ann managed, and Charlie sobbed. *God, if you're going to take her, take her on a Sunday,* she prayed.

And He did. At 11:05 p.m., Brittney took her last breath in T'Ann's arms. Before she cried until her chest bruised, before her sobs announced that Brittney was gone, before anything else, T'Ann was calm.

Defeated.

She looked up through her tears and whispered, "Good-bye, baby. I love you."

Author's note: The process of sharing Brittney's story for the purpose of this book was both painful and healing for T'Ann, but she did it to fulfill the dream her daughter had of helping other children by sharing her story with the world.

A Poem—a Message—to Kids Battling Cancer

by Brittney Wolfe

I think I could help children with the same disease as me,
With tips to make their hospital stay the best that it can be.
This disease can make your life perspective start to change and sway,
But once you have gone through it, not a thing stands in your way.
Nurses will try real hard to keep you happy and content,
When all you need is silence, not another chance to vent.
Doctors act as robots; they find it hard to understand,
What it is that we are going through; they just lend their helping hand.
They tell you things at times that you'd never want to hear,

Which is why it is important to always have your family near.
And when you're bored and antsy, with nothing much to do,
Have your parents bring some movies and CDs from home to you.
Bring your best stuffed animals and blankets from your past,
They'll make you think of family and friendships that will last.
Bring pictures of your friends and your favorite family pet,
Make phone calls to your loved ones every second that you get.
Have your cat or dog come see you, if you think it'd make you smile,
And if the nurse refuses, sneak them in for just a while.
I will talk to kids with cancer because I know I'll help them through,
I'll broaden their horizons and give them strength to hold on to.
It helped for me to know that others had beaten it before,
I stayed positive, courageous, and grew strong forevermore.
After having this bad illness, you will start to understand,
Life and death and boundaries as they rest in God's good hand.

Garrett Stuart

"There are only two ways to live your life.
One is as though nothing is a miracle. The
other is as though everything is a miracle."

—Albert Einstein
(Garrett's philosophy on life)

* 1 *

"**S**OM ORKUN OSH *pi doung jet*," said Suem Pahn, and Dine Tuy translated, "Thank you from my heart."

Garrett glanced across the circle to study Tuy Dien's reaction to Suem's words, his expression, his pain, as Suem shared the story of how she lost her legs after stepping on a landmine in a rice field twenty-two years before. The explosion had sent people from her village looking for her, and she told the story of their rescue and her journey to a hospital in Siem Reap, Cambodia.

"*Pel knom tov pateah ving. Kanom arch tov leng psa ning pateah mit peak. Ka nom mint dek jum pateah teat tey*," said Suem. "When I go back home, I can go to the market or go to see a friend. I do not have to stay in the house," Dine translated.

Tuy, who had removed his sunglasses before joining the circle of others who had lost their legs, sat intently, squinting as though the hot, Cambodian sun was inches from his face. Garrett glanced at Tuy's legs, gone from the knee down, and wondered if every painful wince was a reflection of his own misery—their lives, too familiar; their stories, too sad.

Next in the circle, twenty-year-old Saktourn repeated through tears, "*Orkun, orkun*"—"Thank you, thank you"—after sharing the story of how she was born with only one leg to a family of nine children. Her dream of finishing sewing school and making clothes for a living was becoming a reality.

As tears streamed down her face, Tuy squinted and closed his eyes.

• 135 •

Jo Joan, next in the circle, shared the story of how her leg was amputated after falling from her home, lifted by stilts, when she was a baby. Garrett watched as Tuy looked down, then up again with pained squints.

What's wrong with his eyes? Garrett thought, and then Tuy shared his story.

"*Ka nom taleb jeer jon pikar jeer yoo mok hay,*" he began, and Dine translated, "I have been disabled for a very long time."

Twenty-one years earlier, he stepped on a landmine while collecting wood from the jungle. Before finishing the story of how he rode twenty miles in the back of an oxcart to the nearest hospital, where both of his legs were amputated, he stopped talking and looked deep into the eyes of everyone in the circle around him.

"*Ka nom arch pik van ta ban tey?*—"Can I please put my sunglasses back on?" he asked. "*Komdov preah ar tid tver oy panek kanom chhur*"—"The sun is hurting my eyes."

Why did he wait so long to put them on? Garrett wondered.

It had been forty-five minutes.

Tuy carefully placed the glasses on his face, and as he finished his story, Garrett looked long and slow around the circle, where ten people from the city of Siem Reap surrounded him. Their silence, their devotion to one another's stories, came from a place of great respect, deep understanding. Garrett finally understood why Tuy had listened and blinked with such agony for so long. He wanted no distraction, no barrier between himself and the others, nothing to come between their stories and his undivided attention.

Tuy ended his story with, "*Hay pel nih kor jeer lerk ti moy dell ka nom mean kov ey pika. Ey lov ka nom mint rong jum neak joy krea ka nom tey.*" Dine translated, "This is the first time I will have a wheelchair. Now I don't have to wait for someone to carry me." Now Garrett finally understood how his charity and the work he had done would impact these people's lives.

With his parents and a small crew from Globe Aware, a non-profit that organizes service projects around the world, Garrett had spent one afternoon, a few simple hours in the sun, building wheelchairs from lawn chairs and bicycle wheels, changing the lives of those surrounding him.

Thanks to these efforts, Tuy, Suem, Saktourn, Jo Joan, and six others—including a twelve-year-old girl whose circulation problems left her unable to walk to school and a fifty-seven-year-old father of four who lost his legs to a landmine explosion while collecting firewood—were given the gift of mobility, of freedom, of independence.

Garrett had once viewed his inability to walk as a life sentence, the wheelchair, his prison, secluding him from his world of traveling, rock climbing, bike riding, camping, basketball, and soccer.

As he sat in that quiet hut, words of stories circling his mind—"I can go anywhere, do anything ..."; "I don't have to wait for someone to carry me"— Garrett realized that while these people had spent most of their lives trapped in their homes, within the walls of their villages, his prison had wheels—invisible bars, freedom.

*   2   *

All that was beneath me
Was ten feet of air
Before I knew it
I hit the ground
Crying
With my elbow beneath me
Not being able to move anything
A muscle
A bone
Nothing
—Garrett Stuart, second grade

Voices of children bounced between the sky-high walls of Vertical Dreams, where little hands grabbed and reached, little feet gripped the rock-climbing holds. Eight-year-old Garrett was among them. His arms were toned from sports, his mind was strong as he pictured himself climbing in Costa Rica, rappelling in Utah's Zion National Park—places his parents, Mike and Linda, spoke of often. These thoughts drove his small body to inch forward, one good hold after another, up toward the top of the steep, ten-foot-tall wall to which he clung.

The echoed sounds of kids shouting, parents cheering, were mute in Garrett's mind as his body, shaky with determination, reached higher, grabbed tighter to every colorful hold as he approached an archway near the top of the gym.

He looked to the ground, looked at his leading hand, looked to the top of the archway, less than an arm's length out of reach. He would dyno—jump to the next hold—as he had done a million times before. If he missed, the mattress-lined ground would cushion his fall.

Garrett pushed off from his hold, up the wall. His body flung itself forward, and his fingers gripped the next hold briefly before sliding off as his body joined gravity, the rushing ground, his thoughts slipping away. He hit as fast as he had fallen, his body cushioned, his elbow cracking on the hard ground between mattresses. Pain bolted through his arm, filling his mind and his lungs with screams his parents heard from the tops of boulders they were climbing around the corner.

Mike and Linda leaped down, boulder after boulder, with the skill and precision of professionals, mountain lions, to find their son screaming at the base of the wall, the floor of the gym. Linda scooped him into her arms, and they rushed him to the hospital where doctors reset and cast Garrett's arm.

As nurses inserted an IV, Mike made a face and said, "I think I can see your blood oozing out!"

Garrett looked at his father, the person who had teased, "Get up, walk it off," when they found Garrett on the ground of the gym, crying. He was the one who always said, "Shake it off, you're fine," whenever Garrett fell off his bike, a small smile silently echoing his jovial, can-do spirit.

Garrett, who admired his father, appreciated his wit, found no humor in jokes about blood or IVs. Face white, heart pounding at the mere thought of the word *oozing*, Garrett's eyes fell from his father's as his head jolted toward the ground, his body heaving. Mike stared as his son threw up his lunch and his worries all over the hospital floor.

No more jokes, Mike told himself before doctors placed a cast on Garrett's right arm.

Garrett returned to second grade just a few days later, and six weeks after that, once the cast was removed, he went back to playing basketball, soccer, and T-ball and continued hiking and rock climbing.

On rainy, New Hampshire days, when playing football in the street with his best friend, Travis, wasn't possible, when the rain forced him to stop games of hide-and-seek with the neighborhood kids, abandon the forts he was building, or quit games of tag and basketball, Garrett would invite friends over for games of Yahtzee or ones he made up on the spot.

"Okay, roll the die!" Garrett would shout as he and Travis took turns rolling the die, collecting Monopoly money for every roll. Roll a six, collect $6. Roll a two, collect $2. Garrett's mind, a calculator, quickly added numbers in his head. They became richer faster with the help of six dice, where they could collect as much as $36 at a time. They played Garrett's made-up game for hours, collecting thousands.

He was practicing for the day he would count his millions.

"Did your big check come today?" Linda would ask nearly every day from the time Garrett was three years old.

"Nope, not today," he'd say, closing the door of the mailbox. Never disappointed, he remained hopeful that one day $1 million would appear.

"Check again tomorrow," Linda would say, quietly laughing to herself as she wondered where her son got the idea that someone, someday, would be sending a check in the mail for $1 million.

Garrett was good with numbers, great with math, which, in addition to science, was his favorite subject in school. He was meticulous, careful, and logical about his math homework, and he knew that one day, when he grew up, these skills would come in handy as the owner of a business that would make him a millionaire.

One day, as he hovered over his homework, adding and subtracting on paper with perfect lines, Linda watched over his shoulder and studied the way he wrote his numbers, the pencil sitting strangely in his hand. Elbow directly in front of him, forearm straight, Garret's hand curved slightly outward at the wrist, fingers wrapped clumsily around the pencil.

Over the next couple of months, Garrett's struggle became more pronounced, and Linda and Mike decided that his crooked arm, the way it progressively curled away from his body, must have resulted from breaking his arm.

"Some people just aren't that flexible," an occupational therapist told Mike and Linda after working with Garrett for a year to correct the twist of his wrist. Exercises intended to strengthen the muscles and retrain his arm and wrist didn't seem to be working, and that was the explanation they received.

Remaining hopeful that therapy would eventually work, Linda and Mike, who had received no instruction from doctors to stop their active lifestyle, continued their outdoor adventures of camping, hiking, and climbing with Garrett. Since his arm was still healing, they chose shorter mountains to hike, smaller boulders to climb.

* 3 *

In June, the summer between Garrett's third- and fourth-grade school years, Linda, Mike, Garrett, and his best friend, Travis, ventured along New Hampshire's Kancamagus Scenic Byway and the Sawyer River below and parked at a trailhead leading to a campsite along the river.

Black, distant clouds threatened patchy blue skies overhead, but, as adventure seekers, they loaded their gear, strapped on their packs, and headed down the narrow, dusty trail. Garrett, usually so far ahead that nobody could keep up, slowed the group's pace.

"C'mon, Bilbo," Linda said. "You've gotta keep up with Frodo and the rest of us. Do you need some GORP (good ol' raisins and grapes) or a Starburst for energy?"

Garrett shook his head, looked to the ground, smiled at his mom's attempt to bring lands of Middle-earth, the fictional setting of his favorite book, *The Hobbit,* to life. It was a hiking ritual, a longtime family tradition, to lace imagination with reality.

"I'm so tired," Garrett said, trailing.

Linda darted past a tree.

"Stay away from these trees, Bilbo!" she hollered playfully, continuing the fantasy. "They'll come alive and eat you!"

"We're going too fast," he said.

"Stay away from those berries!" Linda yelled, pointing into the distance, to the leaves of nearby plants, bundles of invisible red berries. "They're poisonous!"

"Mom, I'm serious," Garrett said. "We need to slow down. This pack is too heavy."

This was the kid who, at the age of seven, less than a year before, plunged through knee-high rivers snaking through The Narrows in Zion and hiked Walter's Wiggles, famous for its twenty-one treacherous switchbacks as tired, breathless grown-ups turned back.

He had conquered miles and miles of trails in Moab, Utah, the sweat of 100°F dripping down his back, as he pedaled, his bike stuck in first gear, like crazy, going nowhere—and he did it all with a smile.

As a family, they had hiked all throughout New England—to Arethusa Falls and Frankenstein Cliffs, through Jewell Trail, Old Bridle Path, and the Falling Waters Trail of the White Mountains—and climbed more than 4,000 feet up Mount Lincoln, Mount Washington, and Mount Jefferson.

"Expect pain, endure pain, and don't complain," became the Stuart family motto when Garrett saw and memorized this quote printed on the T-shirt of a stranger during one of their trips. The bigger the challenge, the better.

Linda lifted the gear from her son's back and divided its contents between herself, Mike, and Travis. As they continued walking slowly along the river, raindrops, falling slowly at first, then harder and faster, plopped into the cool water of the Sawyer as it flowed neatly over smooth, giant rocks. Wind tickled the leaves of towering maples, pines, and oaks as sheets of rain fell through their branches.

Mike and Linda stopped to take a picture, their clothes dry beneath protective rain gear, before continuing to the campsite to set up in the rain. Dusk was starting to settle, with the faint glow of lingering sunlight tucked behind dark clouds. Scents of wet soil rose from the ground along with the smell of rain-soaked leaves and dampened earth. The storm had sent everyone to their tents, turning the campground into a wilderness ghost town. Far-off voices and laughter were muffled by rain, and the smoky smell of camping was faint, almost invisible. But it was there.

Where is that coming from? Linda wondered quietly. *How did anyone light a campfire in this rain?*

She peeked from her tent and saw, in the dark distance, flames of red and orange. She trekked through rain to the campsite with roaring fire and asked how fire in rain was possible.

"Birch bark," the camper said, and when Linda told Garrett and Travis about the special wood that makes flames in spite of water, they were off.

In kindergarten, Garrett wore a cowboy hat and boots every day because, in his imagination, everywhere he went was the Wild West. He eventually traded his cowboy hat for coonskin and spent hours in his backyard pretending to be Davy Crockett. On his sixth birthday, Linda took yellow paint to a handful of rocks and buried them in the yard, where Garrett spent months digging for "gold." Searching for fallen Birch bark with Travis was yet another adventure.

Having camped all over New Hampshire with his parents, Garrett could build a campfire with his eyes closed. Using the Birch bark as paper, he placed it into the middle of a perfect tepee of sticks and watched excited flames dance into the night, reaching for black sky.

Linda boiled water, stirred noodles, and mixed meat with sauce for their first night's dinner. As she drained water from the noodles, she lost her grip on the strainer and a pile of hot, wet spaghetti landed in a clump on the muddy ground. She stared at it, head cocked to the side in disbelief, before letting out a belly laugh that made the others gather around.

As a group, they stared, hungry and tired, at the fallen spaghetti. With deep laughter and carefree shrugs, they dug in, sorting through noodles untouched by dirt. As they ate dinner around the campfire, Linda's mind trailed with the flames, thoughts hanging in the air like smoke.

Beneath the stars, sorting through and putting pieces of their lives from the last year together in her mind, Linda began to realize that something was wrong with her son. She suddenly became very aware that the curl of his wrist had nothing to do with the fall. That the funny way he had walked sometimes—with a little bounce, a slight swag—wasn't his way of trying to be cool or silly around his friends. After watching Garrett struggle down the short, flat trail to the campsite earlier that day, she knew in her gut that something wasn't right.

When they returned home, she immediately took Garrett to his pediatrician, who referred them to an orthopedic doctor. Throughout his fourth-grade year, Mike and Linda continued taking Garrett to different specialists, children's hospitals, neurologists, and out-of-town pediatricians, looking for answers to the increasing contortions of their son's body.

One doctor prescribed Ritalin to help with symptoms—body movements, impulsivity—similar to Attention Deficit Disorder (ADD), while another recommended deep muscle massage, which he tried for four painful months. They heard, "This is so strange" from one doctor and "I've never seen this before" from another.

After seeing more than a handful of doctors, one told Garrett that he was pushing his body too hard with physical activity, while another had the nerve to insist he was making it all up, suggesting he visit a psychologist.

"He's too coordinated," the doctor said after conducting a series of standard tests—taps on the knees to check reflexes, challenges to hold his hands in place without moving—tests that Garrett had been through a dozen times.

Making it up? Linda asked herself.

After twelve different doctors—twelve misdiagnoses—and no explanation for the increasingly strange movements of her son's body, she let herself entertain the doctor's diagnosis. *What if Garrett was making it up?*

She let her mind dip into a dark place—*Did something traumatize him that I am unaware of? Was he hurt at some point in his life and I didn't protect him? Was there some behavioral reason Garrett was making everything up, craving some sort of attention?*

Deep down, she knew her son—knew he wouldn't make something like this up. But even deeper down, in the quiet of her soul, she questioned it, questioned why twelve different doctors had not been able to give them a diagnosis.

∗ 4 ∗

Linda, left with her own thoughts, tormented by that doctor's words, watched as Garrett continued his life, despite his challenges. He remained hopeful and joined Vertical Dream's rock climbing team, practicing three times a week, and asked his parents to build a rock climbing wall in their garage. They worked as a family all summer, drilling thousands of holes into plywood, placing endless climbing routes along the walls and ceiling.

Garrett spent hours on that wall, climbing, rappelling, and climbing again. He pushed himself, stretching from hold to hold, perfecting challenging angles, practicing perfect form. He gained strength with repetition, stability by climbing with a hacky sack balanced on his head—an exercise learned from competing on the climbing team—and confidence to maneuver holds, quickly and efficiently, by playing games of tag on the wall with his friends.

Toward the end of fourth grade, Garrett competed in divisionals, hoping for a place in nationals. Climbers from all over New England gathered for the divisional competition with hopes of qualifying for nationals, and Garrett, competing against other kids his age, reached for the wall.

Mike and Linda watched from below as their son climbed with the technique of a professional, the devotion of an athlete. He stretched great distances to reach holds marked with colored tape of the courses he was following, gripped tightly to the most difficult holds—smooth and rounded "slopers"—and reached the tops of every course without falling. As he climbed, dedication dripping down the sides of his face, Linda wanted to scream, "Reach to the left! Twist to the right!"

They could see from below the exact route he should have been taking, the holds he should have been grabbing, the perfect placements for his feet. With every pause, every hesitation, Linda wanted to holler guidance, shout direction. Instead, she watched. She knew what Garrett wanted to do, knew that his body would not listen.

Mike also knew in that moment that his son was not the same climber he had always been, and that he may never be again. It was obvious that Garrett's nimble mind, for some unknown reason, no longer belonged to the same body—this was no longer the body of an athlete, of a competitive climber.

He's done, Mike thought.

Garrett qualified for nationals that day, but while his family and friends rejoiced, he knew deep down, in the depths of his intuition, that competing was not going to be an option. He knew that, while on the wall, his mind had told his body to twist left, and it remained. He had told it to turn to the right, to reach for the next hold, and it did not listen. The twist that had started in his wrist, the involuntary way it turned away from his body, was just the start. He knew his body. He knew the way it should move, the way it should obey. And it no longer did.

In the midst of celebrating his feat, his placement in nationals, there was something unspoken between Garrett and his parents. They all knew that competing was not going to be an option.

That summer, an orthopedic doctor from Boston's Children's Hospital confirmed their concern and, in addition to advising Garrett not to compete, placed him on crutches.

"We need to keep him off his legs," the doctor said.

There was still no diagnosis, no explanation for the way Garrett's body was becoming a stranger to him. The way it moved, the small spasms in his back, the jutting of his legs, and the funny way he sometimes walked remained mysteries.

The Stuarts had always defined themselves as a traveling family, an outdoorsy family, an adventurous family. Garrett was only ten years old and had already traveled to more places than most adults would see in a lifetime. He had canoed and eaten termites in Costa Rica and held koala bears and tasted green ants in Australia. From the time he was a toddler, they had traveled together, camped, hiked, rock climbed, mountain biked, and skied.

It was time to reinvent themselves. Linda cheerfully bought games and set them up every evening. They couldn't play outdoors, so their adventures would continue indoors. They played Yahtzee, canasta, and backgammon. They made popcorn and cookies, signed up for Netflix, and watched endless movies. Garrett, lost in his mother's redefined world, her optimism, escaped to other worlds through books. He joined the adventures of Alex Rider, a fourteen-year-old spy in a series of books by Anthony Horowitz, and followed teenage criminal mastermind Artemis Fowl in a series of science fiction by Eoin Colfer.

On the outside, Garrett maintained a smile and looked untouched by the reality of his situation: not being able to play sports in the street with his friends, ride his bike, live the life of a kid.

On the inside, he was lost. Confused. Anxiously awaiting the day for a diagnosis, a reason for his body's rejection of his mind's instruction.

By the end of the summer—three months of fumbling through the house, through life, on crutches—Garrett's condition worsened. Barely able to walk, Mike and Linda took him to see his primary doctor, Dr. Roger Wicksman, for yet another referral to another specialist. As Garrett lay on the long, cushioned table, Dr. Wicksman's hands digging deeply into his muscles, Garrett grabbed at its sides, tearing strips of thin, white paper lining the table.

As Dr. Wicksman massaged his legs and hips, hoping to loosen and separate the muscles, Garrett ripped big pieces of the paper into smaller pieces, smaller and smaller, until little piles of white formed on each side of the table. This massage, called Rolfing, took place at every appointment and was a painful technique Dr. Wicksman thought would slow the progress and intensity of Garrett's condition—whatever it was.

"Okay, we'll see you in a few weeks," Dr. Wicksman said when he was finished. As the doctor left the room, Mike, Linda, and Garrett stood, and as Mike followed Linda out the door, they turned to see Garrett standing in place near the table.

"C'mon, sweetie, let's go," Linda said.

"Mom, I can't," Garrett said. "I can't move my legs."

He stood as still as an old tree, its roots deep in the ground.

"What do you mean you can't walk?" Mike asked, stepping

toward his son. He placed Garrett's arm around his shoulder for support as Linda held onto the other side of him.

"My legs won't move," Garrett said, panic creeping to the edge of his mind, pushed back by his parents' encouragement.

"You're okay," Linda said calmly. "I'm just gonna go get Dr. Wicksman."

She returned with the doctor, who took one good look at Garrett and said, "He's fine. Looks like he'll just need to use a walker for a short period of time until his body recovers from the intensity of the Rolfing session."

He's fine, Linda thought, mocking the doctor's words. *What do you mean, 'He's fine'? He can't move his body!*

With an arm draped over her shoulder, the other around Mike, Garrett's weight was too much for Linda. She slowly ducked beneath, letting his arm fall, the burden becoming Mike's. She took one last look through tears before leaving the room. Hunched and frail like an old man, her ten-year-old son's feet scratched along the doctor's office floor, barely moving, as Mike guided him across the room toward the door.

There were two escapes from Dr. Wicksman's office, but none from Linda's mind. As she made her way down one of the hallways of the office, Mike and Garrett slowly making their way down the other, images of the way Garrett's wrist had twisted when this all began more than a year ago, the way his body had gradually become a stranger to him, to them all, raced through her head at a dizzying rate. Her tears, which had remained invisible in her imaginary world where everything was okay until now, fell and became real.

This was no magical adventure. There were no poisonous berries hanging from make-believe, human-eating trees in this world. Bilbo and Frodo did not exist. Linda could not laugh or pretend her way out of what was happening. Garrett's response of "fine" when asked how he was feeling could no longer fake its way to "suitable answer" status in her mind. This was real. Her son could not walk.

As a family, they had lived as though the elephant in the room would stomp its feet, crushing them, if they acknowledged that anything was wrong, acknowledged its existence. Videos Linda had taken of her son, proof to doctors who heartlessly accused him of making it up, were sugarcoated with Garrett's attempt to mask the severity of his condition by fighting against his body.

When his leg jutted outward, announcing to the world that something was terribly wrong, he would turn it in, painfully forcing it back to normal. If he didn't look sick, he wasn't. If he remained strong, it might go away. Mike, Garrett, and Linda had kept all their fears, all their worries, inside. Three souls, countless secrets.

If they made cookies and played games, life could remain normal until a diagnosis made its way into their lives. Until then, they were a happy, normal family.

But not on that day. When Linda saw Garrett's body fail him, completely detach itself from his mind, she lost it. Everything became real in that moment, and she could no longer pretend. She sobbed quietly, afraid of the long hallways echoing her cries. But it was too late. Garrett came around the corner, held up by his father, and saw her face.

"What's the matter, Mom?" he said, terrified eyes.

Doesn't he know? she thought.

"Well, I don't know," she said hesitantly, wiping away tears, evidence of weakness. "The fact that you can't walk?"

She posed it as a question, a small part of her hoping that the answer could be changed. But she knew it couldn't.

She reached for Garrett, hugging him tighter than she ever had before, as tears slid down his cheek. They both silently realized in that moment how important her positive outlook, the "Pollyanna" world she had created, was in their lives. He needed her to pretend, and together, in their embrace, they re-entered that world.

Linda never broke down in front of him again.

* 5 *

They left Dr. Wicksman's office, went straight to the pharmacy to pick up a walker, and drove home, where Mike and Linda taught Garrett to walk for the second time in his life. Only this time, he wasn't a one-year-old boy with toddler ambition and a healthy body.

His legs, his body, were broken. Mike and Linda taught him to push the walker forward, then shuffle his legs to catch up. Push, shuffle. Push, shuffle.

Slowly, over time, his mind's determination pushed his leg forward, then eventually forced his feet to motion, heel to toe, heel to toe, and his other leg slowly began to follow. Garrett maneuvered through fifth grade using a walker, crutches, walking sticks, or his own feet, depending on the day.

Over time, the stranger that was his own body, unknown and unwanted, was becoming more understandable. Garrett was learning its spasms, its strange, sporadic, and involuntary movements that completely took away his ability to walk some days, hindering his ability on other days. He was learning to navigate his limitations.

On days his body would allow him to walk, Garrett made his way down the halls of his elementary school backward, chatting with friends as they walked normally, facing him. He grabbed onto walls in class, clutched desks, walked backward, working against his body's desire to contort. As the school year dragged on, his attempt at normalcy became much more painful, the kids at school becoming less and less tolerant, more and more skeptical.

"There's nothing wrong with you," they would say when they saw him running at recess on good days, jumping from the wheelchair to catch a football.

There was nothing he could say to prove something was wrong. Nothing the doctors could say. It had been three years since his body had started its process of becoming a stranger, and there were no explanations—none for Garrett, none for his parents, none for his doctors, none for the kids at school.

On the day Linda took Garrett to get a wheelchair, her voice pushed through the lump in her throat.

"That one looks fun!" she said with as much excitement as her saddened heart would allow, pointing to a red wheelchair that said "Quickie" on the back.

Garrett stumbled across the room and climbed into Quickie, taking off immediately, sending the front end into the air. Arms in full motion, Garrett raced around the room, up and down a long ramp used for learning to ride. He practiced wheelies with the proudest smile.

"I can go anywhere I want!" Garrett hollered to his mom, zooming by. He had never felt so free.

Friends pushed him around campus at school, taking turns "chauffeuring" him around, and the wheelchair allowed Garrett to participate in sports and school activities. It was giving him back his life.

On a field trip to the Museum of Science in Boston, Garrett struggled up and down stairs, on and off subways, in and out of the museum. The twists of his body, the debilitating spasms of his muscles, made walking backward easier than stumbling forward and made running easier than walking in either direction. Getting on the subway to leave the museum, he lunged from his wheel-chair, ran, and collapsed on his hands and knees before crawling quickly, racing against his body's attempt to stop him with involuntary movements.

Dirty looks from strangers, people on the street who were convinced, like the doctor, that he was faking it, followed him around Boston, onto the subway, but Garrett didn't care. At least he was outside, part of the world. He wasn't going to let doubts from society take away the abilities he had left—walking backward and sporadic running. For some reason, his body hadn't yet taken those capabilities away from him.

He was going to hold onto them until the day he knew why his body was becoming an out-of-control stranger—and that day came toward the end of fifth grade.

"I think it's a condition called Dystonia," said a doctor from the Spaulding Rehabilitation Hospital in Boston. He was one of the few doctors left in New Hampshire or in Boston whom Garrett and his parents hadn't seen. The doctor told them he had recently heard of a patient with the disease.

"If you had come to see me six months ago, I wouldn't have been able to help you," he said before referring them to Dr. Nutan Sharma, a Dystonia specialist from the Neuroscience Center at Massachusetts General Hospital.

To a ten-year-old child, an answer meant a cure. The doctor would fix it, and he could continue his active life. To his parents, a possible name attached to his son's condition meant a lot of research and, that night, a lot of tears.

They knew that running a Google search on an illness could potentially come with sometimes inaccurate, frightening information—literature that could kill you with worry. But when they searched *Dystonia* that night, long after Garrett was in bed, reassured that everything would be just fine, not a written word was needed. Pictures of bodies, twisted like pretzels, looked almost inhuman, unnatural, and impossible the way they bent and contorted.

Videos were worse. Mike and Linda watched footage of these twisted bodies attempting to stand and walk with horrific, jerky movement, many of them with progressed Dystonia twisted and bedridden for life. With thoughts of any of these bodies belonging to Garrett, they Google searched and cried, hugged, talked, and cried some more, all night.

Through tears, they read that the neurological mechanism in Garrett's brain, the part that makes his muscles relax when not in use, was not functioning properly. Linda thought back to the time they were camping and Garrett couldn't keep up. It was the start of Dystonia. She remembered how his wrist had started twisting, his leg began jutting. That was Dystonia starting to take over. Garrett's progression from spasms and stumbling to binding him to a wheelchair meant Dystonia was winning.

Linda cried harder than she had ever cried as they continued reading, learning how involuntary muscle contractions force the body into repetitive, twisting movements and awkward postures.

Was this their son's future: lying in a bed and twisting into non-existence?

To uncover the truth, to find the answer, they visited Dr. Sharma, a leading expert on Dystonia and a clinical researcher of the disease. And they trusted her instantly.

"We're going to do everything we can to get Garrett's Dystonia under control," she said to Linda and Mike.

Then she turned to Garrett. "This is what's happening to your body," she said, dark, caring eyes staring into Garrett's frightened face. She drew a picture of the brain.

"This is the part where the brain tells your muscles what to do," she said, pointing, "and it isn't working right, so we're going to give you medicine that will guide your muscles and tell them what to do."

Plain and simple. Pills would make him better. They needed to. But it was not guaranteed.

Medicine was used to mask the symptoms, to place a cover over Dystonia's ugly face, not to cure it. There was no cure.

Dr. Sharma started by prescribing Garrett half a pill. From everything Linda had read online, most patients who were going to respond to the medicine started responding around pill two. After a week of waiting, videotaping, and watching the videos for the slightest improvement, Dr. Sharma increased his dosage. One pill.

Garrett finished fifth grade in a wheelchair and spent his summer taking another half pill at a time. Wait a week, take half a pill. Wait a week, take another. Watching for the slightest improvement, for Garrett's body to move just a little less, bend less, twist and spasm a little less, was pure torment for Linda.

By pill two, she was convinced. This was not going to work.

"It doesn't work for everybody," Dr. Sharma had warned, and those words haunted Linda.

They continued their indoor activities, continued their reinvented life, as they waited and watched, still hoping to reach that magic number—that perfect number of pills that would give Garrett back his freedom.

The magic number was six.

For the first time in months, Garrett could almost feel his brain's signals rushing through his overthrown body; he could almost hear their demands, imagine their shouts—"Move! Do as I say!"

His legs, his hips, and his arms were slowly becoming his again, slowly belonging to his mind, slowly listening to its commands. As days passed, Garrett's body succumbed to a steady flow of medicine, and he no longer questioned whether or not his body would continue to fail him, no longer wondered if he would be stuck in its shell, his mind remaining smart and capable. He no longer worried about living trapped for the rest of his life.

Linda watched with hope as Garrett walked, but he had walked before. That's how the disease had started. He could walk one day and not the next. He could run one day but barely be able to move the next. Was this one of those days? One of those days when, for whatever reason, Garrett's disease let go of its grip for a few moments to tease him with false freedom?

She could not entertain its cruelty. She could not let herself fully believe that Dystonia's voice had been hushed forever. It was time to wait.

⋆ 6 ⋆

"Go, Garrett, go!" Linda screamed from the side of the pool at their resort in Africa.

The hot sun beat down on them, on other tourists, on the free-roaming, wild animals beyond the walls of their resort, but Linda was only focused on one thing—Garrett.

"Go, go, go!"

It had been only a couple of weeks since Garrett started to walk. While Linda was still waiting for the disease to return, stick out its tongue like a mean, teasing child, they left for a trip they had planned months before—an African safari.

Unsure of whether or not Garrett would be in a wheelchair when they planned the trip, still hoping the medicine would work, they had decided that waiting shouldn't mean not living. It was time for an adventure—an adventure that did not include Netflix movies, card games, or baking cookies.

When the sixth pill finally told Garrett's brain to move his body, safely and normally, Linda's skepticism made her drag Garrett's wheelchair from the garage and into the back of their car before leaving for the airport. It was going with them. She wanted desperately to believe that Garrett was finally beyond the reach of Dystonia's arms, but she couldn't.

They hauled the chair all throughout Africa, in and out of the van escorting them between the hotels where they stayed.

"Crazy Americans" was written all over the driver's face.

"We might need it, I swear!" Linda said, feeling like a child explaining her need to drag around a big, heavy, unnecessary toy.

From the time they had left their New Hampshire home, Garrett had walked everywhere. His body, without one flinch, one spasm, one twist or turn, never touched the wheelchair. They spent the first week of their trip at the resort in Nanyuki, Kenya, and the rest of it "glamping"—glamorous camping (hotel-style service in a large, military-type tent, complete with turned down sheets, hot showers, chocolates placed neatly on the pillows, and fresh towels daily). They had booked the trip not knowing if Garrett's condition would allow him to "rough it," so real camping was out of the question.

While he would have preferred regular camping, would have chosen white water rafting down the Zambezi River or climbing Mount Meru, Garrett was satisfied with watching giraffes, gazelles, rhinos, elephants, and zebras from across the river that ran behind their resort.

They saw baby lion cubs nibble one another's tails, playing tug-of-war with small pieces of blankets, and, during a private van safari tour, watched a real-life episode of the Discovery Channel as two lionesses crept low, tracking with laser precision before pouncing on a helpless wildebeest. As Mike watched, enjoying the show, he was glad he had decided to add a little excitement to their trip, as he always did.

He was the reason they had once rappelled down a waterfall in the Dominican Republic, climbed the inside of a ninety-foot-tall Strangler fig tree during a trip to Costa Rica, and ventured in canoes down the Rio Sirena with "Crocodile Dundee of the Osa Peninsula," spotting anteaters and Jesus Christ lizards running along the water's surface before chasing a baby alligator into the unknown. Mike was an adventure seeker with the desire to explore other countries—their people, their land, their ways—and the trip to Africa would be no different.

In addition to taking a hot air balloon ride over a migration of a million wildebeests traveling eighteen-hundred miles from the Serengeti region of Tanzania to Kenya's Masai Mara in search of greener grass, he had researched ways to not only view the country as tourists, but to see it through the eyes of its locals with a private escort to meet Tanzania's Hadza tribe, one of Africa's last tribes of hunters and gatherers.

"How will we find them?" Linda asked before venturing into the wild.

"You don't find them," said their guide, explaining that they are a nomad tribe, a wandering group that drifts like the wind. "They find you."

Linda, Mike, and Garrett became part of the beautiful, red clay African soil, torn by the tires of their Jeep, as it lifted in clouds from the earth and settled in thick, suffocating coats on their bodies and their vehicle. They coughed it from their lungs, wiped it from their eyes, as the Jeep drove further and deeper into Africa's backcountry.

Jutting rocks and dips of potholes forced them to crawl slowly along the road's twists before suddenly, in the midst of their drive, in the middle of nowhere, Linda gasped as a man, toothless and covered only by a small piece of animal's hide, jumped onto the hood of their jeep, dirty hands pressed against the windshield.

She breathed a long, silent exhale as the man smiled, and she repeated the guide's words to herself—"they find you."

They sure do, she thought, laughing.

They pulled to the side of the road and followed the man to his tribe, which consisted of fifteen others. Beneath a tree sat a temporary, igloo-shaped hut made from twigs that would most likely disintegrate in a strong breeze. They spent the afternoon learning to make bows and arrows and following the Hadza to the area's best hunting places. They were fascinated by stories of how the children walked hours to school and back, how the people shared hunted food, and showered only when it rained. They laughed and learned until the sun went down, then danced with the Hadza in the glow of the setting sun.

It was another adventure in their travel logs.

"Go! Go! Go!" Linda continued to shout as she watched Garrett race a little boy in their hotel swimming pool at the Sweetwaters Game Reserve near the town of Nanyuki, Kenya.

The boys had jumped in, side by side, and Garrett, arms and legs tearing through the water, spray shining like diamonds in the sun, swam as though he had never been sick.

His mind had taken back control of his body.

Linda stood from her lounge chair, following the splash of Garrett's stroke, perfect and determined, until his little hand slapped the hot cement on the other side of the pool, twenty-five feet from where he started. She knew he would soon be back to all of his adventures—they all would.

She realized this as she thought of how Garrett couldn't swim five feet just three short months ago. He couldn't even stand in water without Dystonia grabbing and twisting his body, forcing him beneath the water to finish its selfish strangle. She had watched for months as he struggled through swim therapy, trying to let go of the pool's side without going under, trying to stand straight without bending, trying to swim with a body determined to tangle.

The smack of Garrett's hand on the side of the pool was like a snap of his fingers, breaking Linda out of her nightmarish trance— a reality check. Her son was healed. Dystonia was not coming back.

She finally believed.

⋆ 7 ⋆

Garrett walked through sixth grade flawlessly. He excelled in school as always, maintained straight As, and played basketball once again. This time, he could run steadily, controllably, up and down the court, his legs and mind strong. He did not stumble clumsily the way he had in fifth grade, when he was on the floor more than he was on his feet, when standing still to catch the basketball was impossible, when baskets were made by pure luck.

He spent his afternoons swimming in his backyard pool and venturing on bike with his parents through the area's most scenic spots—Lake Massabesic in Manchester, New Hampshire, and Vermont's Killington Peak in the Green Mountains. With his Dystonia still concealed, Garrett continued all the things he loved— spending time outdoors, running around with his friends.

One afternoon, during a game of football with neighborhood kids, Garrett ran the length of the grassy lawn, football cradled safely, touchdown the only thing on his mind. He ran and dodged beneath the bright sun on that free, summer day, when another player, a kid much shorter and smaller than Garrett, crashed into his body, sending a rush of instant, numbed pain.

Garrett walked to the sidelines of their playing field and sat down, holding his left wrist, as sharp tingles took away any feeling left in his arm. It was the same feeling that had washed over his right arm after his fall at the rock climbing gym, the same feeling he had when he was eleven and sprained his ankle after jumping from a picnic table to slam dunk a basketball. He knew the feeling. When his wrist swelled to double, triple its size, he knew it was broken.

Again, his wrist was reset and cast, and while the bone slowly healed, taking back its strength and shape, Dystonia came out from hiding, creeping through Garrett's body like a selfish snake. He remembered Dr. Sharma's words—"Our bodies hold the genes for specific diseases, but most of us go our whole lives without those genes blooming. Injuries can sometimes trigger those genes and activate the disease."

Dr. Sharma was certain that Garrett's first fall, his first break, at the rock climbing gym had released the disease, had enabled its existence. Garrett wondered if this accident, this break, would do the same.

Within a week, he knew.

His body, once again, became uncontrollable, its movements sporadic and infuriating. But this time, it wasn't a stranger; it was all too familiar.

Linda, who worked as a teaching coach in the school district, made frequent visits to Garrett's junior high school and looked through the windows of his classrooms as she walked down the halls. She watched quietly, from a distance, as her son's body jolted in his chair, his head thrown back, his body, once again, out of control.

It was time to increase his medicine. Half a pill, no improvement. One pill, a little. Over time, with more and more pills, the medicine would keep Dystonia out of Garrett's mind until it forced its way back in, only to become defeated again by another pill.

Garrett got better, then worse, better, worse, throughout the seventh grade, until he was taking eleven pills a day. A strong force in his body, silenced but not killed, Dystonia always found its way back in, until Garrett was in the eighth grade and no amount of medicine was working. Its voice, its presence, was too loud, too demanding.

Garrett fought it with all his strength, body versus mind. He could feel the dance of his muscles in class, the way they seized up, clenched, jerked, twisted. With fingertips gripping the bottom of his chair, his back stiff, muscles tense, mind focused, he would hold himself that way as long as he could, until Dystonia squeezed its way through the strength of his mind.

During finals at the end of the year, the disease forced him onto the ground. He took his advanced algebra test on the classroom floor, the only place he could keep somewhat still as his body pulled at him, demanding attention.

Garrett's wheelchair remained in their garage that summer as he fumbled through the house, lunging, jumping, crawling, running clumsily, and holding on to furniture. He used it only in public; his freedom, what was left of it, remaining at home, where there was no shame in crawling down the halls on all fours, sometimes his body's only way of getting from one place to the next.

It was time, once again, to see Dr. Sharma, and though she offered to increase Garrett's medicine, they all knew it was not going to work. Dystonia was determined to own and control his body.

"I want you to consider deep brain stimulation surgery," Dr. Sharma said, explaining that the surgery would involve implanting two leads into Garrett's brain, a wire leading to a battery in his chest. The device would reroute his brain activity with electric impulses.

Brain surgery.

Those two words sent Garrett's head into his hands, elbows to his knees, stomach into his throat. He was either going to throw up or pass out, or both. He sat there for forty-five minutes, speechless, head in hands, face white, sweat dripping down his back. He could not even handle the thought of getting poked by a needle or having his blood drawn. Brain surgery was out of the question.

Mike, who had been to every one of Garrett's doctor's appointments, could not make it to this one, and it was up to Linda to choke down her shock, letting out only words of comfort and encouragement. This was something they needed to consider, or Garrett's fate would eventually lead him to bed for the rest of his life.

It was the biggest decision that they, as a family, would ever have to make. They researched the surgery online, read books, talked to several of Dr. Sharma's patients, each of whom had some level of improvement with the surgery.

"We've been very successful with this surgery," Dr. Sharma had reassured them.

The decision was never far from their minds. Debating it became a part of every meal, every activity, every moment. Did they let Dystonia take over completely, leaving Garrett's body a living shell, a trap for his mind? Or did they opt for surgery, with all its risks, all its possible complications?

During good moments, when Garrett's body twisted less, teasing with false hopes of normalcy, the decision was easy—no surgery. No probing, no drilling, no change. But in the next moment, when he thrashed and twisted and jerked, Garrett knew he had to at least consider the surgery, at least entertain the idea that it might actually work, that he might get his body back, his control.

After a month, they made a decision. Mike and Linda wanted their son to have a good life, and Garrett wanted his life back, despite the risk, in spite of his fear of needles, probes, hospitals, and doctors. He was going to have the surgery. Every day his body was drifting further and further away from him, and if surgery was the only way to get it back, that's what he was going to do.

⋆ 8 ⋆

Garrett thought he could make it through his freshman year of high school and undergo surgery the following summer, but when many of his nights became battles with his body, hours spent pinning himself between his bed and a chair in an effort to stop from moving long enough to fall asleep, he and his parents decided it was time. He was physically and mentally tired of fighting it, only to lose every single time.

They scheduled the surgery for March, four months later, and Garrett, convinced it was going to work, remained determined to live the rest of his life with this disease as independently as possible. He was no longer in the fourth grade with the imagination of a child, the imagination that could turn a wheelchair into a race car. He no longer viewed the wheelchair as freedom the way he had when he was ten—it had become a cage in his mind, something that controlled and owned him.

The pills had made him better for a short period of time, had allowed him to walk and experience life the way he had before Dystonia ever entered it. That freedom had become a daunting tease. For Garrett, being confined to a wheelchair meant reverting, taking steps back in time, back in a direction he never again wanted to go. But while Garrett viewed it as his prison, Mike and Linda, over time, had started to see the wheelchair as his release, a way out, a way back into the world.

A few months before, as his condition worsened daily, they took a trip to Vancouver, Canada, and Seattle, Washington, determined to focus on the things Garrett was still able to do. They had learned over the years to work with what they had, to do what they could do to live life to its fullest. They knew their reinvention as game players, cookie bakers, movie watchers, was no longer enough, so after considering all of their options, they concluded, "Garrett cannot stand, but he can sit. He cannot walk, but he can float." And from there, the idea was born to take Garrett paragliding.

Strapped to an instructor, Linda ran with all her might, feet pounding the earth beneath, eyes on the endless blue sky ahead as she plunged from the end of a mountain where time stopped, life paused, before gliding through the crisp air, white-tipped Mount Rainier in the distance, the city of Seattle below.

She coasted to the ground and watched Garrett, who ran as fast as he could—the one thing Dystonia had never taken from him—as he jumped from the edge, time, once again, standing still, nothing but that moment existing.

He floated, body still, dangling, as his mom watched from below, his dad waiting his turn.

Living by their newfound determination to continue doing the things Garrett could do despite his disease, during their trip they had already kayaked with whales, biked down the Freund Canyon Trail, rafted down the Wenatchee River, and now they were free-falling through time, emotions, reality. Their hope was renewed.

Garrett spent the next few months on his hands and knees, up against his hallway walls, running and collapsing, jumping and crawling, until the first day of ninth grade, a day he had been dreading all summer. High school was a time to impress the girls, hold their hands in the halls, fit in. A wheelchair allowed for none of those things.

As Linda drove him to school that day, wheelchair in the trunk, Garrett stared out the window. He didn't say a word. He spent his first few weeks worrying about how he would maneuver through school—a campus with four levels on one side, five on the other, hallways packed with rambunctious teenagers. His thoughts became less and less about schoolwork and more about how he would make it from one class to the next.

Determined to stay as cool as possible, to remain as accepted as his disease would allow, Garrett tried in every way he could, with everything inside of him, to look "normal," to keep his body from giving him away, from taking away his image, from stealing his high school years.

Leaving his wheelchair, his prison, in class on days his body felt strong, Garrett would walk backwards down the halls, hands on the walls for support, facing his friends, talking and laughing as they made their way to class. He would fight it in class, fight it at home, fight, fight, fight.

For Spring break that year, Mike and Linda decided to give their son a break from fighting with a trip to Belize—a place they had never been before—maintaining their philosophy, "Never visit the same place twice." He could float in the Caribbean Sea and lie on the white, sandy beach. But, as always, they found something more. Despite Garrett's limitations, they found an adventure.

Maneuvering the wheelchair in the sand was nearly impossible, so one afternoon they left their small cabin on the beach and took a boat to a nearby deserted island, Silk Caye, where Garrett leaped from his wheelchair, crawled through the sand to the water, and strapped on a pair of goggles and fins. As Linda walked to the water's edge, she glanced at the wheelchair, abandoned in the sand like a sunken ship, tilted and no longer needed, at least for the moment.

In her optimistic mind, where reality easily became make-believe, that wheelchair would stay there forever. She would pretend it away, smile the surgery from existence, laugh Dystonia from their lives. Just like the wheelchair, they would abandon it all.

She and Mike swam hand in hand with Garrett, away from shore and around the island, away from it all. They pulled Garrett through the water, admiring bright fish and colorful coral below, the sun's heat on their backs. This was their reality for now, but if all went well, everything would change. The surgery could fix everything.

And while, in their minds, it had to, they knew there was a chance it could fix nothing. If it didn't work, if Dystonia won again, this could be one of Garrett's last adventures, one of their last adventures as a family, their "last hoorah." They were determined to make the best of it. They snorkeled and spent hours at the ice cream shop and beach bars, befriending tourists and locals to the area.

When they left paradise and returned home, reality was waiting to greet them. Surgery was one week away. Linda cried to her friends, and the days leading to surgery, she and Mike sent Garrett's mind as far away from reality as they could with endless games of Rock Band on the Xbox with his friends, nights out to dinner, and sightseeing in Boston where the surgery would take place.

On the day of surgery, dressed in blue smocks, fear living inside, Mike and Linda held Garrett's hands as doctors placed a metal "halo" around his head to keep it still, to locate exact areas of his brain. He was fifteen, but the way his blue eyes searched his mom's face, the reassurance for which they begged, reminded Linda that he was still her little boy. She plastered a smile on her face, willing her eyes to communicate, *You're going to be just fine.*

And Mike believed it. Garrett, listening to his iPod, had sung "Beautiful Day" by U2 after being admitted to the hospital.

The words of the song, of falling skies and good days slipping away, circled Mike's head, and he listened.

The sky was not falling today. This was a good day, a beautiful day—a day that would give Garrett back his life.

"Everything's going to be okay," Linda said, just in case her expression, the message in her eyes, was not clear enough, then she squeezed Garrett's hand and left the room.

"We'll see you later," Mike said, smiling. "Good luck."

★ 9 ★

During the five-hour surgery, Mike and Linda roamed halls, paced the floor. In a deli across campus, Mike calmed his nerves with a big Italian dish while Linda drank hot chocolate and chicken broth, the only two things she knew her nerves would allow her to keep down.

They spent most of their time in Garrett's empty hospital room, looking out the window at the highway packed with cars coming and going between New Hampshire and Boston.

Everything will be fine, Linda told herself. *They will take good care of him. He'll be okay.* A pager in her hand buzzed every so often with updates, confirming her thoughts.

"We are starting surgery now," a nurse working with Dr. Sharma texted after they took a CAT scan of Garrett's brain and merged it with results from a previous MRI, creating a perfect map of the area where they would place the leads.

They shaved and numbed his head before starting to drill. Garrett didn't feel a thing. For perfect placement, doctors asked him questions, challenging his brain, making him move his arms and legs, firing neurons. The sound of it, the noise of his brainwaves, rushed through his ears, a soft static swooshing loudly with each command, every movement.

"One side is done!" the pager announced.

I knew it, Linda thought. *I knew everything would be okay. Fake it 'til you make it.*

A few hours later, another message.

"The other side is done—Garrett did great!"

She could finally breathe.

"You can see Garrett in the recovery room," the pager said, and Mike and Linda made their way through the waiting area, a small, warmly lit room with a beautiful undersea mural painted on its wall. Linda thought of their trip to Belize just a week before, filled with ocean adventures, possibly their last journey, their last family trip before the unknown. Now here they were, the words *Garrett did great* on the pager in Linda's hand. As she glanced at the mural, the ocean, one last time, she smiled at the irony.

"It wasn't as bad as I thought it would be," Garrett said, smiling at his parents.

Two days later, brain surgeon Dr. Emad Eskandar surgically placed a pacemaker in Garrett's chest, wire connecting to the leads in his brain, and recovery was more miserable than he ever could have imagined. He slept through as much of it as he could, waking up to throw up, trying to rest during the most intense headaches he had ever felt. But then it was over, and once again, it was time to wait.

They headed home, where Garrett rested and healed, filled his time with relaxation and schoolwork, and a month later, it was time to see if the surgery worked. The incision had healed, the swelling had subsided, and Garrett went with his parents to see Dr. Sharma and nurse Lisa Paul, who would turn on the device that would determine his future.

They wanted the reaction of a light bulb after a flipped switch— instant. But that's not how this worked, and they knew it. It could take up to three months for Dystonia to release its hold on Garrett's brain, which it had been controlling for the past seven years. It was not going to let go easily.

Garrett returned to the ninth grade, in his wheelchair, and waited. He tried almost daily to test his brain, to challenge his body, and to walk. But just as before, Dystonia won every time.

Until one day toward the end of the school year, a day no different from any other, a day that became the next chapter in his life.

It was the end of Garrett's geography class, his last for the day, and when the bell freed the students, they gathered their things and made small talk as they headed toward the door.

Garrett stood, held onto the back of his wheelchair and began to push. There was nothing special about that moment, nothing in his body that shouted "Dystonia will not win this time!" He decided that, if letting go caused his leg to jut or his back to spasm, he would just grab the handles and nothing would change. No one would notice. But the moment his hands let go, his legs moved forward, around the side of the wheelchair, and guided him around the room, all eyes on him.

"Hey, I thought you couldn't walk!" hollered a kid from across the room.

Garrett smiled, beamed, then shouted, "Neither did I!"

He couldn't wait to show his parents. Linda was outside waiting, as she was every afternoon. In his wheelchair, Garrett pushed through the door on the side of the school building and rolled toward his mom, who got out of the car. He stopped the wheelchair and said, "Hey Mom, watch this!"

He stood up and walked around the car, not a hand on it for support, not a falter in his step. He wasn't jolting or twisting, and nothing was jutting—his body seemed out of Dystonia's reach, at least for the moment. With a big smile on her face, disbelief in her eyes, Linda couldn't help but wonder what the next moment would hold. She wrapped Garrett in her arms, expecting to feel a spasm in his back, an involuntary shake or heartbreaking twitch.

Nothing.

They drove home, Garrett planning how he would tell his father, Linda hoping with all her heart that they had just entered the imaginary, perfectly pretend world she had been creating in her mind for so many years.

They pulled into the driveway, and before she could put the car into park, Garrett was out and walking quickly, normally, toward the door leading into the kitchen of their home. He couldn't get to his dad fast enough. Linda watched as he walked through the door, and Mike, who was heading toward the kitchen from the other side of the house, stopped the moment he saw Garrett.

"What the hell are you doin'?" he asked, a smile crawling across his face.

"I'm walkin'!" Garrett shouted, arms thrown out at his side as if to say "ta-da!"

Pure happiness turned Mike's proud smile into a relief-filled grin as he reached out to shake his son's hand. Garrett had been running or crawling or confined to his wheelchair for so many years that Mike had forgotten what it was like to look at him eye to eye. He didn't offer a hug for his little boy; he offered a handshake for the man standing before him, the man who had handled his situation with such maturity, such dignity, such patience, and optimism. As Garrett squeezed back, he realized that this was not a congratulatory handshake, this was a welcome handshake—*welcome to your new life.*

Sand-colored dust circled in clouds through hot air as tires of a rustic, flat-bed truck tore through the dry, Cambodian earth. Garrett watched as it made its approach, and through those circles, swirling and climbing, disappearing toward blue sky, he could see the faces of those that reflected his past—the faces of ten people living the way he had once lived; the faces of people whose lives he was about to change.

Some of them, whose legs were nothing but heavy, numb, useless limbs, scooted with their arms, well-defined from years of carrying themselves through life, along metal to the back of the truck as it came to a dusty halt. Others, legs missing from the knee down, just sat waiting, as they had their whole lives, for arms to lift them.

As Garrett helped them down from the truck, one by one, they looked at him with childlike eyes, much like his own that had once scanned the faces of doctors desperate to help. He smiled and they smiled back, a universal language. With the help of his parents and two others from their Globe Aware group, Garrett placed each person in his or her own wheelchair, and while some took off right away, using their arms to push the large bicycle tires on either side of their seat, others remained still, helpless, unable to grasp the idea that they could finally move freely, on their own.

Garrett watched as they circled, then pushed handles and let go, sending these people into freedom. It had been a year since surgery, a year of independence, a year without Dystonia. When he learned after his surgery that he could make a wish through the Make-A-Wish Foundation, Mike and Linda jokingly said, "We're not going to Disney World."

Garrett had never been, and they were not the Disney World kind of family. They were adventurers, seekers of the untraditional.

"You should consider giving back," Linda had said, and the only thing Garrett could think to give was the best gift he had ever been given—the gift of mobility.

Garrett and his parents had traveled all over the world, journeyed unbeaten paths, taught English and math to kids in impoverished countries, and gained a deep understanding of different ways of life. They had lived in homestays, met locals in different countries, been enriched with firsthand knowledge of other cultures, but they had never fully immersed themselves, connected themselves, to the lives of the people. This was their chance.

"I wish to go to Cambodia and build wheelchairs for people who can't walk," Garrett had announced, and the Make-A-Wish volunteers sat still, smiles plastered, confusion setting in. They had never heard such a wish. How would they go about building wheelchairs in Cambodia? Where would they start? They contacted Globe Aware, a nonprofit that organizes service projects, and Garrett and his parents were on a plane a few months later.

"*Orkun,*" cried one woman, grabbing the bottom of Linda's shirt after she helped her from the back of the truck. The woman looked to the ground, tears landing in the soft dirt after running down the length of her hands, pressed together in prayer.

"*Orkun,*" she cried over and over in her native tongue.

Linda smiled and looked at their translator, Dine.

"Thank you," he said.

"You're welcome, you're welcome," Linda said over and over, but the woman would not let go.

Garrett watched, the woman's intensity rushing through him. He wanted to hear her story, wanted to know what happened to her legs. He wanted to hear all of their stories. As a group, they eventually migrated to a nearby hut with a large, open floor, straw above, a table, and nothing else. They sat in a circle and exchanged stories, speaking slowly, deliberately, as the rest sat in total silence, Dine's voice, his translations, echoes.

As they spoke, Garrett remembered pinning himself between a chair and his bed for hours in the middle of the night. He recalled stares in the halls of his school, disbelief from strangers, running clumsily before falling, learning to live inside his body, a perfect stranger. And then he looked at the faces surrounding him. The faces of people who had spent more than twenty years with broken legs or no legs at all, no means to get around, no "prison with wheels."

Their prisons were their homes, places they stayed, sitting still on dirty floors—for days, months, years at a time. Their prisons did not include occasional running, the ability to jump from a wheelchair and catch a football. Their prisons did not take away their outdoor adventures, forcing them into air-conditioned homes with TVs, games, and books. They had no books. They had no TVs. They had no air-conditioning, despite cruel, hot summers, no electricity, no light.

When each of the ten people finished telling their stories, Garrett and his parents, the only people from the group who asked to visit each home, each prison, bounced in the back of the old, metal truck as it crawled along dirt roads and into the villages where these people lived. One by one, they visited each home as the setting sun chased behind with fiery reds and magnificent orange. Its persistent push limited their visits to just a few minutes each, but it was long enough to see firsthand poverty that Garrett had only ever seen from a distance.

He had once witnessed the slums of Nairobi, consisting of cardboard homes with aluminum roofs, from a highway in Kenya. He had danced with the Hadza tribe—the poorest people he had ever met—admiring their content spirits, appreciating their genuine smiles inspired by living from the land. He had watched the children teeter-totter on tree branches, play in the dirt as though it was sand in a sandbox. He remembered how they only showered when it rained and only ate after a successful hunt.

That was poverty, but this … this was different. This was confinement in their own, dark homes, escape only possible through their minds. Leaving was not an option for them, not without the help of another. There were no cell phones to call for help, nobody to hear their shouts outside of earshot.

Garrett watched as each wheelchair recipient pushed himself or herself freely around the wooden floorboards of their stilted home, and for the first time, it didn't seem to matter that a box in the corner used as a bed was the only piece of furniture in the room. The dust and lack of windows went unnoticed. They could move, and that was all that mattered.

All these people could see was this newfound freedom, and that's when Garrett realized just how much he had—how much he always had. Nothing was taken from him. Without his experience, without Dystonia's firm grip on his life, he would never be standing in the homes of these people, realizing and appreciating every single thing in his life. It was time to start looking at what he had, not at what he did not have. What an invaluable lesson to learn at sixteen. It was his trip, his wish, that taught him that.

Standing in the home of the woman who would not let go of Linda, the woman who was still thanking them, still touching their arms and insisting for them to spend the night, Garrett drank milk from a coconut she had given him and made a decision.

He decided that every vacation in the future would not just serve as a good time, would not just involve exploring and expanding his view of the world. He was going to become part of it—part of the culture, part of the people. His Wish trip opened his eyes to all that he was capable of giving, the difference he had the ability to make. Every vacation would be a "service vacation," and after his trip to Cambodia, Garrett graduated from high school and his first "service vacation" before enrolling at the University of South Carolina to study international business was to teach English to children in Nicaragua. His second was helping at an after-school program for street children in Peru.

After Garrett's Wish trip, he started speaking for Make-A-Wish Foundation functions and fundraisers, helping to raise money and spread awareness of the impact wishes make in children's lives. He gives credit to his doctors for his gift of mobility, his miracle, and thanks Make-A-Wish for letting him pass it on.

Meera Salamah

"My fight with DFL has been long and hard, just like the fight of trees against the forces of deforestation. Trees, I endure, and so shall you."

—Meera Salamah

WAVES ROLLING IN from the deepest part of the Mediter-
ranean swelled and crashed in the distance before meeting the shore with gentle, peaceful ease. With arms stretched like
wings, Meera twirled in dizzying circles through the clear, emerald
green water of Lebanon's Golden Beach, *Shat Dahabee*, and fell into
its warm embrace.

A slight breeze carried the scent of the country's most authentic
dishes—fresh fish caught from the sea, hummus dip, baba gha-
noush—from bamboo-roofed cafes lining the historic peninsula
surrounding them. A vibrant, folksy mix of traditional Lebanese
and Egyptian music flowed from those cafes, creating a cultural,
celebratory vibe for beachgoers, who played soccer and made drip
castles in the sand.

Meera laughed and splashed then soared from the sea as her
grandfather scooped her into his arms and hurried toward the
beach. She knew just what that meant.

"Where are they?" she asked excitedly, leaning over his shoulder
to get a closer look. "I don't see them, Jiddu!"

Ankle-deep, he glided carefully, patiently, through the calm waters.

"There they are," said her grandfather, "Jiddu," as Meera called
him. "See the jellyfish?"

Meera's long, black hair danced in the salty breeze, covering her
face. She quickly swiped it away from her eyes and leaned in for a
closer look.

Hundreds of these tiny, fascinating creatures bobbed gracefully below.

"*Andeel*," he said in his native tongue, and then translated. "Jellyfish. Can you say *Andeel*, Namoora?"

He and the rest of the family had called Meera "Namoora"— the name of a sweet, Lebanese dessert—from the time she was born.

"*Andeel*," she said proudly, excited to add another Arabic word to her four-year-old vocabulary.

———— ✳

"Remember the warm, salty air in your face," Alex whispered into Meera's ear. "The hot sand in your toes. The sound of the waves. You are playing at the beach with Jiddu."

Eyes closed, Meera's father blocked out the beeps, warmed his body in the cold room with thoughts of the ocean's tepid air, breathed in memories of the water's salty scent. His mind took him to *Shat Dahabee*, and he wanted his eleven-year-old daughter there with him.

"Fill your lungs with the warm air," he said, begging.

Demanding.

"Breathe it in, Meera. Just breathe," he whispered.

Her body was giving up, but on some level, she heard the pleas of her father.

Alex found relief every time the numbers on the machine keeping Meera alive would jump as her oxygen level increased, indicating another breath taken. He and his wife, Nita, remained at Meera's side, night and day, giving her orders. When her chest remained still and the numbers dropped and the beeps persisted, Alex took over for the machine.

"Breathe."

She listened and her body responded, fighting for life.

Dr. Robyn Barst, a Pulmonary Hypertension (PH) expert at New York-Presbyterian Morgan Stanley Children's Hospital, who had been working with Meera's doctors from the beginning, knew there were risks of the Extracorporeal Membrane Oxygenation (ECMO)—heart and lung—machine keeping Meera alive for too long. Her body would eventually grow weak, letting the machine take over its organs.

"We need to take her off the machine and get her to New York City," Dr. Barst said.

The first time Nita, Alex, Meera, and her younger brother, Zane, had traveled from their Dallas, Texas, home to New York was in 2004, three years before, when Meera was eight years old and first diagnosed with PH.

"Don't worry, we're going to beat this," Dr. Barst had said.

It was time to find out if they would.

✴ 2 ✴

C'mon, you can do it, Nita thought to herself one morning as she watched her eight-year-old daughter on the soccer field, hunched with hands on her knees, head pointed toward the ground. The other girls on her team sprinted down the field as Meera jogged to the sideline for a puff of her inhaler.

"You okay, sweetie?" Nita asked.

"Yeah, I'm okay," Meera said, panting.

She caught her breath, inhaled once more, and let it out as she ran to join the game. She trudged up and down the field, from goal to goal, on the defense for her team, the Ladybugs.

Icy winds on that late March morning grabbed at her hair, still damp from an early-morning swim lesson, and pulled at her body as she ran against it. Determined, Meera played her heart out, maneuvering the ball with ease, running alongside her teammates, until her run became a trot, and then a gradual walk.

Breathing the chilly air, running through its frigid grip, she came down with a severe cold a few days later. An X-ray to determine whether or not she had developed pneumonia revealed that her heart was enlarged and she was sent to a cardiologist. After hours of testing and numerous whispered conversations between doctors, they asked Meera and Zane to play in the children's waiting area while they spoke to Alex and Nita.

"We've determined that Meera has a rare condition called Pulmonary Hypertension," one doctor said with a calm voice, but there was alarm in his eyes.

Nita spent that night in front of her computer, the light of the screen illuminating the tears on her face as she scrolled and read site after site.

"No known cure."

"Serious illness."

"Progressive heart failure leading to death."

One step at a time, she thought, wiping her eyes. *We will get through this.*

The first step was telling Meera the doctor's orders—no more physical activity, no more soccer.

"No more soccer?" she asked in alarm. Her eight-year-old life revolved around the sport. "Why not?"

Without a full understanding of the reasons she could no longer play, Meera spent her recesses at school staring longingly at the other second graders playing tag and soccer as she and her friends circled the campus, talking and sharing secrets.

One afternoon, she picked a handful of wildflowers lining the fence surrounding the playground and carefully bundled them into a bouquet.

"Treehugger!" her friends teased, and Meera smiled. She could no longer experience the outdoors the same way she once had, kicking soccer balls, running in the fresh air, but she could continue enjoying and appreciating it in the way she had learned to do after joining the school's environmental club earlier in the year.

"All right, we're going to build butterfly houses today," said Mr. VanSligtenhorst later that afternoon during an environmental club meeting. Meera had joined after an environmentalist visited her elementary school and fascinated her with clothing made from water bottles and other recycled materials.

Through the club, Meera enjoyed planting flowers, learning about the rain forest, making paper, and keeping the environment clean by recycling. She painted her wooden butterfly house lime green and lavender and added bright polka dots and pastel flowers.

Once they were dry, Mr. VanSligtenhorst hung all the colorful houses from an oak tree near the playground, and Meera stood beneath them, watching in awe as butterflies fluttered through the windows and out the doors before landing gracefully on the rooftops to rest their beautiful wings. She watched carefully, intrigued by the way they seemed to study their surroundings thoughtfully, deciding what their next destination would be.

When Meera got home, she just wanted to be outdoors, in nature, with the sun and the wind. She wrapped her arms around the forty-foot-tall silver maple in her front yard that she loved for its shade and beauty and whispered, "I love you." Sitting on its bumpy roots, she waited until the late afternoon sun took a dip beneath the horizon before pulling out her finger paints. Resting on its trunk, she began to paint the fire reds and blazing oranges of the setting sun, and it was then that she transitioned from athlete to artist.

Pulling out another sheet of paper, Meera created a colorful trail of hearts all over the page. She wrote inside each heart the timeline of her life, from birth to "Boggess Elementary, PH, Murphy Middle School, high school ... "

Then she predicted her future—"college, medical school, PH doctor"—before writing on the back, "My dream is to become a PH specialist and help the young and old who have PH like me. I would like to help them follow their dreams."

During her battle with Pulmonary Hypertension (PH), Meera created this picture—a prediction of her future, from birth to PH doctor.

She had practiced medicine on her stuffed animals from the time she was just four years old, checking their imaginary heartbeats with her plastic stethoscope, their pretend pulses with a steady hand. She studied the intricacies of roly-polies and Daddy Long-legs as she got older, and for her tenth birthday, Meera's friends bought her a book called *The Human Body* so she could learn the inner workings of the body's systems. But before she could become a PH doctor, she needed to beat her illness.

Three years after Meera's diagnosis, after her days of playing soccer and running with a child's freedom in the sun were seemingly over, Nita and Alex wanted to lift her spirits, and their own, as she lay still, unknowing, in her hospital room. They hung pictures, reminders of their daughter's love for the outdoors, the places they knew she would rather be.

Though Meera couldn't see them, these images captured moments of ocean waves breaking, waterfalls splashing, and birds flying freely, and they brought comfort and peace to their lives. The photos brought with them the warmth of the sun, the serenity of the sea, the calm of the open air—the very elements that had made Meera fall in love with the outdoors at a very young age.

Her favorite place in the world was Maxwell Creek, a gentle flowing stream behind her backyard that crept through the nooks of the earth, twisting through giant maples and oaks, jutting lightly against rocks and branches that got in its way. When Meera wasn't busy in her room with doing homework, practicing the violin, reading, or painting, she spent hours exploring the banks of the creek, learning its sounds, discovering its creatures, releasing her thoughts to the wind. It was there that Meera became at peace with her illness.

Alex glanced between the photographs hanging on the stark walls of her hospital room as he continued to whisper in his daughter's ear, "Breathe."

His strength, his determination, moved through her.

It guided her, as it always had. She took shallow breaths with every command, her father's words keeping her alive when the machine no longer could.

After five days on ECMO, Meera's doctors decided to test the strength of her organs by temporarily unhooking her. Because transporting her on the machine to Dr. Barst's hospital in New York was not an option, they needed to see if her body could stand to make the journey on its own. Alex and Nita watched nervously through the glass window of Meera's room, looking beyond their own reflections, as doctors shut the machine down.

For three days they remained watchful. Meera was on dialysis and her lungs were filling with blood, but, with time, her numbers stabilized and doctors slowly began to wean her from sedation. Alex and Nita sat on either side of her hospital bed, their hands in hers, waiting, until the moment her eyes began to flutter open.

The innocence in them when they finally opened took Nita and Alex back to the day she was born eleven years before. The first time Nita held Meera in her arms, her wide eyes, an intense sea blue at the time, explored her parents' faces, searching for answers, waiting for guidance. Overwhelmed with joy and frightened by how much he could love someone so instantly, so deeply, Alex didn't sleep that night—Meera's big, happy, blue eyes pierced the darkness of his mind every time he closed his.

Meera's eyes searched now, as they had eleven years ago, between her parents.

"Hi, baby," Nita said. "You're okay. Everything's okay."

She squeezed Meera's hands and kissed her forehead as Alex said, "We love you so much."

He struggled with everything inside of him to keep his tears from falling and looked at her with strong, loving eyes as he caressed her face. Through every moment of weakness, every emotional collapse, he had stayed strong in the presence of his daughter. She needed that from him.

It had been five weeks since the start of the nightmare they were living, when Meera's period was heavy and painful and lasted longer than a month. When she started vomiting continuously, their local hospital had sent her to Children's Medical Center of Dallas, where she received two blood transfusions for all she had lost.

After a week in the hospital, Nita, who had spent every night curled up on the small couch next to Meera's bed, woke to a panicked voice at 2:00 a.m.

"Mama!"

"I'm right here, sweetie," Nita said, jumping to her side.

"I need to go to the bathroom."

Nita slowly helped her daughter from the bed and guided her gently to the restroom. With arms around one another, Nita was careful not to trip over Meera's gown or the IVs hanging from her tree.

Meera suddenly began to drag her feet, her arms loosening and crawling slowly down Nita's shoulders, falling away from her body. Limp, she slithered to the ground against the strength of her mother, and Nita hovered above, frantic. She quickly pressed the nurse's button in the restroom and screamed her daughter's name, over and over, before turning to God.

"*Bismillahir Rahmanir Raheem!*" she prayed loudly.

"In the name of God, the Beneficent, the Merciful," Nita chanted, repeating this Muslim prayer.

"*Bismillahir Rahmanir Raheem!*" she continued as two nurses lifted Meera from the bathroom floor and placed her on the bed. They began CPR and chest compressions while Nita's shaking fingers clumsily dialed her husband's cell phone.

"Meera's not breathing! They're doing CPR! She's in cardiac arrest!"

The words pouring from her mouth, the voice repeating them, didn't sound like her own. She felt as though she were watching herself from a distance, from another place, as she paced the room, panicked.

Alex dropped off Zane with his in-laws on the way to the hospital. He kept the tone of his voice calm and his face hopeful for the sake of his seven-year-old son. Zane did not need to know that his sister was dying.

Hands clutched around the steering wheel, Alex disregarded speed limit signs and tore through the streets. He zipped past cars on the dark freeway, tears blurring the headlights and white lines, the words in his head blocking out the sound of traffic.

This can't be it, he reasoned with himself. *They will bring her back. My little girl is not going anywhere.*

He needed this to be true.

Alex quickly parked his car and ran as fast as he could to Meera's room, where nurses still hovered over her body, pounding their fists into her chest.

It had been forty-five minutes.

They're going to hurt her! he screamed in his mind, tears flooding from his eyes, hands desperately pulling at his reddened face, his hair, as he watched his daughter's lifeless body jolt with every attempt to start her heart. He was losing it. The pain was unbearable. He stepped out into the hallway, his sobs echoing outside of Meera's room, and Nita left her daughter's side to join him, to hold him.

"She's going to be okay!" Nita insisted.

Every ounce of her knew that Meera wasn't going anywhere. She knew the doctors who said Meera would have brain damage if she survived at all were wrong. As a mother, she could not lose her daughter, and God knew it. He would not take her from them.

"*Bismillahir Rahmanir Raheem,*" she repeated, and Alex looked down, his tears dripping to the floor, before he closed his eyes and became lost in his wife's prayer.

✦ 4 ✦

"Her heart is beating on its own," said a fellow doctor an hour later. That's all Nita and Alex wanted to hear, but they knew there was more. "We've got her stabilized, but her heart is beating only because of the level of epinephrine we've got her on."

The doctor, whom they had never met before now, delivered the rest of the difficult news with sincere compassion and practiced calm.

"When we stop the medicine, her heart will probably stop, and if not, her brain will most likely be damaged."

When a doctor standing by his side added, "You should start calling your family and friends—there is a good chance she is not going to make it," Nita turned her back and walked away. She had no tolerance for negativity, no matter how much truth was in it. They had come this far, and ending the journey without Meera was not an option.

When Nita and Alex returned to Meera's side, her eyes remained closed, her life dependent on a machine.

"I hope you can hear me," Alex whispered into her ear. "If you can see the angels, they're there to help."

He could not bring himself to tell her to go with them. They were only there to comfort her. The pain he felt swelled in his throat. He paused, gained control, and continued.

"Squeeze my hand if you can see the angels," he said.

Meera's hand, small and fragile, gently squeezed.

Alex looked to his wife with wide eyes, mouth opened.

"She squeezed my hand!"

Her brain was not damaged. A heavy current of excitement and fear flowed through him. The angels were there to guide her, but when Meera woke later that day, he knew she had chosen not to follow.

Meera was responding to commands and began communicating

with her parents by writing notes on a Magna Doodle, a magnetic drawing board that a nurse had given to her. When not answering questions about how she was feeling or asking for ice chips, Meera would draw hearts and write "I love you" to her parents.

The third day after her arrest, Meera was off the breathing tube, reading books, talking, and eating spaghetti and meatballs. Contrary to her doctors' predictions, her heart and lungs were functioning on their own, and Meera became known as "Miracle Girl."

That night, Child Life volunteers from the hospital came to let Meera know about the Make-A-Wish Foundation and that any wish she desired would be granted.

The Make-A-Wish Foundation, Alex thought, staring at the volunteers with resentful eyes. *That's for kids who are at the end of their rope. I don't want to be involved with …*

"What do you want?" Nita asked excitedly, her eyes wide with anticipation. She scooted toward Meera and took her hand. "You can have anything in the whole world!"

Alex stared at Nita's hopeful face, watched as her determined eyes studied their daughter's thoughtful expression.

She's right, he thought. *Meera deserves a wish.*

"You can go to Disney World, meet a celebrity … " one of the volunteers started before Meera answered.

"I want to plant a tree in the rain forest," she said with finality.

"Oh, that's a great wish!" the volunteer said. "What made you choose that?"

"I want a chance to help stop the deforestation of the rain forests that could potentially hold the cure for my disease," Meera said with more maturity than most eleven-year-olds. "I know that planting one tree won't stop deforestation, but if each one of us does our share in planting a tree, we could have a big chance of saving the rain forests all over the world."

Nita and Alex sat in silence with the volunteers. It was the most selfless, generous request the volunteers had ever heard, and Nita and Alex smiled with pride.

Meera imagined her hands in the soil, surrounded by the floral scent of tropic air, her tree becoming evidence of her contribution to humanity for many generations. She had never been to Hawaii, but she imagined that the beauty of the island, the peace and smell of the ocean, would be no different from that of *Shat Dahabee*. Eyes closed, she smiled at the thought.

Meera remained stable for two more days, but by the third, her oxygen saturation numbers had dropped gradually throughout the day. By early the next morning, doctors had decided to put the breathing tube back in and asked Alex and Nita to step into the waiting area.

He comforted his nervous wife with a hug and said, "They're just putting the tube back in. We'll be with her again in just a few minutes."

———————————⋆

The moment Alex and Nita had met Dr. Thompson, they instinctively knew she was one of those doctors who listened. One who paid close attention and spoke with patience, one who cared with a kind heart. They knew she watched her patients' statuses and conditions closely from monitors in her home. When Dr. Thompson wasn't at the hospital, Nita and Alex knew she was watching.

They had known Dr. Thompson for only a day when she saw Meera's oxygen saturation levels drop rapidly from her home monitor. A clear indicator of possible PH crisis, Dr. Thompson raced to the hospital and walked into the waiting area. Her presence brought them comfort, but her words left them panicked.

"Her lungs aren't working," Dr. Thompson said, offering no

other information. Alex could sense she was holding something big back.

"Well, what's going on? How is she doing?" he nearly shouted.

"She's in cardiac arrest and doctors are performing CPR," Dr. Thompson said hesitantly.

She was keeping something from them.

"Is there something we can do, any kind of machine that can breathe for her?" he asked, almost reading her mind.

She nodded her head. "It's a machine called ECMO that will take over and function as her heart and lungs."

Why didn't you tell us that? You're wasting time! Alex wanted to scream.

Her reluctance came from a place of concern. This was a drastic measure, and she reluctantly sought their approval.

"Do it," they said in unison.

"Just keep her alive," Alex demanded.

Dr. Thompson ran down the hall, leaving Alex and Nita alone in the waiting room, where they wrapped their arms tightly, desperately, around each other and fell to the ground sobbing.

☆ 5 ☆

The longest hour of their life passed before Dr. Thompson returned to tell them that Meera was stabilized and successfully hooked to the machine, and that they could go in to see her.

They walked slowly into a large room, half-filled by the machine. Meera was lying beside it, hands by her side with her head tilted awkwardly away from them. Her blood was leaving her body, circulating through the tubes of the machine, and re-entering, oxygenated and filtered. They watched, frozen, as red streams flowed in and out of their daughter. They walked in silence through the cool, iron air and sat by her side, staying there for the next several days.

After all the stress her heart and lungs had been under the past couple of weeks, doctors let them rest for five days before Dr. Barst's orders came to remove her temporarily from the ECMO machine. She did not want Meera's organs to give up the fight to live on their own.

Alex had done his best to strengthen and guide Meera's spirit by bringing her mind back to *Shat Dahabee* through his stories, letting her toes touch the sand, filling her lungs with her mind's memory of the ocean air, but now it was time for her body to follow.

"Temporarily removing Meera from the machine has been a success," said Dr. Thompson, who had been working hand in hand with Dr. Barst since Meera was admitted to Children's Medical Center of Dallas. "So now it's time to make a decision."

The doctors at Dallas Children's had done nearly everything they could for Meera. They could keep her alive but nothing more. They could not heal or save her.

Nita remained by Meera's side, and Alex roamed the halls, tormenting thoughts circling, haunting his mind.

Keep her in Dallas and watch her die or risk transporting her?

This was the decision they had to make.

For the past three years, Meera and either one or both of her parents had traveled every couple of months to New York to see Dr. Barst, world-renowned for her work with PH. She had run endless tests, placed Meera on different medications, and monitored her from 1,500 miles away—but now she needed Meera there.

You know there's a good chance she is not going to make it, one doctor's words echoed viciously in Alex's head.

Though her organs had grown strong enough to function temporarily without the machine, her lungs continued to fill with blood; her kidneys were failing. With no more options in Dallas, getting Meera to New York seemed to be their only option.

But what if something goes wrong on the flight? Alex thought, pacing. He hadn't had more than an hour of sleep at a time in a week. He had never felt physically or emotionally weaker in his entire life. He wandered while Nita stayed by Meera's side.

If we keep her here, she probably won't make it, he analyzed. *Something could go wrong on the flight. But there's not much else they can do for her here.*

These thoughts, these realities, crashed violently in his head, pulling at him, tearing him apart.

I can't make this decision! he wanted to scream.

Alex had been a data analyst for fifteen years, and plugging numbers into spreadsheets, comparing historical data, creating root cause analyses were the only ways he knew how to deal with problems, to find solutions. He had spent countless hours on his laptop, by Meera's side, researching PH, understanding her condition from its core.

He wanted to know why she bled the way she did when she was first admitted to the hospital. He found several causes and traced them, filling in the blanks of his hand-drawn, fish-bone diagram. He created reports using reverse analysis and used his skilled method of data mining to answer questions. He had watched Meera's stats on every monitor, interpreted their sounds with his eyes closed, and created an internal database containing all of her vital statistics.

It had been his only way to process their situation, to feel any sense of control over it, but now none of it mattered. His knowledge of her numbers, the answers he had found, the research he had done, the charts he had created, none of it could answer this question for him.

Tormented by his thoughts, Alex staggered into a waiting room chair and sat, alone, embraced by the uncomfortable silence of the chilly room.

What do we do? he asked himself as his head fell into his hands. His and Nita's support system—their family and friends—was in Dallas. They didn't know a soul in New York City. If they were going to lose Meera, they wanted to be in Dallas, surrounded by family and friends, rather than losing her during or after transport to a city fifteen hundred miles from home.

As Alex cried, the sound of footsteps echoing in the quiet hallway made him look up. Meera's elementary school principal, Mark Speck, walked toward him, a comforting smile on his face, together with the school nurse, Megan Schuler, and the after-school coordinator, Mary Jeanne Higbee, at his side. They had made several visits to show their support for Meera, and in this moment of agony, this raw feeling of anguish, they were exactly who Alex needed.

"I can't do this," he wept. "We need to decide to keep Meera here or transport her to New York, and we could lose her either way. I can't do this. I don't know how to make this decision."

"Would you like us to pray together?" Mrs. Shuler asked, hugging Alex then looking at him through tears.

"Yes, please," he managed, and they took one another's hands and bowed their heads.

"God, we pray for Meera, and we ask that you guide Alex and Nita," Mr. Speck said. "Help Alex and his family make the right decision."

Alex's body warmed, his heart ached, and his mind cleared.

He had his answer—*get Meera to New York.*

It was the clearest message, the most reassuring and overwhelming feeling he had ever experienced, and nothing inside of him doubted the decision he believed was just made for him. Nita agreed, knowing the risk of transporting Meera but finding some hope that, if they made it to New York, Meera could survive.

⋆ 6 ⋆

On transport day, nurses wheeled Meera, intubated but awake and alert, in a stretcher through the double doors and into the sunshine for the first time in weeks. She had forgotten the smell of Texas air, so she took it in, one shallow breath at a time.

"Wind in my face," she wrote on the Magna Doodle before closing her eyes and tilting her head toward the sky, letting the sun calm her, the breeze soothe her. They arrived at the airport safely, and Nita and Meera boarded the plane. Limited space forced Alex to make the flight commercially.

Shortly after takeoff, he gripped the armrests of his chair as the force of a sudden drop thrust his body from his seat, shoving the belt into his gut. The left side of the plane dipped, the right side soared, as it shook furiously before freefalling and leveling momentarily. It swayed and jumped in the wind, danced in the clouds, for the next four hours.

"God, please take all the turbulence from Meera's plane and put it on me," Alex begged, waves in his stomach crashing as he imagined his daughter's plane plunging and swaying to the sky's relentless, violent rhythm.

After all she's been through, just get her to New York, he pleaded.

When he arrived in New York, Alex was relieved to hear that Meera's plane, flying at a much lower altitude, experienced very little turbulence and would arrive shortly. He walked through the hospital as he would his hallways at home and tapped on the office door of Dr. Barst.

After so many years of traveling to see her, just being in Dr.

Barst's office, in her care, relieved some of the pressure in Alex's chest. He could finally start to breathe.

Nita and Meera finally arrived, and ten minutes after settling her into her new hospital bed, Meera suddenly clutched the metal rails as the voices of her family and chatter from the TV blended to the background of her mind's panic.

I can't breathe, she thought. *I can't breathe!*

Her body stiffened with determination to take another breath, but invisible hands wrapped themselves around her small neck, squeezing, suffocating. She thrashed as air crept slowly, mockingly, through its straw-sized passage before Meera's body went limp, her fight dead.

Doctors from the ICU rushed in with a balloon and pumped air into her lungs, but the resistance was as great as the force. As air seeped out, they quickly and frantically hooked Meera up to an oxygen machine, started the monitors, and hovered over her blue body as Alex ran from the room.

"We should have never brought her here!" he yelled in the hallway, punching his fist into the wall. "This is all my fault!"

His shouts became whispers.

"This is all my fault. All my fault," he repeated, pacing the halls, hands in his hair.

"She's going to be okay!" Nita said.

How are you always so sure?! Alex wanted to scream.

But once again, she was right. Doctors discovered a blood clot in her breathing tube that was blocking her airway, and after it was out and a new tube was in, she could breathe, her face regaining its beautiful color.

Okay, we made the right decision, Alex assured himself, keeping his mind in the moment. He couldn't let himself imagine what might have happened if the incident had taken place in the air—in the small confines of an airplane with fewer doctors and less equipment than the hospital they were in now.

Shaking, Alex sat silently, internally thanking God for those ten minutes He had spared.

Over the next several months, Meera had her good days and her bad, an emotional mixture of successful stats, blood transfusions, surgeries, and steadied and crashed oxygen levels. Alex traveled between Manhattan and home, maintaining his career and visiting Zane, who was staying with his uncle in Dallas. No matter which city he was in, Alex found inspiration in the sunrise of the Dallas or the New York dawn. As the sun crept into darkened skies every morning, subtle glow leading the way, Alex prayed deeper and harder than he had ever prayed in his life. He knew God was taking those prayers with Him every night with the sun, delivering hope and assurance with each morning rise.

Through prayer, he kept Meera alive during a series of close calls—a nurse accidentally switching the medicine in her IV, leading to lung failure and paralysis of her GI tract, and her appendix rupturing less than a week later.

Zane flew out to New York to meet his family for the holidays, and on New Year's Eve, Alex and Nita looked out the window to the celebration below with a renewed sense of hope.

"Two-thousand-seven is behind us," Alex said, his arm wrapped around Nita's shoulders. He rested his head on hers as he looked down at Meera in her wheelchair, her little brother by her side. They were a complete family again. "This is a new beginning for us."

He felt it with every crash and color of the dazzling fireworks show in the distance. The black sky sparkled with vibrant colors that eventually faded and vanished into the night. They could hear the cheers and shouts floating from Times Square, and they felt as though they had something to celebrate, too. Meera had held on for this long—had survived two cardiac arrests, a disconnect from a life-supporting breathing machine, a risky transport, paralysis of her GI tract, and a ruptured appendix—and they knew in their hearts that there was nothing their daughter couldn't survive.

But they were not at the end of their journey, and they knew it. Still supported by machines, Meera faced two surgeries in March that, if successful, could lead to her recovery.

———————— ✶

When Meera was still in Dallas, doctors inserted a temporary Flolan line to keep the blood vessels in her lungs and throughout her body open and flowing, which meant limited physical activity and little exposure to water.

"She can't go swimming anymore?" Zane had asked sadly. Some of his favorite memories were playing Marco Polo with Meera in their community swimming pool, having races, and seeing who could hold his or her breath longer under water.

Saddened by the news, he wrote in a spiral notebook, "I wish for my sister to get off of Flolan so that she can go swimming again."

In New York, doctors removed Meera's appendix and placed a feeding tube in her stomach during the first surgery and inserted a permanent Flolan line during the second. She would always have to wear the Flolan pump, an intravenously administered drug, meaning her brother's wish would never come true.

The last time Meera ever swam with her family was the summer before she became ill.

They had traveled to Dinosaur Valley State Park in Glen Rose, Texas, when Meera was eleven and Zane, seven, for their first-ever camping trip. They hiked along the Brazos River, searching for fossilized dinosaur footprints in the slate-colored stone.

Meera stopped at every track, placing her foot next to the giant, three-toed prints as though comparing them to famous handprints on the Hollywood Walk of Fame. They followed the tracks to the riverbank and found a deep pocket called the Blue Hole, where kids jumped from cliffs and families splashed beneath the hot, Texas sun.

Fascinated by the minnows darting past her legs, Meera wanted to watch their activity from a distance. Alex carried her in his arms and trudged through the clear, warm water's edge. He placed her back into the water when Zane wanted to see who could venture further into the water without going under. On her tiptoes, Meera squealed and lunged toward her father, who plucked her from the water and back into his arms.

The memory of that moment made Alex smile as he sat with Meera in her New York hospital room, finally back at her side.

⋆ 7 ⋆

A couple of months passed. Alex and Zane had returned home to Dallas in January so Alex could work and Zane could continue a somewhat normal, second grader's life. It tore Alex apart daily to be so far from his daughter, but knowing she was gaining strength and making progress gave him the reassurance he needed to know she was on the path to recovery.

It was the beginning of March when he and Zane returned to New York and stayed for the entire month. Anticipating their arrival, Meera excitedly said to Nita, "I'm gonna show Daddy how strong I am by standing and giving him a hug and kiss when he gets here!"

When the day in early March arrived, Meera dressed in a snow white robe she had received for Christmas and asked Nita to neatly French braid her long, black hair. Meera sat in a chair and waited patiently for Alex to walk through the door. When he did, she silently pushed at the arms of her chair, concentrating. Slowly and steadily, she stood and raised her chin, looking up at her father, intense pride in her eyes.

He had doubted for so many months that this moment would ever come, and when it did, the pure bliss he felt carried him across the room until Meera was wrapped tightly in his arms. He closed his eyes as they filled with tears.

"I am so proud of you, Meera," he managed.

He sat beside her the rest of the day, listening to stories of how she had grown so strong. She told him about the first time she managed to sit on the edge of her bed, the moment she was able to get out of it, the exercises she had done and the therapy dog, a big, black poodle named Scout, that helped to mobilize her arms.

"I dressed Scout in bandanas and sweaters," she said, giggling. "She even let me paint her toes pink."

As Meera spoke, the hope she felt poured into Alex. He knew life would not be the same—she could no longer swim or play sports or live without some worry—but she was alive, and that was all that mattered.

———————✳

After Meera's two successful surgeries in March, Alex and Zane returned to Dallas. On Zane's first day back to school, Alex walked him onto the campus and into Ms. Adams's second-grade classroom, the same room where Meera had spent her second-grade year—the year she was diagnosed with PH.

Alex pictured her sitting in one of those small desks, raising her hand. He remembered the homework he and Nita helped her with and the stories she would write. Ms. Adams could see the pain on Alex's face as he remembered the day Meera graduated from fifth grade. The halls had been lined with parents and teachers, clapping and cheering as their soon-to-be middle schoolers proudly paraded down the halls.

The moment Alex and Nita had learned about PH, Meera's future had become uncertain, the severity of her condition unknown. Graduating from fifth grade was a milestone in her life, and as Alex pictured her smiling face as she walked with her friends down those halls on graduation day, Ms. Adams put an arm around his shoulder and squeezed.

"Those are the memories you should cherish," she said with a small, encouraging smile.

Blinking back tears before they fell, he knew she was right, but those memories made Alex want Meera home that much more.

———— ✳

On April 16, 2008, Meera was finally released. The automatic doors of the hospital entrance slid open, and she closed her eyes from the shock of the bright sun and lifted her face toward it. She had been in New York for six months but never had a chance to inhale the scent of the city, the smell of freedom, until that moment.

Planters of tulips with rainbow beauty surrounded Meera as Nita wheeled her alongside them. The closest Meera had come to feeling nature's embrace was the sun's warmth pouring in through her hospital window during naps she took with Nita on a small couch beneath the window.

On this very special day, she savored every smell, every bird chirp and rustle of leaves, because she knew that the next month would be spent in a New Jersey rehab facility. During that month in New Jersey, she grew strong enough to return to Dallas, where Alex and Zane were waiting.

A group of "Welcome Home" balloons peeked from behind tall, cement pillars in the baggage claim area of the Dallas airport, swaying in the light breeze of scurrying crowds. Alex gripped the balloon strings and a bouquet of flowers in his hand with anticipation, Zane's hand in his other.

As Meera and Nita approached, they jumped out from behind the pillar and hollered, "Welcome Home!"

Meera, who had always welcomed surprises with as much enthusiasm as getting blood drawn or taking a math test, couldn't contain her smile. Wrapped in her father's arms, she was finally home.

When they pulled into their driveway, twenty neighbors and friends waited with a sign Alex had made in the colors of Meera's bedroom—lavender and lime green—that read, "Welcome Home, Meera!"

Meera's smiling eyes were back and so was her laugh. The celebration of her return home continued at school when she went back the very next week, just two weeks before the end of sixth grade.

"We missed you!" and "Welcome back!" her classmates hollered, arms in the air, as she walked into her classroom for the first time. They stood and cheered as her jaw dropped, and she covered her cherry-colored cheeks with her hands.

Meera had been out of school for most of the sixth grade, but after a meeting with her parents and teachers, Principal Ann Aston decided to let her take a placement exam to determine whether or not she needed to repeat the sixth grade. Meera couldn't imagine her friends moving on without her.

She passed the test with high scores and was placed in seventh-grade honors classes.

Alex and Nita believe it was the work Meera had done with

Mary Hennigan, an Irish teacher at the New York-Presbyterian Hospital, who helped Meera escape to other places—back in time to the Renaissance, into the magical world of *Harry Potter*—with her readings and lessons.

"She's been back ten minutes and she's already showing you up!" teased her sixth-grade math teacher, Mrs. Crawford, who had supported the decision to let Meera take the placement test. Mrs. Crawford had put a problem on the board and let Meera, the only student with a raised hand, share the answer with the class.

⋆ 8 ⋆

Life was moving forward, but something invisible, unexplainable, was holding Alex back. He needed some kind of closure from the nightmare they had lived through, and the only place he could think to find it was at Children's Medical Center of Dallas, where Meera had started and nearly ended her battle. He needed to stand in the waiting room, peek into the ICU to reassure himself that it was really over.

During a routine visit, Alex, Nita, Meera, and Zane made their way to the twelfth floor of the hospital, got off of the elevator, and headed down the empty, quiet hallway toward the locked doors of the ICU. The doors suddenly swung open and out walked Dr. Thompson, who slowed in pure shock at the sight of Alex and Nita.

She looked at Meera with disbelief—like she wasn't the little girl who had failed kidneys and lungs filled with blood the last time she had seen her.

Dr. Thompson's glossy eyes lit up with her smile as she reached out her arms and hurried toward Meera and her family. She bent down and squeezed Meera's small body in her arms before looking up at her parents.

"I will never be able to repay you for what you did for our daughter," Alex said, hugging Dr. Thompson.

"You can repay me by inviting me to her high school and college graduations," she said with the same confidence she always had when telling Alex and Nita that their daughter would be okay.

"I also want an invitation to her wedding," she added softly, winking down at Meera.

The thought of walking his daughter down the aisle brought tears to Alex's eyes, and he could not speak.

Dr. Thompson's words, her belief in Meera's future, were exactly what Alex needed. When they left the hospital, he knew he could finally move on.

Over the next six months, Meera continued physical therapy and made frequent doctor visits, regaining all of her strength and most of the weight she had lost. She walked proudly through life with the Flolan pump attached to her waist, the only reminder that she was ever ill.

In seventh grade, she continued playing the violin and enjoyed Girl Scouts, which she had been involved with since she was eight years old. She never lost her love for science and won first place in the school's science fair that year—taking her to the district and regional fairs—with a project comparing the UV blocking capabilities of different materials and the energy conservation of each.

Her life, which had nearly ended just a year before, was before her, waiting. She had made it this far, and she was determined to attain every goal, reach every dream. She knew she had survived for a reason—to become a PH doctor and to find a cure for her disease.

* 9 *

The breeze, dampened with the scent of ocean and hibiscus, brushed Meera's skin as she hiked with her family through trails of Iao Valley in Maui, Hawaii. The clouds had parted earlier that morning, rain ceasing nourishment to its forest below for a few short hours. Sunrays stained the blue sky, pouring in streaks from the heavens, breaking through thick, white puffs still hugging the tip of the Iao Needle.

Mist and rainbows lingered in the high skies, but the delicious air surrounding them remained warm and calm and welcoming as they came to the spot where Meera's young tree would start its new life.

She placed the three-foot-tall native Ho'awa tree on the ground and plunged a shovel into the moist, Maui soil. After a few digs, she handed the shovel to Zane, who plowed into the ground with full force. They removed the tree from its container and placed it into the ground, pushing on its roots, breaking its perfect form, letting it—letting them—become part of the Hawaiian earth.

After planting Meera's tree, she and her family stood back to look at it, proudly placed along a paved path of Iao Valley State Park, where thousands of field trip students would see it and become inspired by the story of its existence.

"This tree was planted by Meera Salamah in partnership with the Make-A-Wish Foundation," a plaque staked near the tree announced to the world. It would be there for decades of time, for generations of people to see.

I want a chance to help stop the deforestation of the rain forests that could potentially hold the cure for my disease. Meera's words repeated in Alex's mind as he recalled his daughter's wish from her hospital room more than a year before.

She's going to change the world, Nita thought proudly, and this was the first step to fulfilling her purpose.

Planting the tree connected Meera and her family to the Hawaiian life they had been experiencing over the past week with luaus, helicopter rides, dinner cruises, submarine rides, whale watching, and walks on the beach. Inspired not only by the beauty of the island but also by the feeling of liberty that signified their entire trip, Alex and Nita gave themselves something they were denied sixteen years earlier.

They had met and fallen in love while attending the University of Texas at Dallas, both studying electrical engineering. Disapproval came from both families—hers from India, his from Lebanon—so they went against their families' wishes and eloped, giving up their dream of a big wedding.

Now, sixteen years later, love had gotten them through everything, and with the Pacific Ocean as their backdrop, the palm trees spying from above, their two beautiful children by their sides, they decided to renew their vows, barefoot in the sand.

They all dressed in off-white, Alex and Zane in suits, Meera and Nita in flowing dresses, with matching leis of bright, plum-colored flowers. Arms outstretched, hands linked in front of them, Alex and Nita stared at each other and repeated after the preacher.

Alex heard the words his wife was saying, but the true message behind their love, their marriage, was unspoken. The same strength that had gotten him through Meera's illness poured from Nita's big brown eyes and into him, and he felt like the luckiest man on earth to have her as his partner through this life.

Alex realized in that moment that some marriages might have fallen apart in the middle of everything they had gone through to save Meera, every difficult moment, every impossible decision, but they had survived.

After the ceremony, the four of them created a single jar of sand together, simultaneously pouring layers of different colors, watching them flow and mix.

Later that day, they walked down the beach as a family, until

Zane ran off to explore and Meera lingered behind, feeling the tickle of the sea between her toes. She watched the waves roll and crash, and while she longed to jump into them, to be part of them, she was just thankful to enjoy them from the shore.

Alex watched as the breeze caught Meera's dress, her hair, and he knew it was time to let go. Meera was free. It finally felt real that there were no more numbers to watch, no more beeps to interpret, no more stats to worry about. The whole family was free.

Watching Meera walk along the sand, Alex remembered taking her mind to the beach with his words when she was ill, and now, here they were, at the place he believed kept her alive. He had reminded her to breathe, to take in the ocean air, and now he could finally do the same.

They all could.

Dakota Hawkins

"I have fought the good fight, I have finished the race, I have kept the faith."

—2 Timothy 4:7

"**O**NE … TWO … three … four … " Dakota said, breathing in slow, steady breaths, air crawling gently, obediently, through his mask.

"Five … six … seven … eight … " Riley continued.

Dakota remained calm, focused, as his eyes sent an unspoken message to his younger brother.

Keep counting, they commanded, his smile, provoking and competitive. Eyes locked, a silent understanding between them, Dakota and Riley continued to count, a fight against the other's will.

"Nine … ten … eleven … " Dakota continued.

They weren't on the football field, or racing quads, or preying on the same seven-point deer in the woods. This wasn't a game of baseball or basketball or "Underwear Olympics" that they played nightly with their father, Henry, in the hallways of their cozy, Cabot, Arkansas, home.

This time, Dakota and Riley were on the same team, fighting the same fight—but it was in their nature, their blood, to keep the competition alive, even during a transplant from one brother to the other.

"Twelve … " Riley nearly whispered into his mask, eyelids pushing down against his mental strength.

Keep counting, he demanded silently. He couldn't let his brother win.

Dakota had always been the kid in track and field who pulled ahead of the other runners and stayed that way past the finish line.

He was the star of every team—scoring the most goals, the highest points, the greatest touchdowns. He was a born athlete, a natural leader who was used to winning, addicted to victory.

Not today, Riley thought, but his words were floating away, leaving him.

"C'mon boys, keep counting," he heard from one of the doctors, whose voice, encouraging competition, became whispers, clouds in his mind.

Dakota's face, his stark blue eyes that were once paired with hair as fiery as his spirit—hair now gone—remained still and just as strong as Riley faded into the darkness.

"Thirteen … fourteen … " Dakota continued, but once he knew Riley was completely under, he closed his eyes, sinking heavily beneath the wave of anesthesia flowing through his body, letting it carry him away.

Dakota and Riley lay side by side, in silent peace, as the process began—the process to save Dakota's life.

★ 2 ★

A year and a half earlier, Dakota ran beneath the white glow of towering stadium lights, which pushed against cold, black air, lighting up the small, all-American, football-loving town of Cabot.

Bleachers surrounding the field rumbled beneath pounding feet, shook with excitement, as eleven-year-old Dakota and his team, the Green Bay Packers, took on the undefeated Dallas Cowboys in the last game of the peewee championship.

A cool, November breeze carried the scent of fresh-cut grass and powdery chalk into the stands, where dozens of familiar faces screamed and cheered for their boys, who, for that one night, were NFL players in the Super Bowl.

Dakota was on fire. His cleats tore into the earth, heart pounding with every step, as he made every pass, every tackle, every play with perfection.

He had grown up on the sidelines, mapping out plays in the dirt for Henry, loosening the hillsides playing one-on-one with Riley. He spent years studying his father's coaching technique, memorizing tactic, internalizing strategy, until Henry, who had played football for Arkansas Tech University and was an assistant coach for the Cabot High School football team for the past fourteen years, determined he was old enough to play.

The night of the last championship game, Dakota was unstoppable. He scored two touchdowns before the ball, leather spinning in a perfect spiral, landed in his arms at the twenty-yard line. He looked up from under his helmet, eyes of a cat before pouncing, and ran with the breeze down the length of the field, zigzagging, dodging, sprinting, until he was safe in the end zone.

He smashed the ball hard onto the ground, letting it fly, while his teammates stormed and the crowd went wild. They had won the game and the championship. At the end of the night, Dakota and his fellow Green Bay Packers smacked high fives into the crisp air and wrapped their arms around their hard-earned trophy.

"You played your heart out, buddy," Henry said, hugging his son after the game. "Three touchdowns!"

"Yeah, that was an awesome game!" Dakota shouted, and Henry reached for Dakota's forehead to find it warm, clammy.

"How are you feeling?" he asked.

"Fine, Dad," Dakota said.

"Are you sure?" Henry asked, concerned.

It was hard to say whether the fire beneath his hand was fever or the game's intensity. He let it fall from his son's face, remembering the strep throat diagnosis Dakota's doctor had given the week before.

Antibiotics she prescribed were not working, and Dakota's fever was persistent. Until the big game, his body had been weak, lethargic, but that night, Henry and Sharon, Dakota and Riley's mom, saw the first sign of energy, the real Dakota, that they had seen in several days. They saw his face crease with determination as he sprinted down the field, his spirit as strong as ever.

During the weeks following the game, Dakota's walk gradually became slower, his skin whiter. Sharon tried to keep things as normal as possible for her boys as Christmas approached—a smile on her face, traditions alive—but her insides ached with every forced smile, every attempt at normalcy.

Why are the antibiotics not working? Why is he so weak? she questioned, the thoughts heavy on her mind, the answers unknown.

They baked cookies together and delivered them to retirement homes as they had every year, watched the town's annual Christmas parade, attended their church's cantata, and participated in their schools' holiday programs. They put up their Christmas tree, hung ornaments, decorated their home, enjoyed the peace of freshly fallen snow, and counted the days until Santa arrived—but rather than a jolly heart, Sharon's was heavy.

Her mother's intuition, an internal knowing, grabbed at her stomach, made her ache with worry.

His bruises are probably from playing football, Sharon told herself as she stayed up late at night researching the symptoms her son had shown for weeks, but she couldn't convince even herself. The symptoms were too close, too familiar.

She read: "Leukemia—headaches, lethargy, bruising."

A few hours after Christmas Eve dinner, Sharon stood in the kitchen with her older sister, Regina.

"Oh, my goodness, what will I do if my Dakota has leukemia?" she sobbed into her sister's arms.

The rest of their family was on the other side of the kitchen doors, laughing, celebrating, opening gifts, while Sharon remained in Regina's embrace, their tears flowing together, dripping down linked arms.

"Oh, Sharon," Regina managed. "I'm so sorry, I just don't know what to say."

She didn't want to give Sharon false assurance with "It's going to be okay" or "I know everything will be just fine" because, the truth was, she didn't know. Instead, Regina hugged her tightly, feeling her sister's pain deep within her own gut—a feeling of absolute desperation.

"I just don't know what to say," she cried, almost whispered, into her little sister's ear.

⋆ 3 ⋆

The next night, at their church's Christmas program, Dakota's pediatrician, Dr. Ruth Ann Blair, stood beside Sharon in the choir loft, getting ready to sing their first song. Dakota walked down the aisle, toward the front of the church where he always sat, and as he took his seat, Sharon leaned over and whispered to Dr. Blair, "Does Dakota look pale to you?"

Friends and family agreed that, over the past few weeks, his skin had turned the color of gray sheep's wool, but when Dr. Blair's eyes studied him from a distance, squinting with concentration and then with concern, Sharon had her answer. That dark answer, lurking behind every thought, creeping through every part of her mind, was stepping into the light, standing directly before her.

"Yes, he looks pale to me," Dr. Blair confirmed gently. She had diagnosed him just a few weeks before with strep throat and could see that the antibiotics were not working. "Have him come see me after Christmas."

The music started, the soft, sweet sound of praise and rejoice. Sharon stared at her songbook and then blankly into the eyes of the congregation, and she knew hers were empty and deeply sad.

She glanced at Dakota, and the words, her voice, flowed heavily, resiliently, around the heavy lump in her throat. She made it through the cantata as she had the rest of the Christmas season, with a forced smile and a sickened heart.

———— ✷

"Mama, can we go home to play with my new toys?" Dakota asked the next day. It was 1:00 p.m. on Christmas afternoon, and the family had just finished eating a big, traditional meal at Papaw's, Henry's father's, home.

The adults had gathered in the living room, drinking coffee and squeezing dessert into their stuffed bellies, while the kids played with their new toys. Sharon looked down at her son, who loved playing with his cousins, especially on Christmas, and smiled as best she could.

"Sure, baby," she said, keeping her tears tucked away.

"Jingle Bells" and "Deck the Halls" swirled softly around the car on their drive home as Sharon glanced at Dakota, whose head was resting on his seat, eyes opening and closing slowly.

"Mama, thank you for a wonderful Christmas," he said, looking at Sharon as she kept her eyes on the quiet, open road, not a soul around.

She looked at him with smiling eyes full of tears that she quickly blinked away when she turned her head back to the road.

"This was the best Christmas ever," he added.

She couldn't look at him again. She stared at the highway,

reached a hand over, and squeezed Dakota's knee, pursing her lips into a half smile, just in case he was looking to her for a sign that everything would be okay.

She knew this wasn't his best Christmas ever. In her mind, the piles of toys in their trunk should have made him feel better. The distraction of family, the excitement of the holiday, should have been enough, but it wasn't.

It was Christmas, and he wanted to go home and rest.

"You're welcome, baby," was all Sharon could manage, the lump in her throat suffocating.

The sweetness in Dakota's voice, the kindness in his eyes that afternoon, would live inside of her forever. She believed it was his way of telling her that, somewhere, deep, deep down, he knew something was terribly wrong.

They both did.

★ 4 ★

"The doctor needs to speak with you," a nurse said the next day at Dr. Blair's office. "Dakota, sweetie, come with me to watch some cartoons."

Sharon didn't know this nurse, but even the eyes of a stranger could not conceal such a dark, unwanted secret.

God, this can't be happening, Sharon pleaded. She wanted to stay right there, in that moment, before another word was spoken. She clung to those last few seconds of not knowing, of having an ounce left of hope. She wanted to live in that moment forever.

"Sharon," Dr. Blair said when she walked into the room. She spoke as gently as she could, and Sharon closed her eyes. There was no easy way to say it. "Dakota's white blood cell count is through the roof. I'm afraid he might have childhood leukemia."

There they were: the words she knew were coming. Dr. Blair wrapped her arms around Sharon as she slipped through them.

"No, no, no, no, no ... " she sobbed.

Maybe if she said it enough times, if she squeezed her eyes tight enough, shook her head back and forth hard enough, this would all go away.

"This can't be, this can't be ... " Sharon cried.

Dakota doesn't have cancer, she told herself, hardly able to even think the word.

Her body, her mind, numb.

She couldn't live without Dakota, so the only option was to beat it.

Dr. Blair immediately sent her, Henry, and Dakota to Arkansas Children's Hospital for blood tests and draws, and that day, it was confirmed. Dr. David Becton, the hospital's chief oncologist, gave the news to Dakota in a way a child could understand.

"You have leukemia," he said to Dakota, who suddenly turned from a growing eleven-year-old back into Sharon's baby boy.

She watched as her son studied the doctor's face. She wanted so desperately to wrap him in her arms, to protect him from the world, from cancer, from the rest of what the doctor was about to say, but she knew she couldn't. This was in God's hands now.

"Leukemia is a type of blood cancer," Dr. Becton continued, "and the bad guys are fighting against the good guys in your immune system. We are going to annihilate the bad guys with chemotherapy, which we will start you on tomorrow."

He didn't tell Dakota that he suspected Acute Myelogenous Leukemia (AML), one of the most destructive, hard-to-beat cancers rarely found in children. He wanted to keep it simple but real.

"It's going to make you sick," he said. "And ... " Dr. Becton paused.

He looked at Dakota's beautiful, thick red hair and added, "Your hair will come out."

"Son … " Henry said when Dakota started to cry. As his father, he needed to stay strong, even if his insides were falling apart. Henry placed an arm around Dakota's shoulders and spoke his language. "We are in a marathon, and we are going to cross the finish line, and then we are going to keep running and running. We're gonna keep our eye on what's ahead, on the finish line."

Dakota, blinking tears down his lightly freckled cheeks, looked at his dad and nodded.

"Will I ever play sports again?" he asked, turning his reddened face to Dr. Becton.

He smiled at his little patient.

"Yes, you will."

★ 5 ★

Dakota was admitted to the hospital that day, and two hours after he got settled into his hospital bed, a Child Life volunteer at the hospital brought Dakota a stuffed toy, Doc, one of Snow White's Seven Dwarfs. Dakota placed the doll on his lap, making room for a sheet of paper, and began to draw.

Slowly, meticulously, he sketched an outline of Doc's body, then filled in the details of his face. Beside Doc, he wrote, "I can beat it," and at the top of the page, added, "I can do all things through Christ, who gives me strength—Philippians 4:13."

Sharon's eyes welled up when she saw the picture. She immediately thought of the time Dakota had brought his small *New Testament Bible* to show-and-tell in kindergarten.

Dakota drew this picture the day he was admitted to the hospital
after being diagnosed with cancer.

"How many of you go to church?" he had asked his classmates, holding the Bible high into the air. A few kids raised their hands, most didn't, some looked around, uneasy. His teacher, Mrs. Melder, who attended the same church as Dakota and his family, stood in the corner, watching, smiling.

"Well, if you don't, you should consider it," Dakota finished and sat down.

Even with news of cancer and within the confining walls of a hospital instead of a football field's freedom, his faith was still alive, and so was his will.

The next day, after Dr. Becton confirmed to Sharon and Henry that Dakota had AML, a bag of red chemotherapy, the meanest, most intense and aggressive form of treatment, hung beside Dakota, dripping its life into his veins.

"I will beat this," Sharon read again, and she pictured him at two weeks old, lifting himself with his arms when most babies couldn't even lift their heads.

He's a fighter, she thought, suddenly seeing the significance, the irony, of his name—Dakota, Native American for "Strong Warrior" in the Sioux tribe—she had always been told.

After two weeks of chemo, Dakota was in full remission. It was the end of January, but to make sure every cancer cell was gone, defeated, doctors continued his intense protocol for the next four months.

Most treatments kept him in the hospital for a week at a time before he was able to go home, where Sharon, his "codoctor," administered natural remedies she had researched to keep him fighting—Shiitake mushrooms to build his immune system, oxygenated water to supply his blood, green barley for its natural healing ability, and milk from a local goat farm for his bones.

After learning that sugar can potentially feed leukemia cells, she kept Dakota on a low-sugar diet, had him take as many herbs and vitamins as possible, and eat fresh, raw vegetables to build up his weakened immune system. These remedies seemed to keep away the fever and infection that many leukemia patients developed, but Dakota still had good days and bad—days when he couldn't get out of bed, days he couldn't keep anything down, quiet days of sickness and sleep.

One morning during a hospital stay, Dakota slept soundly, peacefully, as the sun rose and poured in through his window, crawling slowly across his face and onto his pillow, revealing the undeniable sign that they were actually going through this, cancer's most irrefutable presence—a beautiful lock of strawberry hair lay, detached, inches from his head.

This can't be! Sharon wailed in her mind, silent tears and whispered sobs escaping her uncontrollably. *This isn't right!*

It didn't take long before every strand, falling out by the handful, was gone.

When Dakota saw the sympathy, the sadness, in Henry's eyes, he teased, "Daddy, you always said hair was way overrated."

Dakota looked at his father's balding head, sensed from his smile that he was warming Henry's broken heart.

"Now I look like you!"

He was easing Henry's pain, softening the severity of his situation, as he had tried to do from the beginning when he said with determination, "I can beat this."

During hospital stays, Dakota had good days and bad. On good days, when chemo would release its firm grip, even momentarily, Dakota would roam the halls and even leave with doctors' permission to go to the movies, race go-carts with Henry and Riley, and make visits to Toys "R" Us, before returning for more treatment.

"I'll be in here!" he whispered to his parents loudly one afternoon on a good day, crawling into the medical closet of his hospital room.

He had filled two syringes with apple juice and closed the door behind him, waiting patiently to hear the voice of one of his nurses.

"All right, Dakota ... " she said before he threw open the door, aimed and squirted the juice, his laugh filling the room, the halls, the lives of other families nearby who needed the sound of a child's laughter.

Dakota had pulled his first prank at six years old while visiting

Sharon's mom, "Mama Lamb," on her farm at the end of a dirt road in Delight, Arkansas. Mama Lamb's tiny washroom was in the corner of the barn, the clothesline outside. It was a breezy day and clothes flapped in the wind as Dakota helped hang them with wooden pins.

When Mama Lamb entered the barn, darkened without the help of the sun peeking through its door, Dakota used all his weight to swing it shut, locking her tightly into that dim, smelly barn.

"Dakota, if I ever get a hold of you, I'm gonna wear you out!" Mama Lamb shouted, and Dakota chuckled, just the way he did when he squirted apple juice at his nurses or put Riley in his place in his hospital bed, shocking the nurses when they'd pull back the sheets.

On days when Dakota wasn't feeling well, when it took all of his energy to get out of bed, he would pile games, books, puzzles, and video games from friends, family, and church members into the hospital's red wagon—the wagon used to discharge kids once they got well—and drag his IV pole with its hanging bag of fluid to distribute the gifts to the other sick children on the third floor.

Dakota visited a two-year-old little girl with leukemia down the hall one day and told his parents about how happy he had made her. He imitated her smile, mimicked her laugh, reliving the girl's joy when he handed her a "Dora the Explorer" balloon. "Oooh, Dora! I love Dora!"

He created smiles with jokes, laughter from words, and hope with his presence in the hallways coming and going from his hospital room.

★ 6 ★

Dakota remained in remission but struggled against the tight grip of chemotherapy, its cruel demands, relentless misery, until May, when he received his final treatment and a "last chemo party" in the oncology department's outside courtyard where he was showered with love and gifts from friends and family.

The courtyard's water fountain, its colorful flowers and small wooden bridge, had been a place of escape, of make-believe, for Sharon and Dakota throughout his treatment. They had left the doors of the cold, sterile-smelling hospital every day to enter this place of peace, where they shared their thoughts, sat in silence, read books, and made plans for when Dakota came home for good.

Sky-high glass windows with peeking patients surrounded them, reminding them of where they were—in the middle of this nightmare. But in those moments, in their minds, they had left the hospital and entered the outside world.

The day of the party was a day when the door opened, even just the slightest bit, to that outside world—that world filled with family and friends and a future without cancer. Dakota had undergone his last treatment that morning, and in his twelve-year-old mind, "last" meant forever. But for Sharon and Henry, "last" signified only a moment in time—the "last" treatment in a month, a year, a lifetime? They didn't know.

All they knew was they had this moment, this very special moment that brought Dakota, weak and sick from chemo, out of his hospital room and into the sunshine, where six of his best friends gathered around and performed a humorous jingle they wrote about Dakota and his love for sports and life.

Bless his heart, Sharon thought. *He just doesn't feel good.*

She could see the misery in his face, the weakness in his eyes, but, as always, the joy he had in his heart, the hope and happiness he felt in his soul, lived in his smile, which reached from ear to ear as he received gifts and hugs from his friends, his family, his doctors, and his nurses.

A hole of uncertainty ached in Sharon's heart as she watched her son's happy but pained face, and while the reality of possible relapse would inevitably live in the back of her mind, she decided to view this moment as a milestone, the first step in possibly beating cancer forever.

The peace that surrounded them that day—their family and friends, the bridge and the trickle of the fountain, the place that had provided hours of respite for Dakota and his mom—would soon become a memory for them to hang on to. A memory of the place they left, the door they stepped through, to re-enter life.

When the party was over, that's where Dakota went, to the outside world, the real world—the world he had wanted to rejoin for the past five months. He had the entire summer before his seventh-grade year to let his body heal from the damages of chemotherapy. After a few weeks, Sharon, who hadn't left Dakota's side since December, knew she needed to let go.

She, Henry, and Riley drove Dakota to church camp at Camp Wyldewood, about thirty miles away, where she and her siblings had spent their summers growing up. Dakota walked beside them, bald head held high, a proud cancer survivor. The camp nurse was aware of his condition and would administer his doctor-prescribed medicine, as well as Sharon's natural remedies, during the week he was gone. She felt confident that he would be in good hands but said a little prayer anyway that God would take good care of Dakota while he was out of her care.

Giddy with excitement and anticipation of long-awaited freedom, Dakota eagerly followed his parents to the cabin where he would be staying and listened as they shared Dakota's story with his bunkmates. Certain that church camp was the safest place for their son to enjoy himself without getting teased for having a bald head, Henry and Sharon wanted to make sure that the other kids understood and treated him kindly—treated him the way they would treat any of the other children at camp.

Sharon set up Dakota's bed with his pillows and blankets from home. After he placed his favorite stuffed animal, a black Labrador named Trouble, on top, Sharon smiled and hugged her son, embracing him with all the love inside of her. She saved her tears for the car ride home, focusing, in that moment, only on Dakota's happiness and his freedom, the greatest gifts she could ever receive.

When they returned a week later to pick up Dakota, he ran from his cabin, tearing down the dirt trail, a big smile leading the way, and skidded to a dusty halt in front of his parents.

"I have hair!" he yelled before wrapping his arms around them. The fuzz tickled Sharon's chin as she embraced him with all her might.

He has his life back, she thought, tears dripping into her smile.

When they returned home, Dakota spent every day that summer playing football and basketball in their front yard with Riley and the other neighborhood kids. He dribbled and passed as though he had never been sick and chased runaway balls down the street and into the woods. He returned to school that August and tried out for basketball, making the seventh-grade team.

Dakota played with all his might, with every ounce of vigor as any other player on the court. The first point he made that season was a free throw. Standing at the foul line, looking down at the ball intently, he dribbled in place, looked up at the hoop with determined eyes, and …

Swoosh.

The crowd erupted, Dakota shot a smile at his parents, and Sharon dropped her head into her hands, sobbing right there in the stands, right there in the middle of the wild crowd.

She didn't care. Her son was back.

Dakota was excelling in all of his pre-advanced placement classes, learning as much as he could to pursue his dream of becoming an engineer, a missionary, or the President of the United States. He thrived in math and had a passion for history, which started as a child when he spent hours creating homemade Civil War and John Wayne movies with neighborhood kids. Dressed in boots, holsters, and bandanas, Dakota would use his parents' camcorder to film scenes with his friends, rolling handwritten credits at the end on rolls of paper towels. Dakota was the star of every film—always the toughest soldier, always John Wayne, always the last one standing.

Two weeks after the seventh-grade basketball game, Dakota relapsed.

Sharon could feel it in her bones on the way to his routine checkup. The anticipation of every appointment sat heavy in her chest, nestled deep into her heart, but this appointment was different. Dakota's color wasn't quite right. It hadn't been for two weeks, and his energy had dipped with his spirit.

"I'm afraid to tell you this," said Dr. Becton after returning to the tiny room where Sharon and Dakota waited, hours after he drew Dakota's blood. Every tick of the clock, every minute it had taken to comprise those hours had settled miserably into Sharon's gut, second by second, and she knew what was coming. She knew that any sign of cancer, any glimpse of its existence, required multiple tests, trips to pathology, second and third opinions—required time.

After those long, torturous, unsettling hours, Dr. Becton's eyes, usually radiating strength and confidence, looked down, troubled, before looking up at her, this time strikingly sad. "The leukemia has returned."

Sharon's heart folded over itself, fell into the abyss of the pit in her stomach. The pain of it pounded into her chest so violently that everything else went numb—her arms, her legs, her mind. Dakota dropped his head to look at the floor, and Sharon wrapped him in her arms.

"We're going to get through this again, son," she reassured him. "We'll do whatever it takes. We're going to get through this as a family."

You're the mother, she thought to herself. *Keep it together, stay strong. Save your tears for later.*

When Dakota called to tell his father the news, Henry closed his eyes. He pictured the bruises on Dakota's knees—bruises he had convinced himself were from kneeling on the basketball court during season pictures, bruises that could indicate the return of cancer, bruises he wished he could pray away.

"I hate this, Dad," Dakota said. "But Dr. Becton said we can beat it again."

"You bet, son," Henry said, his voice unwavering. "We will beat it again."

And he already knew how.

Nine months earlier, when Dakota was in remission from cancer but still undergoing chemo, Henry, Sharon, and Riley had all been tested as potential bone marrow donors—for the possibility that cancer would return, for this very moment.

It was Valentine's Day 2003 when Dr. Becton skipped into the room where Sharon sat, waiting for results. He was barely through the door before nearly shouting, "Riley is a perfect match! If we ever need him, if it ever comes to that, he may be Dakota's lifesaver."

Lifesaver.

Sharon let that word, with all its hope, all its promise, rise up and float there. She closed her eyes, breathed out, silently thanking God. It was no coincidence to her that on this day of love she found out her son, Riley, could possibly give the gift of life to his brother.

She couldn't get to Riley's school fast enough, where she knew he was celebrating this very special day in his fourth-grade class, opening tiny, stuffed envelopes with messages from Scooby Doo and Elmo, eating heart-shaped candies etched with "I love you" and "Hug me."

She led him by the hand and into the hall, then hollered, "Riley, we've been given the greatest gift of all today! You're a perfect match for Dakota!"

Riley's face beamed, radiating happiness, but he remained silent in shock as his mom squeezed him tight, grabbing and kissing his face all over.

Finally he spoke.

"Let's go!" he shouted, leading Sharon back into his classroom, where he told his teacher and made an announcement to the class. The words *cancer* and *transplant* probably meant nothing to that room full of fourth graders, but Riley's excitement, the smile that stretched across his entire face, sent his classmates out of their seats, their hands pounding together, their cheers filling the halls.

⋆ 7 ⋆

Cancer had made its return, but before Riley could save Dakota's life, Dr. Becton had to get him back into remission, at least partially.

As before, Dakota had good days and bad. And while his body was tired, weakened by such an intense first round of chemo, he resisted the treatment's misery and remained hopeful and spirited. His hospital stays were longer, darker than before, but he still made rounds to eagerly awaiting children, still tricked his nurses with apple juice-filled syringes.

After just a few days, two Child Life volunteers made a visit to Dakota's room and told him about the Make-A-Wish Foundation—told him that he could ask for anything in the world, seek anything in his heart's desire, and his wish would be granted.

Anything—that word would stretch any twelve-year-old's imagination to its limit.

A trip to Australia, Dakota thought. *Meeting Brett Favre from the Green Bay Packers . . . No, the memories will fade.*

Sharon and Henry leaned forward, wanting desperately to read his mind, to hear his wish.

"I want something that will last," he finally said.

Dakota closed his eyes, remembering a moment just a few weeks before, when he was living a cancer survivor's dream—remission— still living his answered prayer.

It had been a brisk, October morning when he, Riley, Henry, and Henry's father, Papaw, rode their ATVs through the silence of the woods, the sun still resting peacefully beneath the horizon, the freedom of the wilderness stretching endlessly ahead, dark and adventurous.

It was the first day of deer hunting season, and at the ages of ten and twelve, Henry decided it was time for Riley and Dakota each to have his own deer stand. Hunting from the time they were toddlers and shooting with their own guns starting at six and eight, their senses were trained, their instincts polished.

They were ready.

Riley's eyes looked up the length of an oak tree at his deer stand—one of the tallest he had ever seen—placed, from his point of view, sloppily up top. A steep, skinny, worn ladder led toward the sky and into the stand, which offered no place to sit.

"I don't want to go up there," Riley said, keeping his wide eyes on the stand.

They had just come from looking at Dakota's stand—300 yards away—a shorter, more solid-looking tree house–type structure with a chair.

Dakota looked at his younger brother.

"Papaw, Riley can have my stand."

They got settled into their own stands, sat, and waited in the silence, the serenity, of the forest. Endless stars dotted the black sky while a light breeze danced peacefully through the trees, the only sound for miles. After fifteen minutes, a sudden bang cracked that silence, its echo a warning to all wildlife.

"He got a deer," said Henry, who was about 300 yards away.

Riley also heard the shot.

"It's a seven-point buck!" Dakota yelled, hovering over his fallen prey.

He smiled in his hospital bed at the memory and decided in that moment what his wish would be.

"I wish to have an ATV," he said proudly.

Not only was he choosing something he knew his parents could not afford to buy for him, he was choosing a wish of freedom, of independence, of adventure. He would use it to maneuver the thick woods, haul animals, explore.

He brainstormed aloud all of the desired features for his ATV—its speed, capability.

"We've never met anyone who knew what he wanted quite the way you do!" said one of the volunteers, laughing, charmed.

In between IV drips, blood draws, chemo, trips home, and back to the hospital, Dakota was attached to his laptop, researching every detail, every function, of his new, personalized ATV. Nurses continued to poke and prod, change medicines, switch arms for IVs, but he would work with them, using his good arm to run the mouse, peek around them politely to see the computer screen.

He never stopped researching—color, speed, engine size, brand, model, accessories.

His thoughts went from leukemia—from chemotherapy and test results and transplant—to riding the ATV through the forest, hunting, life after cancer.

Dakota settled on a John Deere Gator HPX 4x4—it went one mile an hour faster than the rest.

⋆ 8 ⋆

When he went into partial remission—enough for a transplant—it was time to get Dakota and Riley to Houston, Texas, where the bone marrow transplant would take place. Obtaining doctor's approval of Dakota's wish, getting every detail of his special order just right, took a significant amount of time, which volunteers with the Arkansas Make-A-Wish chapter suddenly ran out of when they learned that Dakota was in partial remission and leaving town very soon.

Knowing the family was heading to The University of Texas MD Anderson Cancer Center in Houston on Saturday morning, it was a small miracle that the chapter received the Gator in time. They quickly made sure it had the correct hood, windshield wipers, doors—every detail—before covering it with bows and balloons and taking it to Dakota's home Friday night.

Sharon and Henry, who knew it was coming that night, hosted dinner for a house full of loved ones, their closest family and friends, telling Dakota they were there to see him off before their eight-hour drive to Houston the next morning.

The smell of wholesome Southern cooking lingered in the kitchen after dinner and followed the group into the game room, where they laughed, chatted, and played pool until a big, dark, quiet figure snuck up to the glass patio doors that lead from the game room to the pitch blackness of the night.

"No way!" Dakota yelled when the porch light illuminated two Make-A-Wish volunteers pushing his Gator, his wish, his freedom, toward the closed door. His beaming smile pierced Sharon's heart as he ran past her, opened the door quickly, and crawled inside the Gator.

"Who wants to go for a ride?" he asked excitedly.

Everyone gathered around as Dakota checked the wipers and the hood, opened and closed the doors, and gave the Gator a full inspection. The volunteers handed him a pile of John Deere clothing, which he layered with his own before heading out into the cold, January night. The summer sounds of crickets and bullfrogs had been hushed for months, the absence of lightning bugs leaving the moon and stars to light the way.

Dakota took one load after another of friends and family for a ride, and as Sharon and Henry watched, the Gator disappeared time after time into nothing but the sound of its own hum, taking the silence of the night with it. They had never seen him happier, or, after everything he had been through, more free.

As excitement and adrenaline sizzled inside of Dakota later that night, thoughts of all the places he would ride on his Gator dizzying his mind, he forced himself to fall asleep so he was ready for the big day ahead of him.

When he, Henry, Sharon, and Riley arrived at MD Anderson Cancer Center in Houston the next day, Dakota was immediately started on chemo, hoping to wipe away any remaining leukemia cells and demolishing his old immune system to replace it with Riley's.

A month later, with Dakota's numbers moving in the right direction, his condition improving just enough, it was time to harvest Riley's cells, time to start the process of saving Dakota's life.

Sitting at the foot of Riley's bed, Dakota watched as hospital staff placed a mask over his younger brother's face—something he had been through a hundred times—and he instigated a competition that he knew would take Riley's mind off of being put under.

"Let's see who can count longer," Dakota said right before the machine was turned on.

When Riley got to twelve, Dakota pushed even further.

"Thirteen ... fourteen ..."

Riley's eyes closed against his will, and Dakota closed his, too, saying a silent prayer that the cells they were taking would save his life. On transplant day, when doctors hung a bag of cells, Riley's lifesaving cells, above Dakota on his IV tree, Sharon prayed over them—prayed that those cells would work as God's army, march into Dakota's veins, swim through his blood, give him back his life. Each drip crawled through the clear tube, forcing its way into Dakota's body, demanding acceptance, creating life.

Dakota's eyes moved up and down with every drop, watching intently as Riley's cells fell into his body. His parents watched, too, and Sharon took her eyes away only to look at the sun as it crawled in through the shaded window, warming the room and her spirits. It was the first time in a long time she had actually noticed the sun, cared about its existence.

Things of beauty had been hiding for months beneath the selfish darkness, bleeding agony, which had consumed them. Sharon paid close attention to the movement of the sun, its morning dance, as though it were the first time she had ever seen it. This was a good day, a day of renewal, of new life. She felt it in every ounce of her being.

They all did.

When the last drops seeped in, the bag above hanging clear, it was time to wait. At 4:30 every morning, nurses came in to draw

Dakota's blood, and again, Sharon prayed. She prayed for signs of Riley's cells in Dakota's blood, and after twenty-one days, that prayer was answered—his red blood cell count was going up.

After a month and a half, with counts continuing to increase, Dakota could leave the hospital with daily visits. It was his first step toward getting back to the Gator. Thinking about the friends he would take and the places he would go, kept his mind clear, free, during those long days and nights at the hospital, just waiting.

"I can't wait to take Zach and Brandon and Riley and Justin on long rides," Dakota said of his brother and best friends. He talked every day about riding into the woods, hunting with his Gator, and visiting Moccasin Gap in the Ozark Mountains.

When Dakota was released from the hospital, he, Riley, and their parents stayed in what they called The Treehouse, a small, above-garage apartment at Sharon's brother's Houston home. Its soft white walls were somehow different from the bright, sterile shade in the hospital. This white was inviting, as was the old-fashioned, claw-foot tub in place of a cold, tile shower; books that had nothing to do with cancer; contemporary art hanging on the walls rather than posters of the body's systems; and meals served on plates rather than trays. The Treehouse was just minutes away from MD Anderson, making daily visits easy and convenient.

The normal life Dakota was about to re-enter started in Houston, where he hung out and watched *Survivor* every Thursday night with good family friends, the Johnstons, played games and ate pizza with his Grandma Pat and Pa Pa Tom every Sunday night, and spent the weekends—when his counts were good and his energy was up—riding go-carts, visiting the zoo, going to the park, and playing golf, the only sport he never had to give up.

One day, he got a call from The Point, a classic rock radio station based out of Little Rock, Arkansas, during its annual Make-A-Wish

Foundation fundraiser. Dakota Hawkins had become a household name across the state of Arkansas, with local and statewide news coverage of his condition, his progress, and his story.

At the MD Anderson clinic, where he went for regular tests and blood draws, Dakota sat at the nurse's station for a phone interview with the radio station's DJs about his progress, his transplant, his wish, and all the specifics of the Gator.

"You know, man, it's like a pimped up four-wheeler," Dakota said, smiling at the nurses surrounding him, who threw their heads back with laughter, clapping their hands, catching their breaths.

"A pimped up ... " the DJ couldn't even finish the sentence. He and the other DJs were in hysterics at the description.

When the laughter faded, Dakota looked down at the ground, fingers intertwined in the cord of the phone, his face serious.

"I'd like to thank Make-A-Wish for making my wish come true," he said, and Sharon's heart instantly became filled with happiness. She imagined her son's voice in the ears of thousands, driving their cars, sitting in their offices or homes, listening to his story. The sincere gratitude in her son's voice reflected how strongly he felt about the gift he had received and echoed his love for the Gator with which he would soon reunite.

★ 9 ★

Everyday checkups at MD Anderson turned into every three-day checkups, and after one hundred days, Dakota was released and sent home. The cancer was gone, his counts were up, and his organs were healthy.

Two weeks after settling home, he and his family went to Colorado on an all-expense-paid, five-day trip to a dude ranch near Steamboat Springs with nine other families, a doctor, and a nurse from MD Anderson. With the other kids, Dakota and Riley explored the mountain ranges on horses during the day, played kickball in the evenings, and enjoyed cookouts, barn dances, and dips in their cabin's hot tub.

On their bus ride back to the airport, as they made their way toward Denver, nearing the Continental Divide, small, white flurries turned into what looked like the insides of a Christmas snow globe.

"Stop the bus!" Dakota shouted, and the driver slowly pulled to the side of the road. "Let's have a snowball fight!"

That's our Dakota, Sharon thought, grinning.

He and the other kids, all cancer patients, survivors, poured from the bus and into the snow, shoveling handfuls into balls and launching them like little cannonballs. They dusted the bus, its driver, the doctor, and nurse, one another, in white—all while laughing, living in that moment, undefined by cancer, in its cool freedom.

Sharon and Henry watched, smiles dancing on their faces, frozen in that moment of time. And while nothing could take away Sharon's happiness, the heaviness in her chest, its pull through her belly, was something she could not deny. They were about to return to MD Anderson for a bone marrow aspiration—the deepest, most accurate cancer-detecting test—and all she could do was pray for good results.

Once again, her prayer was answered. Dakota was still cancer-free and Riley's cells, in all of their determination, remained a friend to his brother's body. Dakota could go home and continue that life of normalcy, of freedom, that had started in Houston just a few months earlier.

A peripherally inserted central catheter (PICC) line in his chest was the only thing keeping Dakota from enjoying one of his favorite past times—swimming—so he had a decision to make. He could leave it in as a way for doctors to insert medicines and draw blood every month without having to poke him, or he could have it removed and get poked for those purposes every month.

He wanted it out—needed what was, in his mind, permanent detachment from cancer.

After healing from surgery to remove the line, Dakota went with Sharon to his friend Chad's house for an afternoon dip, his first swim all summer. Chad and his family, who welcomed Dakota to their home at any time, were not home that afternoon, so Sharon soaked in the enjoyment of watching her son dive from the board, flip from the sides, and plunge deep into the water.

"I feel so free," he said with a smile, looking right at her before ducking under the water, swimming quickly to the other side. He got out of the pool, stood on the diving board in his bright yellow swim shorts, and smiled again at his mom. A soft layer of golden hair that had just started to grow back gleamed like the sun, mirrored his shorts, became living proof that her Dakota was here to stay.

He's the picture of health, Sharon thought to herself, smiling through tears as Dakota jumped back into the pool.

———————— ✳

As a family, they traveled to Silver Dollar City theme park that summer, the resort town of Branson, Missouri, and to Moccasin Gap—a place where Dakota, Riley, and Henry rode four-wheelers— with its endless streams and twenty-eight miles of ATV and horse trails weaving through the hills and hollows of Arkansas's Ozark Mountains.

As they did every year, Dakota, Riley, and Henry prepared for the upcoming deer hunting season at a deer camp in south Arkansas. They searched for signs of deer, inspecting bushes for places they might have rested and trees for traces of rubbing. They scoped out areas close to water that would quench the deer's thirst and analyzed trees for their height and potential for deer spotting. Dakota would bring his Gator to collect their fallen prey, and his anticipation for October, deer hunting season, started on their three-hour drive home.

When the summer was over, Dakota registered for eighth grade and, once again, excelled with straight As, advanced placement classes, and a position on the varsity basketball team. He attended school dances, birthday parties, church on Sundays, and rode his Gator often with friends. He had returned to his old, normal life, where cancer was just a nightmare from which he had woken.

During Dakota's next five monthly appointments, he received a clean bill of health—his cells were dead; Riley's were thriving. The front door to cancer's old home was closed, but like a sneaky robber, a malicious intruder, it found its way back in and hid behind corners inside Dakota's body.

"It's like hide-and-seek," Dr. Becton explained to Dakota and Sharon during their sixth monthly checkup, where cancer cells had slowly come out from around those corners. "We found little, bitty cancer cells hiding within your cells."

Cancer cells. Those words were supposed to be gone from their lives. *How can this be happening again?*

Sharon didn't speak her thoughts; she didn't mutter a word. And neither did Dakota. They sat in silence, the heaviness of Dr. Becton's words setting like stone in their hearts.

It was time for chemo, once again.

✷ 10 ✷

They tried for two months at Arkansas Children's and another two at MD Anderson in Houston, where doctors determined that those tiny cells had multiplied and cancer had taken over 100 percent of Dakota's body.

After realizing that chemo wasn't working, they exhausted every experimental and compassionate drug and determined a second transplant would most likely be fatal.

"I'm afraid Dakota doesn't have long to live," said Dr. Michael Rytting, one of Dakota's doctors from MD Anderson, whom Henry and Sharon had grown to respect and trust over the course of the past year. He was one of those special doctors who treated patients the way Sharon imagined he would treat his own child. He was Dakota's favorite doctor, he had years of experience, he specialized in cancer treatment, and he had an MD behind his name.

Henry and Sharon, however, had never made decisions based on statistics or speculations, and they weren't about to start. They trusted the man standing before them, but trust only went so far. They needed to know if it was time to start seeking other options, finding other solutions. They were not going to give up.

"How long?" Sharon asked. "A month, a couple of months, years?"

"I'm thinking less than a year," Dr. Rytting said sadly. "Single digit months."

Dakota's blood had become a river of cancer, but his organs were still healthy, and Henry and Sharon were not going to wait around for their son to die. They stayed up late each night, got up early every morning, to research any other possibility, any other solution, to save their son.

A friend at church told them about a missionary from Little Rock who was receiving treatment in Jerusalem, Israel, from Dr. Shimon Slavin, who, according to all of their research, was world-renowned for his work, untraditional and sometimes experimental, with cancer.

"Blood cancer doesn't scare me," Dr. Slavin said to Sharon when she called to explain Dakota's situation. "If his organs are good, get him here healthy, and I can help him."

His unwavering confidence rushed through the phone lines and into Sharon and Henry's ears, into their hearts. They needed to get to Jerusalem.

"He's your best option," Dr. Rytting confirmed. "If Dakota was my son, I would do it. I'm not saying it'll work, but it's your best option."

They had one week to return to Arkansas from Houston, get passports, and collect the money to pay Israel's Hadassah Medical Hospital upfront—$175,000. Henry and Sharon planned to mortgage their home, but instead, word of mouth in the small town of Cabot spread like wildfire through every home, store, restaurant, and church.

In one Sunday, their home church offerings raised $40,000, while other community churches raised a combined total of $40,000. After golf tournaments, school fundraisers, and personal donations, Henry and Sharon needs were met—ample enough to cover all expenses in one week.

In Cabot, coming together as a community was a way of life. Aside from leaving for a few years to go to college, Henry grew up there and had never left. Cabot was home, and its people were his family. Local media had covered Dakota's story from the beginning, keeping everyone in town up-to-date on his condition, encouraging endless support, welcoming love and prayers. But Henry, overwhelmed by their generosity, never imagined they would come together in such a powerful way for their son.

They had returned from Houston to Cabot on a Thursday, and within one week, they scrambled to pack and obtain all necessary medical releases and passports before boarding a plane from Little Rock to Jerusalem, where they would live for nearly four months. Dr. Slavin's plan was to perform a transplant on Dakota, but not with Riley's cells this time. Wiping away Dakota's blood to replace it with his brother's was no longer a solution—he was going to use Sharon's cells, a partial donor.

He would replace half of Dakota's blood with hers and let the battle begin with a graft-versus-host situation, where the healthy cells would fight against the remaining cancer cells, hopefully victoriously. It would be a fifty-fifty war, with well-planned strategies by Dr. Slavin and complicated manipulation tactics that would potentially wipe out the cancer cells.

During the first several days in Jerusalem, Dakota and his family felt like they had stepped back in time and into the pages of the Bible. In between blood draws and preliminary tests, Dakota remained well enough to see many of the places he had studied in Sunday school since he was a little boy, turning scripture he had read and pictures he had seen into something real.

Together, Dakota and his family walked along the edges of the Dead Sea and the Sea of Galilee, and visited the Valley of Megiddo, Nazareth, and the Jordan River. The day before entering the hospital, they went to the Garden of Gethsemane, where Jesus prayed his last prayer before crucifixion. They went into the Church of All Nations, a monastery that enshrines a piece of bedrock where Jesus had prayed. They walked along the quiet, marble floors, admiring the beautiful, floor-to-ceiling murals and mosaics, until they reached the center of the church, the Rock of Agony.

Taking turns, Dakota, Riley, Henry, and Sharon leaned down and placed their hands on the rock, closing their eyes, saying the same prayer.

Dakota's transplant, his last chance, was the next day, and as they walked quietly from the church and into Jerusalem's warm, promising air, Dakota sat without a word on the steps outside the church.

Henry and Sharon looked at each other and tugged at Riley's arm, motioning him away. They gave Dakota the space he needed, the quiet he craved in that very moment where, though she will never know for sure, Sharon assumed her son was talking with the Lord, praying for His healing, moved by the burden Christ must have felt when kneeling at that very rock the day before His crucifixion.

Elbows resting on his knees, head in his hands, Dakota looked out over the old City of Jerusalem and wiped his tears.

"I want to be with Jesus," Dakota said.

He was ready.

They had been back from Israel for more than nine months, where a transplant with Sharon's cells had failed and another using Riley's cells for rescue wasn't enough. Riley had given his brother life for the second time, just enough to bring him home to enjoy a couple of months, once again, in remission, his future unknown.

Dakota wrote these words for his brother, Riley, after Riley gave his bone marrow twice to help save his big brother's life. Riley framed the words and placed them in his room, where they would remain a reminder of Dakota's battle, his strength, his love, and his life.

A few months after writing those words to his brother, graft-versus-host disease (GVHD) sped along cancer's mission of taking Dakota's life, which it did on March 2, 2006, when he was fifteen years old, four years after his diagnosis.

During the last few months of his life, as Dakota suffered through GVHD with respiratory syncytial viruses and lung and skin infections, he came to peace with thoughts of Heaven as his new home and God and angels, his new family.

Sharon had prayed on the hillsides of Jerusalem in the early mornings that God would take her life instead. But when they got home and Dakota's condition worsened, pain and misery defining his life, hope was no longer something to hold onto, so she made one final plea before accepting the destiny her son had already accepted.

"Please just give Dakota the thirty-three years you gave to your own son, Jesus," she asked, but she knew that God had His own plan, His own reason for taking Dakota.

From the day he took his last breath in Sharon's arms, she struggled to see that reason—struggled to recognize God's plan, to know His intentions, to understand His purpose for Dakota in the lives of others. But she never doubted.

Less than a year later, she became involved with the Keep The Faith (KTF) Foundation in memory of Dakota and two other children who lost their lives to cancer, as a way to keep the spirits of those children alive and to carry out what she believed was their purpose—to help other families with what hers had already been through.

With annual fundraisers and contributions, the Foundation raised more than $100,000 in its first six years to help families of children with cancer. In addition to helping families through prayer and encouragement, they also help relieve financial burdens by paying medical bills and other expenses accrued through cancer diagnosis and treatment.

A true believer that no tears exist in Heaven, Sharon knows Dakota is watching from above, unable to see the wretched pain of loss she and her family live with every day. He cannot hear the sadness in their voices, feel the pain in their hearts. He can only smile, and she gives him plenty of reasons to do so through KTF and its largest fundraiser, Pennies from Heaven (PFH).

She and KTF volunteers place buckets in schools, businesses, churches, and civic organizations all over town annually on March 5—the day they buried Dakota—and their first goal in 2008 was to collect one million pennies in one hundred days. They collected 1.1 million pennies—$11,000. They have collected a few thousand more every year, and in 2011, when they launched PFH statewide, the program raised $21,000.

Sharon asks no questions, has no doubts, when pennies cross her path on the sidewalk or appear strategically placed on Dakota's tombstone—they are small, shiny reminders that he is always with her.

And over the years, with each fallen penny, Sharon, Henry, and Riley have slowly learned to see the world again through their tears, feel again through their constant ache, enjoy moments through their grief and pain, their forever loss.

They have realized that Dakota is always with them, sending reminders with pennies on the street or memories with the Gator he left behind—a gift for them, a gift that will forever give.

On the afternoon of Dakota's death, Riley rode the Gator deep into the forest, through its endless trees, into the serenity his brother had always found in the woods. He found peace in the

Gator's hum that day, guidance in its freedom, hope that riding the Gator would always bring a sense of comfort, of closeness, to Dakota and his love for his Gator.

———————— ✳

Adventures on the Gator would not end that day, and it didn't take much time for the Hawkins family to realize what a true gift it really was. Over the years, Henry, Sharon, and Riley have traveled hundreds of miles on the Gator, in the presence of Dakota's spirit, through hills and forests, rain, mud, and the Arkansas sunshine. It has been stuck, rescued, and the saving grace on good hunting days.

When Dakota first made his wish, Sharon was certain it was for him. It was for his freedom, his need to explore and was his way of getting something he knew his parents could not afford to buy.

But every treasured moment on the Gator has revealed to Sharon and her family Dakota's clear intent; his wish was for them—he had chosen something he could leave behind.

———————— ✳

Three years after Dakota's death, Sharon and Henry received a clear message from God, telling them that, even in grief, even with holes in their hearts that could only be filled by Dakota, they still had love to give. After months of family discussion and lots of prayer, they called a local adoption agency to foster a child in need. They received a phone call one day about a two-year-old little boy waiting for a good home, and as soon as they heard the boy's birth name— Dakota Quinn—they knew in her hearts that it was providential.

Sharon sat, silenced, on the phone, eyes filling with tears, heart filling with God's message. This little boy, Dakota Quinn, was meant to be with them. Sharon, Henry, and Riley opened their home and their hearts to the boy, who they decided to call Quinn, and a year later, adopted him into their family.

There was no doubt in their minds that Quinn was sent from above—a gift that they knew Dakota would smile about from Heaven. God had given his parents this gift, just as Dakota had given the Gator, a gift that would keep on giving; a gift for his brother, Riley; his parents; and now their son Quinn.

Tien Leou-on

"I will always remember my wish, even if I get Alzheimer's."

—Tien Leou-on, age twelve

P*ARIS*, Tien thought.

Lights twinkling from the city to the sky. Streets filled with people on bikes, pedaling through the smell of rising dough, of baked croissants and French baguettes from local patisseries. Dogs sitting proper at the heels of their owners at café-lined roads packed with cars and honking taxis, people blowing cigarette smoke from their lips, words in French rolling from their tongues.

Will I speak French by then? he wondered.

Would Tien's father, Bruno, have taught him more than simple words like *bonjour* and *merci*?

Would he be able to say to a waiter, "*Je voudrais le poisson frais du jour*"?— "I would like the fresh fish of the day"—and compare its flavor to that of the fish he had pulled from the South Pacific in Tahiti with his family when he was younger? Would he be able to ask for frog legs and escargot with, "*Je voudrais les cuisses de gre-nouille et les escargots*"? He wanted his taste buds to learn the differ-ence between France's beef bourguignon and his father's, wanted to see if its chefs could perfect an egg the way Bruno perfected an egg.

Tien wanted to immerse his senses in the city's tastes and smells, its sounds and feels. He wanted to see the rolling hills of France's countryside, hills that, in his mind, were like those of Napa Valley, endless green waves of mountains. He wanted to climb the Eiffel Tower and compare the City of Lights to San Francisco, the biggest city near his Berkeley, California, home. He wanted to compare his hometown's Victorian houses to the old, historic homes of Paris, see the differences between ancient cathedrals and the Catholic church where he attended Mass with his mom, Lillian. He wanted to hear the city's live music pouring down its busy streets and taste the flavor of fresh crêpes and *coq au vin* that he would learn to make.

During the nine years of his life, Tien had spent many of them imagining such a place, dreaming of going there. His older brother and sister, Yune and Vanina, had traveled to Paris before Tien was even born. Their experiences fueled his desire, ignited his imagination, with stories of cruising the Seine by boat, staring the Mona Lisa in the eye, indulging in French food, and viewing the lights of Paris from the observation deck of the Eiffel Tower.

When social worker Steve Baisch asked Tien what he would wish for if he could wish for anything in the world, he didn't have to think twice.

Tien smiled.

"I want to go to Paris, France," he said weakly, and Steve thought, *Really? Paris?* "That sounds wonderful!" he said, smiling, as technicians hooked Tien up to the machine.

It was time to start dialysis.

⋆ 2 ⋆

Before making this wish, Tien listened to the wishes other children on dialysis were making.

"I'm going on a Macy's shopping spree," said one little boy, hooked to another dialysis machine near Tien, just a few days before. "When my dialysis is done, I'll get out my laptop and show you pictures of the things I want to get."

Tien smiled, imagining what it would be like to wander the endless aisles of the department store, clothes, shoes, and toys at his fingertips. But then, through his imagination, came the sounds and scents of Paris, the stories from his siblings, the voice of his grandfather telling him how he had met Tien's grandmother in the world's most romantic city.

While studying law at the University of Paris, Tien's grandmother, Theresa, met his grandfather, Yin, when Yin was attending École Nationale Des Ponts et Chaussées—National School of Bridges and Roads—the world's oldest civil engineering school. They had both grown up on the small island of Tahiti but had never met, and together, learned about and fell in love with the foods of France, a passion they passed down to their nine-year-old grandson.

As Tien's dialysis machine grabbed blood from his body, circling and placing it back inside his veins, his mom watched and thought of her own mother, Theresa, who had passed away before Tien was born. Twenty-two years ago, when Lillian left her Berkeley home to live with her mother for a month in Hawaii, where Theresa lived the last of her days near her sister and her best friend, Lillian never imagined that two decades later, she would be holding the hand of another loved one hooked to dialysis, the small hand of her young son.

Lillian thought of her mother fondly as she remembered the serious, intellectual nature of Theresa, the goody-two-shoes reputation she had as a devout student at the University of Paris. Her father, Yin, on the other hand, was a shoot-from-the-hip kind of guy, a man who loved life and didn't take it too seriously unless he needed to.

Brought up on a French-speaking island by parents who spoke only Chinese, Yin could trick his parents into believing his grade school progress. He'd offer up phrases like, "*Vers le haut de la colline, un, deux, trois, quatre, Napoléon est parti en Egypte*"—"Up the hill ... one, two, three, four ... Napoleon went to Egypt"—disjointed sentences combining unrelated words spoken with beautiful French pronunciation—when his parents insisted he demonstrate his progress of learning the language. They believed every word.

Yin's blood ran through Tien, even as it left and re-entered Tien's body. Forced to sit for three-hour stretches every day, Tien suppressed his love of playing games and running outdoors with his friends. He needed to push those thoughts, that life, away for those hours. Just like his grandfather, he was serious when he needed to be, and he was devout like his grandmother.

With his head tilted perfectly still, blood flowing, Tien sat for every long dialysis session, studying with his hospital teacher, Alice Cassman, listening to stories from his mom, his favorite about how his grandfather fooled his parents into believing he could speak French.

Tien laughed, shaking just slightly to avoid disturbing his central line, as this story took him out of the world he was in and into the "normal world," the world he had fully been a part of just a couple of months before—a world where evenings were spent playing games with his family and the biggest concern of the day was deciding which friend to play with after school.

Now, every Monday, Wednesday, and Friday, when Lillian or Bruno took Tien to dialysis, they left that world when the hospital doors slid closed behind them, leaving "normal" outside along with the bright, California sun. The sounds of cars taking people to and from work and school, dance lessons, and soccer were on the other side of those doors as Tien and his parents made their way to the pediatric dialysis center, where this other world existed.

Dreaming of Paris or a day at Macy's brought these kids to that other world, that "normal" place, and kept them there through their long hours hooked to dialysis machines.

"I want a French culinary experience," Tien had said to pediatric nephrology doctor, Dr. Anthony Portale, before sharing his wish with Steve.

Their parents found different ways to cope and bring "normal" back into their lives when they could. From the time Tien was admitted to the hospital, Lillian had found comfort in the other families who were part of this new, unfamiliar world, a world where life could be taken at any moment, where a single moment could change everything.

Lillian was fascinated during long, sleepless nights by another mom with a sick child, who told stories of her truck-driving days— the night she ventured down haunted sections of highway, the time she carried a light truckload of ping-pong balls through a windy section of the Rocky Mountains.

Small talk in the halls, hugs from other parents who had a deep, mutual understanding of their situation, bridged the gap between these two worlds for Lillian and Bruno and became necessary distractions.

Visits from strangers and new friends in the dead of the night reminded Lillian and Bruno that they were not in this alone. The night they got a phone call telling them to rush their son to the nearest emergency room was not uncommon in this world, nor were sharing their concerns and telling their story to other families living similar nightmares just down the halls.

Tien, Lillian, Bruno, Yune, and Vanina left the comfort of their safe, normal world, their previous life, abruptly with no warning.

★ 3 ★

A few months before, Tien had slowly placed his hands, palms down, on the flat, hard, wooden surface of a table in the middle of the gymnasium. Blocking out the stares of his teachers, the voices of other performers, Tien slowly pushed, the strength of lifting all his weight shaking in his arms. Legs moving toward the ceiling as if being pulled by rope, Tien's body became a flawless, still line as he perfected his well-practiced handstand.

He held his position as the teachers of his circus class stared, his sweat dripping, before slowly, gracefully lowering his body and standing upright on the ground to receive smiles and applause. The teachers, who were part of Splash Circus, a group of young performers that entertained audiences throughout the Bay Area, were auditioning for new members. They wrote quiet notes as Tien prepared for the next act in his audition. He walked to the long, thick ropes hanging from the ceiling and grabbed on.

Looking up, he focused as one hand reached above the other, one at a time, slow and meticulous, until he reached the top. Using the same strength it took to climb, Tien slowly, gracefully, lowered himself down the length of the rope. He climbed up, down, up, down, demonstrating the poise and endurance of any other nine-year-old circus performer before moving on to his final audition performances.

From the age of three, Tien had practiced Capoeira, a Brazilian art form combining martial arts, music, and sport, and the technique, dedication, and strength it gave pounded through his body as it flipped, end over end, hands leading the way, across the floor in perfect back handsprings, twirled with perfect cartwheels past the teachers, and balanced perfectly on the shoulders of others during partner acrobatics.

When he was finished, Tien stood proudly before his teachers, panting and smiling, hoping they would select him for the circus.

After the audition, Tien gathered his things and walked to meet his parents as a pain, achy and familiar, crept through the heel of his foot, traveling slowly, purposefully, through its length to his toes. He grabbed at his foot midstep, massaged it quickly as it reached for and touched the ground, and then he grabbed for the other. It was a pain that he had learned to ignore, learned to live with over the past several weeks, because though it would go away briefly, it would always make its return.

He had learned to run through the pain during games of zombie tag at recess with his friends, let it dangle when hanging from the monkey bars, and kick through it during gymnastics and circus class. It would leave and return in the heat of the day as Tien played outdoors with his neighborhood friends, the hot sun pulling at the pain, intensifying it.

His feet would ache during bamboo sword fights and throb during "survivor," a game he and his friends made up that involved eating cherry plums, sour grass, and dandelion leaves from their backyards in order to survive.

One morning a few weeks after auditions, after learning that Tien had been accepted into the circus, Lillian gently touched his cheeks as his eyes slowly opened from the night. Beneath her fingers, Tien's skin, warm from sleep, puffed around his chin, his forehead, and the area below his eyes. She squinted and looked closer and felt deeper, as her fingers sank into the soft yet firm skin on his face.

She called Tien's pediatrician, Dr. Randy Bergen, and scheduled an appointment for later that day. Something wasn't right. His achy, swollen feet and puffy face were trying to send a message to Lillian and Bruno but not a clear one. Tien was enjoying third grade, loving the math club he had joined, and playing with his friends after school every day—*what could be wrong?*

"It's possible that you have lupus," said Dr. Vivien Igra from Dr. Bergen's office, the only doctor available to see them right away.

Lupus, Lillian thought, her body and heart instantly numb with worry, sickened with fear. *Flannery O'Connor.*

Through the American novelist's words, Lillian had learned in high school about life's cruelties and hardships, many of them derived from the author's experience with the same disease—the one with which her son had possibly just been diagnosed.

Sisters from Lillian's Catholic high school had read O'Connor's work to their students, opening their eyes to life's realities, from serial killers to human greed to morality and ethics. The moment Dr. Igra uttered "lupus," Lillian instantly thought of the fourteen-year-battle O'Connor had with the disease. She remembered how lupus sometimes became a character in O'Connor's writing because of its dark, cruel existence in her life. At the time, Lillian was intrigued by the disease's benevolence, its loosened grip on O'Connor's life during remission, until it took it from her in 1964.

O'Connor's death was all that Lillian knew about lupus.

She didn't know that her son's body was about to turn against itself, eating away at perfectly healthy tissue and functioning organs. She didn't know the disease's potential to wipe out any part of the body, from the skin to the joints to its most important organs.

Lillian didn't know that the rashes forming on Tien's skin, rashes she and Bruno thought must be from Tien's allergies to strawberries, chocolate, and citrus—*maybe Tien drank a glass of lemonade*—combined with his puffy face and aching feet were all indicators of lupus.

"Can you move this for me?" Dr. Igra had asked Tien before suggesting he had lupus. She moved Tien's feet gently, touching the small joints near his ankle bone. He sucked in his breath, pain rolling beneath the doctor's fingers.

The pains Tien had been experiencing in his feet could have stemmed from anything, Lillian and Bruno had told themselves—playing in the dirt, tripping over rocks, climbing and falling from the branches of trees. He was a classic boy, an active nine-year-old. He was playing soccer in a summer soccer camp program for the third year in a row, and he was one of his team's best, most aggressive players.

"Does this hurt?" Dr. Igra asked, tugging at the joints of his hands.

The small bones throbbed with the doctor's slightest touch.

Aches in the small joints of the hands and feet, rashes, a swollen face—lupus.

She ordered labs to be done, an Antinuclear Antibody (ANA) test that would indicate the presence of an autoimmune disease, so Lillian took Tien to get his blood drawn later that day.

"We'll call you with the test results," Dr. Igra said, adding that, if the ANA test came back positive and they determined he had lupus, treatment would involve ointment for the rashes, medicine for the aching joints. Simple.

Even if the results came back positive for this disease with no cure, the treatment would be easy and Tien would be fine. Lillian was comforted by the doctor's words. O'Connor's suffering would not be her son's.

The next step was waiting, the step after that, dealing with those results. Lillian had built her life around taking one step at a time— it was the only way she knew to function, a way of life echoed from past generations in her family. As a young girl, Lillian's mother had shared stories with her about the hardships her mother and grandmother faced in China—hunger and war—and the way they shepherded their families, did what they needed to do, and faced what came their way with unending strength and courage.

Having never thought about where it came from, Lillian journeyed through life the same way, from the time she went through law school in the early 1980s and faced the challenges of being a female law student at that time to the situation they were in now.

This would be no different.

For past generations, taking one step at a time meant figuring out how to put meals on the table. For Lillian during law school, it was studying as hard as possible and passing the bar exam. Now, it was getting through one test, one lab, one result at a time.

* 3 *

They got Tien's blood drawn for the ANA test on Father's Day 2008. After their hospital visit, they went out to celebrate the day with brunch in Walnut Creek, a city near their hometown of Berkeley. As waiters placed plates heaped with delicious-looking food in front of them, as Bruno opened his handmade card from the kids, Lillian had to work every second of that day to keep her mind present—there with her family, not at the hospital where her son's blood was being processed, not drifting into the unknown future.

She spent that day and the next living with her mind in two places, split between thoughts, consumed by two different worlds— the world where Tien lived as a healthy child, growing and exploring, loving life, and the other world with the disease that killed Flannery O'Connor.

Lillian blinked at the thought—hard—and refocused, turning toward the laughter pouring from the kitchen as the sound, blending with the scent of fresh fruit, teased her senses. Peeking around the corner of their home's small kitchen, she heard the sizzle of bananas dancing in a butter-lined pan as Tien and Bruno tossed and turned them, perfecting Bruno's fried banana recipe.

Cooking together in their pajamas, whether making fried bananas late at night or breakfast crêpes first thing on Sunday mornings, which they had done together since Tien was six, was his and Bruno's favorite pastime, their most treasured time together aside

from assembling five-hundred-piece puzzles and playing complicated board games.

Once the bananas were on the plate, Tien, who enjoyed presenting meals almost as much as he did creating them, shook the
bottle and formed a whipped cream happy face over the top of
the bananas; one that made Bruno and Lillian laugh before eating the dessert and heading to bed.

Hours later, in the middle of the night, the phone rang. Lillian got up
to answer it, her voice heavy with sleep, eyes only half open. "Hello?"

"I'm calling from Kaiser regarding your son's labs. You need to
get him to the nearest emergency room right now."

Her eyes shot open.

The words *high potassium* snuck into her mind, dancing with
her thoughts, distracting her panic, but those words and *emergency
room* were the only ones she managed to hear.

*We just need to get him in for some medicine that will lower his
potassium*, Lillian repeated to herself as she hung up the phone
and rushed to the bedroom to tell Bruno about the phone call she
had just received. Though it came sooner and more abruptly than
expected, this was their next step.

Get Tien to the hospital.

Lillian and Bruno tried nudging seventeen-year-old Yune and
fifteen-year-old Vanina first with slight nudges that didn't rouse
them, and then they pushed harder, keeping fear as far away from
their voices as possible as they said softly into quiet rooms, "We are
taking Tien to the hospital."

"He'll be fine," Lillian reassured when the eyes of her two older
children looked at her with question and concern. "His potassium
is high, and they need to bring it down."

She hoped it was as simple as that.

Tien crawled into the backseat of their car, and after placing a jacket over him, Lillian and Bruno drove straight to Kaiser Permanente Oakland Medical Center where they admitted Tien and doctors immediately hooked him up to a blood pressure machine and a heart monitor. Tien had never in his life had more than typical childhood illnesses—colds and the flu.

Lillian and Bruno watched as they took his vital signs, then handed him cup after cup of Kayexalate, a thick, brown, pasty medicine to help lower his blood pressure and potassium level. Tien closed his eyes and swallowed, one gulp after another, his mind working hard at convincing his stomach to keep it down.

"You've gotta keep drinking this!" a nurse shouted at Tien after noticing that he had sat it down on the little table beside him. He needed a break. Lillian and Bruno studied her, trying to analyze the panic in her voice.

It was 5:00 a.m. He'd been drinking the liquids for more than two hours. Tien slowly blinked his tired eyes, picked up the cup, and squeezed them shut once again as the bitter, chalky taste invaded his mouth, and swallowed. It seeped in, ventured slowly, working against Tien's body to lower its potassium.

———— ✶

After five days of getting Tien and his potassium level stabilized, doctors released him from the hospital with a strict regimen of oral steroids to help keep his body's blood pressure and potassium at the levels they were when he was released.

Unlike cancer and other diseases with clear warning signs, easy diagnoses, lupus remained a mystery in so many ways to doctors, the sneaky way it maneuvered through its prey, the way it avoided showing up in some tests, tricking the results of others. After numerous tests and a constant decrease in Tien's potassium level, doctors determined that this ugly autoimmune disease had zeroed in on Tien's kidneys, determined to shut them down.

But they weren't going to let it. They sent Tien home that day to continue his normal, active life, with daily doses of steroids and plans to monitor and frequently test that his kidneys were surviving in the midst of this disease.

⋆ 4 ⋆

The next morning, Tien woke up with a headache, a feeling that his head was splitting in two. It pounded violently as he pressed on each side, hoping for some relief.

"It sounds like your blood pressure might be high," Lillian said, and she took him to see a nephrologist later that morning.

"His blood pressure is fine," said the doctor, who sent them home with peace of mind and an order to take Tylenol for Tien's headache.

Tien ventured up the wooden stairs of their home to his bedroom and sat on the floor, waiting for his mom to return with the Tylenol.

"Mom, my head hurts *so* bad," Tien said as Lillian sat beside him on the floor. He held his head in his hands, squeezing gently and scrunching his eyes, his pain pouring into his mother. She rubbed his shoulders and draped an arm around them before placing two pills on Tien's tongue.

"This should help," she said, lifting a glass to Tien's lips.

Water glided gently down the clear glass, but before it reached Tien's mouth, before the pill was washed away, taken into a body so desperate for relief, Tien looked to the ceiling, a place of concentration, Lillian assumed, but then his eyes kept going.

They reached the ceiling, then looked further back, further and further, until only the whites were showing, and then his eyes began to shake, then his face, his arms, his legs, his body.

"Tien?" Lillian asked quickly, unable to chase panic away with calm thoughts. Looking ahead to the next step, to the future rather than the moment, was not an option. This was the moment they were in, the moment they were forced to face, the moment they needed to get through.

"Tien!" she almost screamed, her voice echoing down the hallway. "Bruno, call 911!"

Tien's body violently convulsed in Lillian's arms as Bruno clumsily pounded the numbers into the phone. Immediate screeches of sirens rolled like waves through town from the fire station that was just two blocks away, pouring down city streets, crashing between houses and into Lillian and Bruno's neighborhood. After three minutes, a lifetime, of shaking, Tien's small body rested, his mind, gone. When Bruno heard paramedics plunge through the front door, he carried his limp son down the stairs and watched as they placed him into the ambulance.

Ten minutes into the drive to the hospital, every minute filled with a deepening sense of worry that Tien might never wake up, Tien's body began to move with more than just the motion of bumps in the road.

"What happened?" he said, eyes hiding halfway beneath their lids. "Where am I?"

"You're in an ambulance," Lillian said gently, rubbing his face, leaning in to kiss his cheeks.

"I'm fine; let's go home," Tien said.

One of the EMTs asked, "Can you see me?"

"Yes," Tien answered, eyes closed. "You're a man."

Lillian smiled with relief. Despite his closed eyes and his weak voice, Tien's sense of humor was already surfacing.

"How many fingers am I holding up?" the paramedic asked, dangling three fingers in front of Tien's face.

"Four," Tien guessed.

"Nope," the EMT said, holding another hand in front of Tien's closed eyes, two fingers showing. "How about now?"

With everything inside of him, Tien tried to open his eyes. Fingers moved and blurred as one, jolting with the bumps in the road, trailing across the slight vision his mostly closed eyes would allow.

"Three," he guessed again.

This guessing game kept Tien's spirits up until they pulled into the hospital, where paramedics wheeled him inside and another seizure took over his body. Lillian watched as her son's eyes rolled back, wanting desperately to snap him from what she knew was coming.

"Tien!" she nearly screamed.

"Tien! Tien!" she repeated, hoping her voice, its panicked plea, would be enough to stop the seizure. She rubbed his back gently, hoping to soothe it away.

But nothing worked. His body jolted and shook with more vigor for more minutes than the last. With one quick movement, nurses snapped the metal rails of Tien's bed into a higher position to keep him from falling, and Lillian stood with them, waiting for this dance, this victory dance of his disease, to end.

When it did, they wheeled him into his own room, Lillian trailing behind. She never left his side. She stared at the vacant face of her little boy until the wee hours of the morning, waiting for Tien to wake up. This kept Lillian's mind where it needed to be—right there with her son. Tears would not cure him or change what was happening. Keeping a strong mind and moving forward were her only options, her only ways of getting through this.

Bruno had gone home to be with Yune and Vanina through the night, and every ounce of him ached with the hope that Tien would turn his father's words into reality when he returned the next morning.

"He'll be fine," Bruno had tried to reassure Lillian before leaving the hospital. "He'll wake up and everything will be okay. He has good color in his cheeks, see?"

Lillian rubbed Tien's cheeks, kissed him, and thought only of him as his room quieted from the sound of nurses coming and going. It had been only a week since Tien was running on the soccer field, kicking the ball, cheering with every goal made. *How did we get here?*

Their family had entered a nightmare.

And now it was just the two of them—Tien and Lillian—in the dead of the night, waiting. On some level, Lillian knew her son was fighting hard against his body, against its disease, pushing his mind to resurface through its consciousness, waiting to wake up.

———— ✦

At 4:00 a.m., it did. Tien wiggled the way he had every morning of his life, wiggling from sleep, from dreams, and on that day, from a short-lived coma.

"You're in the hospital," Lillian said gently, almost immediately as Tien's eyes scooted around her face. But he didn't look around the room with questioning eyes as she had thought he would.

In her imagination, she pictured Tien waking up disoriented, scared, and full of questions, but instead, he woke up like he had every other morning of his life, ready to embrace the day, make it as good as possible, and enjoy every moment. He was the kid with a child's heart and, at times, an adult's maturity.

"You had a couple of seizures," Lillian explained gently, "and the doctors are trying to figure everything out."

It was 4:00 a.m., and doctors and nurses had started coming

and going, smiling at their little patient who had pulled through the seizures, who was sitting up in bed with tired smiles and a sense of peace about his situation. He and Lillian spent the rest of the morning talking, playing board games, and watching TV, their minds taking them from the confines of Tien's hospital room to other places, places of "normal."

⋆ 5 ⋆

For the next two weeks, doctors filled Tien's body with high levels of liquid steroids, decreasing his immune system's response to lupus by wiping out his red blood cells. Transfusions every couple of days replenished his supply, red life seeping from bags into Tien's body.

Each steroid "pulse" caused hours and sometimes days of lethargy, days of rest—making Tien still and inactive in a way that Lillian and Bruno could hardly recognize their son.

On other days, on "good days," Tien roamed the hospital's halls, IV pole attached, visiting other children, walking with Josh, his roommate and new friend, to rent movies from the movie cart. Josh, who suffered from spina bifida, had lived a good portion of his life in hospitals and knew how to make time pass seemingly fast. He knew how to make the best of it, and he shared his knowledge with Tien every day.

Together, they spent hours playing video games and board games such as *Life*, *In a Pickle*, and *Scrabble*.

"Rostov," Tien declared one afternoon, finishing his word with a perfectly placed letter "v," the letter that would let him win a game of *Scrabble* against his mom.

"That's not a word!" Lillian challenged.

"Yes, it is," Tien said, explaining that Rostov was a make-believe place in one of his video games.

"Take a look at this, Dr. Rostov ... " said an attending doctor to another as they caught the tail end of Tien and Lillian's conversation. The doctor squeezed her eyes shut, shook her head, and said, "What am I saying? You're not Dr. Rostov! The word *Rostov* is on my brain, and Tien, you have me saying it!"

He bursted with laughter.

"See? I told you it's a word!" Tien shouted, and Lillian laughed.

The next day, Tien's eyes remained closed through the morning hours and Lillian knew it wasn't going to be a good day. They remained that way until midafternoon, until heat began to crawl slowly beneath Tien's skin, boiling in his veins, agony forcing him to leap from his hospital bed.

"I feel like I'm on fire!" he screamed.

Lillian watched in horror, helpless, as Tien ran toward the sink, toward water that might put out the invisible flames dancing inside his body. With a loud swish, Tien leaned in to let it stream from the faucet and onto his head, face, and hands. He closed his eyes as water splashed against his face, held his breath as though being submerged. It dripped down the back of his neck, beneath his gown, but not deep enough, not where it belonged—in his skin, through his veins, pushing back against the violent waves of pain rushing through his body.

Tien paced his room, crawled into bed, splashed at the sink, paced again. Nothing worked. He could not escape his body's fire, the internal flames. Lillian followed her son around the room, comforting him with hugs, wishing more than anything that she could put out Tien's fire, ignite it in herself.

After what seemed like forever, doctors slid a needle beneath the surface of the flames, and like sand choking fire, a cool numbness flowed through Tien's body, morphine taking the heat, the flames, the misery, with it. His eyes grew heavy as the fire died, and finally, they shut. And so did Lillian's, pure relief flowing just as heavily through her.

During the past week, Lillian and Bruno had watched their son jump from his bed the very same way, racing to the sink, screaming as though being burned alive, every day. Every time they witnessed it, the pain that tore through his voice reached into their minds and their hearts, and all they could do was watch in pure agony. The chemo-like drug used to keep lupus as far away from Tien's kidneys as possible had been working so far, and while the process felt like death, he was still living.

But just a few days later, with news from an attending doctor on duty, they weren't sure for how long.

"Tien's kidneys are failing," said Dr. Laura Christie to Lillian only a couple of weeks after she and Bruno learned that their son had lupus.

There they were—words that could not be taken back, ever— four words that changed their lives forever. Their son was dying.

Earlier that day, after an exhausting night of Lillian watching Tien suffer through a high fever and watching and praying away rolling pain that had consumed his back and abdomen, doctors pumped Tien's body with morphine and took an ultrasound of his kidneys.

A nephrologist at Kaiser had slowly slid a transducer across Tien's stomach, his face serious, eyes, not blinking, studying the machine, and Lillian knew something was wrong. Very wrong.

Lupus, a serious yet mysterious disease, had been diagnosed, but the reason for Tien's seizures, his high potassium and blood pressure, and elevated levels of creatinine had remained unknown. At the sound of the words *kidney failure*, Lillian's strong outer shell finally cracked—crumbled to pieces in the area just outside of Tien's hospital room, an area used for "privacy," for receiving and dealing with unwanted news.

Until that moment, the moment Dr. Christie's eyes revealed Tien's critical situation long before her voice did, the moment that turned Tien's illness from serious to life-threatening, Lillian had been able to keep her mind, her thoughts, and her emotions pointed in the right direction. She had been able to focus on taking steps, one foot carefully in front of the other, never looking back.

But in that moment, all she could do was turn back. Time worked against her as images consumed her mind, mental pictures of Tien—her healthy, soccer-playing, food-loving, full-of-life little boy who had always dreamt of traveling to Paris. That little boy now lay still, comatose, in a hospital bed with failing kidneys.

Lillian sobbed deeply, invisible pain smothering her chest, her stomach, her body.

"I need to call Bruno," she managed, and when he arrived at the hospital twenty minutes later, she buried her reddened face into his chest and he looked straight ahead, silent, her tears enough for them both. He needed to be the strong one in that moment, the one to look only at the next step as Lillian always had. That next step, whatever it might be, needed to remain Bruno's only focus.

"We need to get him to UCSF Medical Center," said Dr. Christie. "We put a call in to Stanford University Medical Center and to UCSF, the only two hospitals in Northern California equipped with pediatric dialysis, and UCSF can admit Tien now."

University of California, San Francisco, Lillian thought. This was a whole new playing field. They were being transferred from a reputable hospital with an excellent pediatric unit to a research-based hospital known for providing the highest level of care to critical patients.

Their son was the critical patient.

"Should we call Yune?" Lillian asked Bruno, looking up at him with eyes full of tears, her face, red and broken. She had planned to travel that summer with their oldest son, Yune, to Romania and Paris to visit family, but when Tien became ill, she canceled her plans and encouraged Yune to go without her.

When Yune left, Tien was at their local Kaiser hospital, a place Yune assumed would send his brother home the next day with some medicine to fix his high potassium. He never imagined Tien would become so ill. When Yune heard the news, he locked himself in the small bedroom of his cousin's home in Paris where he was staying. He remained there for days, not speaking to a soul, then made his way to Notre Dame de Paris, walked through its towering cathedral doors, and knelt.

Yune closed his eyes and blocked out the hushed voices of locals and tourists, removed himself from the cathedral's beauty—its golden murals, floods of rainbow pouring through stained glass—and entered a place in his mind, his heart, that would let him connect to Tien from five thousand miles away.

He prayed with everything inside his soul, asking God to save his little brother, heal his kidneys, and bring him home. He felt the heat of the tiny candle in his hand, the dance of its flame, connect their spirits, an ocean apart. He had bought Tien a miniature sculpture of the Eiffel Tower, a small piece of Paris, which he prayed he would be able to place in his brother's hands and see the smile it would bring.

From the time he was a young boy, Yune and Vanina had taken Tien on imaginary trips to Paris with their stories; they let him taste the food, see the sights, experience the culture. And as Yune sat in the serenity of Notre Dame, amid the enormity of its healing presence, he prayed with everything inside of him that Tien would live to one day visit Paris himself.

The power of Yune's prayer traveled across the ocean and into Lillian's heart, where the prayers of many others were living. From the moment Tien had become ill, friends and family from Berkeley to Tahiti, from all religious backgrounds—Buddhist, Catholic, Wicca, Jewish, Tibetan Buddhist—were praying for him. Naama, a friend Tien had since preschool, traveled with her grandmother to Jerusalem, Israel, where they made a special trip to the Wailing Wall to pray for Tien.

In his or her own way, each family member and friend had been praying to their higher power for Tien's healing. Deep down, Lillian and Bruno believed those prayers would be answered.

They had to.

Until that day came, Lillian knew she needed to continue marching through the unknown with one foot in front of the other. Unable to fully wrap her mind around everything, she focused on the next step—getting Tien to UCSF. She couldn't focus on anything beyond. It would kill her, and so would the "what ifs"—*What if Tien doesn't wake up? What if the doctors at UCSF can't do anything for him?*

Let's just get him to UCSF, she told herself. That was the next step.

* 6 *

It was midnight when they got Tien transferred and admitted to UCSF, where he remained in a deep sleep, despite the war taking place inside of his body. Lillian stayed at his side, his hand in hers, for the next several hours until Tien's eyes scooted beneath their lids, dancing as though dreaming, before flittering open, slightly, to look at his mother.

"What, sweetie?" she asked after Tien mumbled something so

quietly it sounded like a whisper, a secret. Was he talking quietly or was her mind, awake for the past two and a half days, trying to sort words through fog?

"What did you say?" she asked, getting so close that the warmth of Tien's breath tickled her ear. She desperately wanted to know.

"Why are you so close?" he whispered.

"I want to hear you, and you're talking very softly," Lillian said, smiling, rubbing a hand over his soft, black hair.

"Really?" he asked, his voice much louder in his mind. "Can I have a hug?"

Lillian smiled and reached down, wrapping her son in her arms. She never wanted to let go. Eyes closed, she held him tight as he whispered, "Mom, I can't feel you."

Lillian opened her eyes as the past few weeks flashed before them. In all the years she had spent watching her children and their friends rehearse and perform circus acts, she had always been the most fascinated with tightrope walkers, the art of pure concentration, unwavering focus.

For the first time, in that very moment, Lillian realized how their lives had become a similar act, a delicate balance, one foot carefully placed before the other.

One stumble and the only way was down; for circus performers, down meant landing safely in a net—for Tien, down meant death. Lillian and Bruno had kept their chins high, their eyes looking only at the safety platform on the other side. Looking down had never been an option.

But when Tien closed his eyes once again, entering another world, a place where no one else was allowed, Lillian wondered if Tien was about to fall. Was that moment his disease's way of letting his spirit—the part of him that could no longer feel her touch—wake up to say good-bye?

She was not ready to look down. They hadn't made it this far to fall. The new walls surrounding them, the new doctors and nurses, the new ideas and untried treatments, let her mind take another mental step forward to stay safely on the rope. This hospital—this new team of doctors trained to care for the most critically ill children—would be a new beginning for them, a new set of options, the next act.

Lillian held Tien the rest of the night.

The following day, Bruno and Vanina called to tell Lillian they were going shopping. They were going to buy something they knew Tien would love very much—a Nintendo DS.

They arrived at the hospital and presented Tien with their gift, their incentive for him to wake up.

"If you wake up, you can play!" Vanina and Bruno teased.

Tien's eyes had danced beneath their lids several times since then, his body almost twitching awake, but he remained nearly lifeless in his hospital bed. His face, his hands, and his body, succumbing to the cruelty of his disease, became puffier, less recognizable, by the day.

"Wow! Look at this!" said Dr. Allon Beck, an intern whose booming voice echoed in Tien's room, into his ears and through the waves of his brain. "Let's turn it on!"

Somewhere, deep within, the doctor's words triggered something that ignited Tien's mind and awoke his passion for games. He wanted it so badly that his mind finally shoved its way through, commanding his arms, his legs, his voice.

"Wow, Guitar Hero!" Tien said, groggy, squirming in his bed.

It was the second night after being admitted to UCSF, and he woke up long enough to see the DS, to imagine pushing its buttons, playing its games. And then his eyes shut once again. But that was enough. Tien was still there—somewhere in the depths of his mind was Bruno and Lillian's son, Yune and Vanina's little brother.

★ 7 ★

Other than the brief moment when Tien, unable to feel his mother's hug, had, in Lillian's mind, woken to say good-bye, it had been days since his parents had seen any sign of life in him. When they admitted him to UCSF just a couple of days before, his body had started the process of surrendering to its attacking disease. His stomach had begun leaking fluids; his skin had turned pale, puffy, and cool to the touch.

Day after day, Bruno and Lillian watched Tien sleep, subtle twitches of his body the only indicator that he was still there, his mind still close to the surface. He hadn't yet fallen into the depths, the static slumber of a long-term coma, and every movement, no matter how small, gave them hope that he would soon wake up.

When little, involuntary movements in Tien's body gradually became intentional, Lillian and Bruno knew that, even in sleep, Tien's body and mind were pushing back against his disease.

Doctors at UCSF had immediately started Tien on dialysis with hopes that his body would respond, and they had all waited patiently through days of failed dialysis, watching for a single drop of urine in Tien's Foley catheter, any indication of kidney function.

Nothing.

On the third day came the first drop, the first indication, dripping into Tien's Foley bag. The liquid was black, darker than blood, but it was there. Lillian watched as it fell, one drop after another, slow and murky, into the clear bag. She and the nurses had never been so excited over the sight of urine.

Dialysis was not yet working, but those drops, combined with Tien's increased body movements and eventual ability to speak and sit up with help from his father and his nurses, gave them all hope that soon it would. To test for the possibility of kidney regeneration, doctors performed a biopsy and stared in disbelief at the results.

"We believe Tien has a disease called Antiphospholipid Antibody Syndrome, or APS," a group of doctors from the hematology and rheumatology departments of UCSF said to Tien's mother. They had taken Lillian from Tien's room and into the common area where all bad news was delivered. Before a word was even spoken, their faces, grim and gray, looked as though they were about to reveal news that Tien had only minutes left to live.

Instead, they told her that the biopsy revealed millions of micro clots in his kidneys, indicating APS.

Millions, Lillian thought. How could millions of *anything* possibly exist inside the kidneys of a small child? She knew the danger of one clot, a single threat, lodging itself in an inoperable location, but the thought of millions inside her son's body, threatening release at any moment, was unfathomable.

The doctors explained that, while it is not uncommon for people with lupus to develop APS and for those with APS to develop lupus, the two do not always go hand in hand.

"Tien has unfortunately pulled a terrible roll of the dice," said one of the doctors.

Lillian tried to absorb the doctors' words, understand their meanings, before Dr. Paul Brakeman came in a while later to talk with her about the next steps for Tien. After breezing by the mention of two other patients with these simultaneous diseases, Dr. Brakeman tried to continue talking about what was next for Tien, but Lillian stopped him.

"What happened to those other two patients?" she asked, fearing the answer but at the same time needing it. "Did dialysis and plasmapheresis work for them?"

Sensing his hesitation, Lillian stared him down.

"They didn't respond to treatment," the doctor said simply, offering nothing more, but there was nothing simple in his answer. Was Tien's destiny also death?

Every set of lab results were coming back with black and white, numeric proof that Tien's kidneys were not improving, his lupus had not been quieted, and dialysis was not yet working. Even if dialysis started to work, making Tien well enough to leave the hospital, lifelong treatments or a kidney transplant were his only options of surviving.

As if the odds against him were not bad enough, his body was now attacking from another angle, with another autoimmune disease, one determined to fill his body with clots that could lead to a stroke or heart attack at any given moment.

But in spite of his diseases' attempts to completely take over his body, Tien, who was taking liquid steroids and sitting through three hours of dialysis a day, in addition to two hours of plasmapheresis—a process to clean antibodies from the blood—seemed to be improving daily, with an increasing ability to speak, sit up, and roam the halls in a wheelchair, despite his numbers and the results of his tests.

"We need to knock out his immune system," said Dr. Portale, explaining that a chemo-like medicine would work to wipe it out, taking away his body's attempt at attacking any more of its major organs.

But Bruno and Lillian were not ready for that. They saw the look in their son's eyes, the way he had improved slowly but steadily in the past week, the way his spirit had woken up, the way his body was fighting back—despite what his labs were saying.

"Just give us a little more time," Lillian said, speaking from her heart, where intuition, her mother's gut instinct, lived and screamed, *Just give him a little more time!*

One more day.

It was Tuesday, and Dr. Portale, who also maintained hope based on Tien's visible improvements, was giving him until Wednesday to let the progress that appeared on his patient's face, in his eyes, and in his smile, show up in his blood and translate to acceptable numbers on his charts.

And the next day, they did.

"His labs are getting better," said Dr. Portale of Tien's very next set.

He smiled down at paperwork in his hand that proved they had made the right decision. It was the end of their second week at UCSF and the first bit of good news they had received since Tien's very first seizure, his body's first defeat.

⋆ 8 ⋆

Tien continued taking steroids and sitting still for three hours a day as dialysis and plasmapheresis cleaned his system, filtered his blood. On August 8, 2008, he was sent home to continue with medications and visits to UCSF three days a week for three hours of dialysis per visit.

The moment the hospital doors slid open after Tien was discharged, he was wrapped in the city's foggy embrace. He smiled as the smell of San Francisco's thick, cool air teased his imagination. He knew that just beyond UCSF was a big city to explore, a city he had rarely visited—a city he knew he'd be visiting three times a week for dialysis. It was a city waiting to be discovered.

For several weeks, Lillian and Bruno helped nurses lift Tien from his wheelchair and lay him gently on the bed next to his dialysis machine. After three hours of lying still, dreaming of Paris, remembering his grandmother through his mother's stories, and catching up on homework with his pediatric dialysis teacher, Alice Cassman, Tien would venture into the city with one or both of his parents.

They visited its giant malls, got lost on its twisted streets, ate in its big restaurants, sat in its unruly traffic. Coming from the smaller, suburban city of Berkeley, Tien felt like a big city boy. He left his Berkeley home every Monday, Wednesday, and Friday, early from his fourth-grade class, to drive to the big city and undergo dialysis before exploring this other world.

His schedule, which instantly became his life, blended many different worlds—the world where he was well and the one where he was ill, the one with his Berkeley home and the one with the big city that became his home away from home, his world full of teachers and friends and "normal" things like school and homework, and a world where the kids around him were making wishes through the Make-A-Wish Foundation because they had beaten death and lived to do so.

The kids at school lived "normal" lives and didn't know anything about staring death in the face, while the kids in dialysis talked about making wishes that would allow them to feel part of that "normal life" again.

After talking with social worker Steve Baisch about his desire to visit Paris, France, for a culinary experience, Tien and Lillian got a visit from Dr. Portale, who was a master of breaking bad news in the best way possible—with just the right amount of sympathy and the necessary amount of truth.

"There's no way you'll be able to go to Paris," Dr. Portale said gently. It hadn't been long since Tien had started dialysis, and his body was still very weak from its fight to hush lupus. "It's too far and you're really in no condition to travel. If you'd like to go somewhere, the furthest you can go is a couple of hours away."

"Ooooh, maaaaan!" Tien said, smiling, trying to roll with this news, as Lillian rubbed his head, lips pressed together. He was alive and responding well to dialysis, so nothing, aside from bad news about his health, could bring Tien down. "That's okay, I'll think of something else!"

A few months later, volunteers from the Make-A-Wish Foundation called with the next best thing. "We know you wanted to travel to Paris, but since you can't, we want to bring Paris to you," they said.

Tien smiled the same smile that snuck across his face with every thought of Paris lights and the city's smells and food. He didn't know exactly what that meant—all he knew was that Paris was coming to him.

Tien had been on dialysis for six months, long enough to return to fourth grade and run and laugh through life the same way his friends and classmates did. He had gone from being wheeled into dialysis every day to walking in, went from pausing on the landing of his stairs at home to racing up and down them. He wasn't well enough to travel to a country across the world, but he was finally well enough to experience it.

A couple of weeks after talking to Make-A-Wish volunteers, Tien was touring Paris through the sights and scents of its most delectable food, living the dream that had lived in his imagination for so long—the dream that had started as a very young child and continued through his long hours in dialysis. He was suddenly in the place he had visited through his brother's and sister's stories, the place from which Yune had sent healing prayers when Tien went into kidney failure. His dream, his wish, was finally coming true.

Paris was still 5,000 miles away, but its heart and soul were in the very kitchen where he worked with French-born Chef Roland Passot, owner of the area's La Folie and Left Bank restaurants, as he prepared food for the annual Make-A-Wish Foundation Wine & Wishes fundraising event on Treasure Island.

Tien was finally standing beside a true French chef, a master of foie gras and frog legs, soufflés and escargot: the country's finest cuisine. Knee-deep in Chef Passot's white coat, its sleeves rolled up high, tall, white hat proudly atop Tien's head, he was finally a chef, and finally, in his mind, in Paris.

The evening, a black-tie affair, brought in dozens of the area's finest restaurants, which displayed hundreds of exquisite samplings, from uniquely prepared starters, to meats, salads, cheeses, and desserts, such as French macarons and puff pastries. Tien and his family strolled slowly from vendor to vendor as though roaming the streets of France, tasting the country's most delicious food from sidewalk cafés selling crêpes or sandwiches to people on the go.

But helping Chef Passot add the final touches to plates during Wine & Wishes was just the beginning. Another two visits to Paris awaited.

✳ 9 ✳

The second of three visits came a few days later as Tien, once again, stood beside the chef, this time, the experience taking him to the heart of French cuisine, the place it all begins—a true French kitchen.

A sleek, black town car had swung by the Hotel Sofitel San Francisco Bay, where Tien and his family were staying for the night. They had checked into the hotel—the fanciest Tien had ever seen—and enjoyed macarons and a rich, flowing chocolate fondue that welcomed them to their room.

The town car, following dancing lights of red and blue from four police cars leading the way, took them to a place that would reveal how these and other of life's most delicious foods were made—Chef Passot's Left Bank restaurant. The closest Tien had ever come to a police escort was riding in the back of an ambulance on his way to the hospital; and the nicest restaurant he'd ever been to would not come close to the restaurant he was about to experience.

In the middle of Left Bank's kitchen, Tien stood in awe as the hustle and bustle of a busy, French restaurant came to life before his eyes with the infectious chaos of knives chopping, pans clinking, flambés firing, shouts of dinner orders echoing. Tien watched as food in every form, from raw ingredients to pans sizzling to perfect plate placement, made its way from the loud kitchen to the dining area, where guests sipped on wine, enjoyed one another's company, and pleased their taste buds with dishes that originated halfway around the world.

Standing over a hot griddle as food on plates carried by the careful hands of prep chefs and waiters flew by, Tien remained focused on the task he was given—flipping crêpes. Left Bank's industrial kitchen had different demands than his kitchen at home, where he had spent every Sunday morning cooking crêpes with his father from the time he was six years old.

Tien had hung a sign on the kitchen door every weekend announcing "Crêpe Day Sunday" to the rest of the family, and he and Bruno spent hours making dough from scratch, flipping and filling them with jam or eggs and cheese. They laughed together as Tien learned to keep the crêpes from flipping onto the floor, and now, beside Roland Passot, the chef watched as Tien perfected the flip—quickly adjusting to the fifteen seconds it took to cook each side as opposed to the two minutes it took in his kitchen at home.

They flipped and stuffed crêpes together, fulfilling the orders of customers ordering any kind of crêpe imaginable from the special, one-night-only, "Tien Menu." Not only was Tien a chef, but also he was a chef with his own menu. He smiled more than he had smiled in months as a long table filled with police and firefighters sat and indulged in his creations.

Touched by the spirit of this young, bright, and healthy child, the officers and firefighters passed around a hat to collect money for Tien—half of which he used to buy board games for himself, the other half he spent on buying games for the children in the pediatric ICU at UCSF. Three days a week, he was still one of those children, but on that night, he was a chef in Paris.

✻ 10 ✻

Tien's tour through France continued two months later in a limo to the Culinary Institute of America in Napa Valley, where he witnessed a very different French restaurant culture from that of the pleasantly chaotic kitchen of Left Bank. The quiet, laid-back style of restaurant or bakery he imagined existing in Paris existed in the kitchen of the Culinary Institute, where Tien got to quietly learn from one of its students the art of making croissants and baguettes.

He helped make dough from scratch for the baguettes, which he rolled out and placed in a machine that molded and folded it into perfectly shaped bread. Fresh from the oven, Tien and his family gathered around a large, wooden table in the main dining area and enjoyed a feast that included Tien's fresh-baked baguettes and other French-inspired foods, such as steaks they could slice like butter, mini quiches, delicious vegetable creations, and traditional desserts like crème brûlée.

Tien left the last trek of his trip to Paris with a bag of baguettes— the way he had always imagined people in France carrying the long, skinny bread from boulangeries to their homes or offices.

Just like them, Tien was heading home. His trip to Paris was over, but through the three experiences that allowed Paris to come to him, the city would live inside of Tien forever.

———————— ✳

Tien returned to the fourth grade, maintained good grades, and signed up for his school's end-of-the-year play, where he auditioned and got the part of the grandfather in a play about the Oregon Trail.

On the night of the play, Dr. Portale gave his "okay" to let Tien leave dialysis a few minutes early as long as everything looked alright. Twenty minutes before Tien's dialysis session was over, Dr. Portale looked at the numbers, checked his blood pressure, looked at the anticipation on Tien's face, smiled, and set him free.

Lillian drove Tien back to Berkeley, straight to his school, where volunteers were able to quickly paint an old man's beard across Tien's excited face and send him onstage. It wasn't the circus—he wasn't tumbling or twirling or flipping or turning cartwheels—but he was back on stage; back in the spotlight, back where he belonged.

The audience, many of them the parents of Tien's friends, cheered wildly at the end of the play, loudly in celebration of Tien's return. He smiled and bowed with the rest of his classmates, then returned home to start his summer vacation.

Tien spent the next six months going to dialysis three days a week, living in between his old, "normal" world and his new world, a world he had learned to adjust to, to live in, because there was no other choice. He no longer had working kidneys, but he was alive.

One day after treatment, Lillian and Tien ventured into San Francisco as they did every other day of dialysis and enjoyed a little piece of France—crêpes in a small, quaint restaurant. Just like every other customer in the restaurant, Tien enjoyed every bite, but now he knew what went on beyond the swinging doors of the kitchen. It was another life back there, another culture, one that the Make-A-Wish Foundation had let him become a part of.

That day was a day like any other, but when Tien and Lillian returned home that night, Lillian opened the backdoor of their house and knew that everything was about to change.

Inches from where she stood were silent flutters in the cool, dark night; black wings of a bat danced wildly, momentarily, before scurrying clumsily back into the night. Staring at its tiny body, its beady, mysterious eyes, and snout face before watching it fly away, there was a moment of truth between them: a clear message delivered from the depths of folklore—bats were symbols of transition, of change, and initiation—out with the old, in with the new. As the wild animal's dark body merged with the night, taking "the old" with it, Lillian knew in her gut what "the new" would be.

After nearly a year of keeping Tien on dialysis, carefully and occasionally broaching the subject of "transplant" with each other, Lillian and Bruno had finally made a decision. Despite its possible complications, they knew that keeping Tien on dialysis was not a "forever" solution. He could not live the rest of his life being kept alive by a machine, having his "normal" world constantly darkened by this other world of dialysis, a constant reminder that he was still ill.

He needed a transplant.

⋆ 11 ⋆

An hour after the bat fluttered into the night, the phone rang and Lillian knew exactly why. Tien had been on the transplant waiting list for less than a month, and as the bat predicted, the words, *We have a kidney for Tien,* were proof of the change the bat promised was on its way.

"Come now," said a woman from UCSF.

Lillian closed her eyes, creased with lines of both happiness and sorrow: happiness for Tien and sorrow for the family that had just lost a loved one, making this transplant possible. She shared the news with her family—Tien was getting a new kidney.

The predicted three-hour surgery ("if everything goes well") was a little less than three hours. It was late at night, and Bruno had returned home from the hospital to be with Yune and Vanina. As Lillian paced the halls, thinking, praying, hoping with all her might that the surgery would go well, keeping her mind free of the haunting "what if" thoughts that easily could have seeped in, she was finally able to breathe when doctors announced that the surgery was a success and Tien was heading to recovery.

"I'll be here when you wake up," Lillian had whispered to Tien when doctors announced, "It's time," before wheeling him back to the operating room. As a family, Lillian, Bruno, Yune, and Vanina had remained strong, patient through months of waiting on test results, kidney function, a transplant, and the fight of Tien's spirit to pull him through.

Finally, as Tien crawled slowly from the grip of anesthesia in the recovery room, the wait was over. They, as a family, had won death's battle, and after Tien's successful surgery, they knew he would have a full life ahead of him, a life that did not require machines to keep him alive, a life he would be free to live to its fullest.

———✦

More than two and a half years after Tien's transplant, he is enjoying middle school, learning to play the drums, and performing once again as part of his school's drama club. Other than a few hospitalizations for different viruses and bacteria and the worry of his body's rejection to its new kidney, Tien's mind is consumed with childhood joy, such as playing with friends after school and coming up with new dreams, new places to imagine visiting, because Paris no longer lives within the limits of his imagination.

He has been there.

A place that only his mind once had the power to take him had come to him through the Make-A-Wish Foundation. It had led him through the double doors of a true French kitchen, let him stand side by side with a true French chef, and allowed him to taste hundreds of authentic French foods.

He hadn't traveled the streets of Paris to arrive at such restaurants, hadn't walked the sidewalks or seen the buildings or heard the accents. But that didn't matter; he had experienced so much more. Rather than eat the food of French chefs in Paris, he had gotten to work with them. Rather than sit in fancy French restaurants, he had gotten to cook in them. Rather than breathe in the scent of crêpes and baguettes and croissants floating down the streets of Paris, he had gotten to make them.

He had visited Paris through his brother's and sister's stories, inherited his love for the city from his grandparents, developed an appreciation for its food from his father, and finally experienced its culture through a gift from the Make-A-Wish Foundation. And if the day never comes to cross the ocean and step onto the streets of Paris, the city, the experience of that city coming to life in his hometown, will forever be with him, will forever be enough.

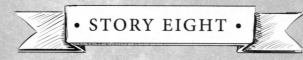

Serena Butler

"Music is an emotional healer that starts from deep within the soul. Without music, all we have is silence, and what is silence but the audio form of darkness? It wasn't until the past decade that I discovered the true power of music."

−Serena Butler

$\star$ 1 $\star$

"It's cancer," Sedra said to her fifteen-year-old daughter, Serena. She turned around in the front seat of the car, eyes filled with tears. "Pull over, Kevin," Sedra added quietly to her husband.

They were somewhere between Lincoln, Nebraska, and Beaver Dam, Wisconsin—a solitary stretch of Iowa or Missouri highway—on their way to Serena's grandfather's funeral. Loose, black gravel crunched beneath the tires of her parents' chili-red SUV as Serena's father slowed to a halt.

In the weeks prior to her grandfather's death, Serena had been through endless blood tests, biopsies, and sonograms, and she knew the results were waiting for her around a dark corner.

Always finding hope and inspiration from the music of Michael Jackson, she had turned to him as she neared that corner, every morning and every evening, gaining strength from his song, "Will You Be There," living by its message to fight until the end.

If this is cancer, I will fight, she told herself from the time an enlarged thyroid had become a cancer threat. *I will fight till the end.*

They had been waiting for biopsy results for more than a week, but when Serena's grandfather passed away, her mom had called the doctors and told them to wait until they returned home to Nebraska to deliver the news.

The message was clearly lost, and the news came crashing in with an unexpected wave against an already saddened family.

Diagnosed with the same cancer nearly ten years before, Sedra knew deep down what the biopsy would reveal. Sitting in the SUV, consumed by memories of her father, she had looked down at her cell phone on its first ring to see Dr. Olson's office on the caller ID.

By the third ring, she knew she needed to answer. She listened quietly, and after hanging up, she finally repeated the words that haunted her—"It's cancer."

Serena looked out the window, past the highway, and into a sea of calming yellow—where towering corn husks danced to the gentle music of the breeze. She closed her eyes as her mother crawled into the backseat, wrapping both arms around her body as her dad pulled back onto the highway for the remaining four hours of their drive.

Small talk of work, school, and everyday life had filled the first four hours, letting Serena, her parents, and her older sister, Seanza, escape the reality they were about to face. Sedra had just lost her father; the girls had lost their beloved grandfather.

The silence surrounding Serena, the thoughts of death and cancer circling her mind, became dark, dizzying. She pulled out her laptop, turned it on, and hit "play" on "Affirmation," her favorite Savage Garden song, the voice of lead singer Darren Hayes engulfing the car.

Serena sank into her mother's embrace, letting his voice fill and free her.

Every line, every message, started with "I believe." When the song faded to silence, to darkness, she hit "play" again, listening to its message about not appreciating love until you've been burned.

I've just been burned, Serena thought. Tears crawled down her face, and she turned from her mother.

The words flowing into her ears, through her mind, quickly carried those negative thoughts like a gentle yet determined wave. *Mom beat this,* she thought instead. *So can I.*

"If the biopsy reveals cancer, just remember," Dr. Olson had said, "this is the good cancer—the best kind of cancer." In Serena's mind, no cancer was "good cancer."

The SUV remained as silent as the countryside outside its windows. Miles of farmland, green pastures, and quaint country homes stretched as far as Serena could see. She longed for the simplicity, the tranquility, of her surroundings—the peace and certainty her life had just five minutes before.

As "Affirmation" continued with reminders of the importance of family, Darren Hayes's message was clear.

I can beat this, Serena thought. *My family and I will get through this. But first we need to get through grandpa's funeral.*

⋆ 2 ⋆

They pulled into her grandfather's driveway, and as her parents and sister crawled slowly from the SUV and gathered their things, Serena stared at the front door of his small house. It was always unlocked with the anticipation of family's arrival. That day, she knew he wouldn't be there to leave the door unlocked—he didn't know they were coming.

He wouldn't be sitting in his recliner, iced tea in hand, watching the playful ripples of Beaver Dam Lake, where he had spent many years fishing and exploring by boat. He wouldn't greet them with the boisterous, "Well, hey there!" with which he had greeted them every summer for the past fifteen years.

He simply wouldn't be there.

A deeper sense of emptiness than she was already feeling from hearing the word *cancer* settled over Serena as she pushed open the door and made her way into the house. Inside, she mingled politely with members of her family who had traveled from all over the country for her grandfather's funeral before making her way as quickly as possible to the screen door leading to the big, grassy backyard filled with her childhood memories.

She needed to be alone, to feel his presence. She sat on the water's edge and watched the sun sink into the darkened waters across the lake, setting it ablaze with deep orange and golden rays. Leaves of giant hickory trees whispered above as she picked up their fallen nuts and skipped them across the lake, just as she had done when she was a little girl.

One, two, three, four, five, she counted the times the hickory nuts jumped across the surface of the water before sinking into its darkness.

If she closed her eyes, she could hear the echo of her and Seanza's giggles carrying across the lake when they were kids, sitting with their grandfather, Red, on his fishing boat, poles in hand.

The rock of the boat always upset Serena's stomach, sending her to the shore most of the time. As she sat there, in the very spot where she had sat and fished for so many summers, she recalled her grandfather and Seanza floating by, laughing and talking. She smiled at the memory of one particular afternoon, one with the three of them and one lost wish.

Serena was about nine, her sister, twelve, and a ladybug had landed on Seanza's hand.

"That's good luck! You can make a wish, but your wish won't come true if she doesn't fly away," Red had warned.

The small boat rocked as Seanza flung her arm crazily through the air, whipping her hand back and forth, flicking her fingers. "It won't come off!" Seanza playfully screamed.

The ladybug clung to her thumb, refusing to spread its wings. Seanza blew on her finger, determined to see it fly, to take her wish with the wind, until the bug's small legs lost their firm grip and she fell into the water and bobbed, wings becoming drenched by the lake. Small ripples carried her further and further from the boat, and as Seanza and her grandfather watched it kick and fight, the ladybug never left the water, and then it was too late.

"Your wish will never come true now," Red teased.

———— ✶

Five years had passed since Seanza lost her wish on Beaver Dam Lake, so now it was time for a new one to come true. Fifteen-year-old Serena and her family had been home from Red's funeral for several weeks, and the surgery to remove her thyroid was a success. Standing in her sister's hospital room, Seanza looked up to find five little black and red spotted bugs crawling on the ceiling.

It was late fall, and Nebraska's snow season had already begun. Spring and summer had passed—*so what are ladybugs doing out of hiding?* Seanza wondered. She had seen two in the car on the way to visit her sister in the hospital, and now there were five on the ceiling of Serena's hospital room.

"I feel like grandpa is here," Seanza whispered to Sedra as they walked in and stood beside Serena's bed. Their red polka dots somehow calmed her, gave her a sense of peace. Their grandfather was there with them.

Everything is going to be okay, Seanza insisted to herself, quietly wishing for her sister's successful recovery. Knowing that the ladybugs surrounding them would eventually fly, she thought, *This wish will come true.*

After prepping Serena for the surgery, doctors had wheeled her back to the operating room, the blinding lights above blending quickly as she passed beneath.

That's strange. There's music playing in here, Serena thought as the gurney jiggled and thumped to the unexpected beat, coming to a halt in the operating room. *I never imagined there'd be music in a hospital.*

Music always seemed to find her, to follow her.

The chill of the operating room, the smell of it, was unfamiliar, uncomfortable. *This is the beginning of the end of my journey,* she thought grimly.

Doctors sedated her, but before she fell into a deep sleep, before the room around her dimmed, one last song came through the hospital speakers before her world was silenced—"I Knew I Loved You" by Savage Garden.

Serena closed her eyes before the medicine closed them for her, and as the song reached its chorus, her tight grip on the gurney rails had loosened and the butterflies in her belly rested.

Darren Hayes, the voice of Savage Garden, had found her again. She had listened to this song a million times, gotten lost in its music, inspired by its lyrics. Any song out of thousands, possibly millions, could have drifted into that cold, lonely room at that moment, but it was this one—this very special song that brought hope, peace, and comfort to a young girl facing cancer and surgery. Eyes still closed, Serena smiled, her mind rested, before it left the room.

⋆ 3 ⋆

The day after surgery, Serena was home with her family, on the road to recovery. Listening to music, watching movies, and playing video games kept her busy, and most importantly, still. Sleeping in her waterbed risked tearing the stitches in her neck, so her parents pulled a mattress out of the basement and set it up for her in her dad's office.

The second night after returning home, Serena stayed up late, chatting online with friends from other countries, testing out games on the family's new Xbox, and surfing the net. When she saw that a preview to Michael Jackson's upcoming release "Cheater" was available online, she immediately hit "play."

The song's slow, playful intro dragged her in, the snapping of fingers enticing her as they led to the heart of the song—a cool, steady drumbeat and the artist's signature "Oh!" echoing in the background. She closed her eyes and let the power of the lyrics, the strength and familiarity of his voice, seep in.

It was well past midnight and quiet in the house save for the subtle sound of voices coming from the TV in the living room, where Seanza was watching and dozing on the couch. Lost in the words, consumed by the music, Serena tapped her thumb on the desk, oblivious as silent, invisible hands crawled up her back and clung to her neck.

She shot her eyes open and inhaled short, quick breaths. Panic rushed through every limb, into her heart, her mind, to the ends of her fingers, which clutched the arms of her chair as she sat up, fighting the urge to run into the cool, Nebraska night to take in all its air.

Instead, she walked into the living room with a hand clutched to her ribcage and looked at her sister. "What's the matter, Rena?" Seanza asked, standing immediately.

"I'm … "

Serena paused, closed her eyes. She hunched over her arm, wrapping it even tighter around her ribcage, before taking in another short breath. "I'm having trouble breathing."

"Oh, God," Seanza said. "Go sit down in the office and I'll wake Mom and Dad."

She came to the office a few minutes later, alone. "How are you doing?" Seanza asked.

"It comes and goes," Serena said, waiting for the next suffocation. Her lungs seemed to tighten and loosen with every attack. "Where are Mom and Dad?" she asked.

"I can't wake them up," Seanza said.

Their father had always been a heavy, comatose-type sleeper, and Sedra was exhausted from a long night at the hospital and taking care of Serena during the days following surgery. Their bodies had moved fluidly beneath Seanza's fingertips, their ears deaf to her pleas, until she finally gave up.

"I'll try again in just a little bit."

For the next several hours, she talked her sister through the panic and into the calm, reminding her with soothing words, "in through your mouth, out your nose."

During moments when air cleverly maneuvered more freely through its constricted passageway, giving Serena momentary relief, she would nearly whisper, "It's not working."

The hours passed—2:00 a.m., 3:00 a.m.— and with more failed attempts at waking her parents, Seanza knew it was up to her to keep her sister calm. She knew something was terribly wrong, but, in her seventeen-year-old logic, not bad enough to call an ambulance or use force to get her parents out of bed. She just needed to get her sister through the night.

They talked, played video games, listened to music, anything they could to keep Serena's mind in the right place—a place of survival, of taking one more breath. It wasn't like other nights they had spent staying up late together, Serena draped across her sister's bed, talking and laughing while Seanza created some form of artwork—a painting or drawing—that illustrated her vision, her interpretation, of the world.

Her sister was known as "the artist," Serena, "the music buff." They had grown up with music filling the rooms of their home—from Michael Bolton to Green Day, Eddie Money to Motown—and the lyrics had always spoken to Serena, inspired and enticed her.

Serena spent hours as a little girl, tucked away in her bedroom, placing vinyl on her record player—Cyndi Lauper, Michael Jackson, Madonna—which her mother had given to her. At the age of five, Serena knew words to songs by The Cars, Tina Turner, Rush, and Billy Ocean.

Her grandfather Red worked a laundry route in the 1950s, when Sedra was just a little girl, driving between diners, stores, factories, and service stations throughout Loves Park, Illinois, to collect old towels and dirty dishrags. When owners of those diners updated their jukeboxes, they'd give Red piles of outdated forty-fives, which later ignited a passion for music in Sedra that trickled down to Serena and ran through her blood. Her exposure to it—the old vinyls, her growing collection of CDs, the instruments her father dabbled with here and there—prompted her to sign up for her school's orchestra in the fourth grade.

Branching out from the guitar and drums her father, Kevin, had introduced her to, she decided to play the violin when Red gave her one that had been passed around his family for more than one hundred years. The violin's nostalgia, its history, wasn't enough to keep her playing. After a year, she found the instrument tedious, its sound, monotonous.

In fifth grade, she changed to the drums and immediately connected to the strength of the instrument, the heartbeat of music, but the school band bored her instantly with its setting and structure. Serena stuck with it but decided to further her instruction at home, in the basement, working out rhythms, learning—by ear rather than sheet music—the beats to her favorite songs. The first song she taught herself was Michael Jackson's "Billie Jean."

That freedom of song choice, those lyrics crashing in her mind, was liberating, addictive.

Through middle school and into high school, Serena's CD collection continued to grow, with albums of U2, Prince, Justin Timberlake, and Eminem becoming part of her musical family. Posters of her favorite artists—namely Michael Jackson—began gracing her bedroom walls. Researching music, writing it, absorbing it, became her inspiration, an expression of who she was.

The night Serena became absorbed in the lyrics of "Cheater," the night that death wrapped its bony fingers around her ribs and up to her neck before squeezing, ended the next day in the emergency room. Seanza had talked her sister through the night, soothed her mind, her spirit, until 6:00 a.m., when Serena decided that a warm bath would calm her panicked, shaking body. She sat in the suds, wrapped in the steam's threatening embrace. The warmth of it seeped into her lungs, pushing against the relentless wall determined to keep air from its deep, natural motion.

When panic resurfaced, threatened, she crawled slowly from the tub, wrapped her body, her pain, in a towel before opening the bathroom door to find Sedra standing directly on the other side.

"Oh, my God," her mother said, cupping her mouth. Serena's skin was the color of clay. "We're going to the hospital—NOW."

After hours of tests, CT scans and X-rays, shallow breaths, and moments of panic, doctors finally determined what had kept Serena and her sister up all night—a blood clot in her lungs, a pulmonary embolism. Over the next twenty-four hours, Serena's inhales finally steadied from calmed panic as her passageway, with the help of clot-dissolving shots in her stomach, expanded, letting tired air through.

She could finally breathe.

* 4 *

After three days, Serena was discharged and sent home with her family. Doctors put her on blood thinners for the next six months to keep clots from forming, and placed her on a low-iodine diet before starting her on radiation to kill any remaining cancer cells. To eliminate vitamin K, which helps blood to clot faster, from her diet, she lived on a very strict, mostly fruit diet, and then it was time for radiation.

The threat of radiation would be present at all times; it could seep from her skin and into the bodies of others. It was a medical necessity that Serena enter seclusion, locked away, for days, sometimes a week, at a time. She could spend no more than two hours at a time with family members, three feet of space separating them at all times. No long car rides, no hugs, no good-night kisses.

Her bedroom door felt closed to the world, where she was locked inside with her thoughts and her music. Confined to total solitude other than leaving to eat a meal from paper plates that nobody else would touch or using the restroom—her own—Serena began to feel like a stranger in her home, an outsider looking in.

She spent hours staring out her bedroom window, imagining the endless rows of corn and farmland and green pastures that existed beyond her neighborhood. When the smell of spicy nacho sauce, drenching salty tortilla chips piled with guacamole and sour cream, would creep down the hallway and under her door, reminding her of all the food she was no longer allowed to eat, she'd become angry with her situation, homesick with thoughts of Tucson, thirteen hundred miles away. She resented those yellow rows beyond her window, dancing, teasing, those pastures covered in winter white, those smelly farms.

I hate corn, she thought. *I hate snow, I hate train tracks, I hate farms, I hate Nebraska.* They had lived there for a year and a half, her old life remaining in Tucson, Arizona, where she was born and raised. Moving at the end of middle school would have been difficult enough for any kid, but being rejected by the town, the people, the culture, had made it even worse.

Seanza was pulled into the assistant principal's office on her first day of eleventh grade. He carefully studied her clothes, her style, before bluntly asking, "Are you goth?"

Seanza looked down at her jeans and colorful T-shirt. She wasn't wearing black. Her face was not white. Her eyes were not hidden in the shadows of dark makeup, and she had no spikes around her neck. Her fingernails were not black, her lips not blood red.

"No," she answered sharply.

It was one of her and Serena's first experiences with the town's small-mindedness, its spirit of disapproval for newcomers—especially newcomers who did not go to church, did not play a single sport, and cared nothing about labels on clothes. They didn't fit the mold.

Serena had never turned a head in Tucson with her brown hair dyed bright blue or red or green—or all colors of the rainbow at the same time. Anything out of the norm, expression of who she was through the colors in her hair, was something to be questioned, laughed at, in this small town they now called "home."

When Serena entered high school, she remained true to who she was. She sported her "I wish you were a piñata" T-shirt, which she was forced to cover with her hooded sweatshirt, and dyed her hair bright blue with gold tints. Accused of craving attention, the word *loner* was thrown at her, settling beneath her thickening skin, but she walked through the halls proudly, spoke up in class, and held her own.

One day during speech class, she decided to let her assuming classmates all the way in, to risk total rejection, and to express her love for music. She presented the history of some of her favorite bands and artists—Culture Club, ABBA, Darren Hayes—adding her love for their music, their influence on the world. When she heard a classmate whisper, "freak," her mind's volume cranked to high.

She stared long and hard into the eyes of her fellow ninth graders. Some stared back, disgusted; others scribbled in their notebooks, pretending the room's thick tension was a light, comfortable breeze.

Serena was going to spend the next three years with these students, trying to make this her home, but it was then that she realized she was as much a stranger to them as she was the day she stepped foot on campus as "the new girl" in that small town.

She finished her speech and sat down, deciding in that moment that acceptance, approval, didn't matter. Remaining true to herself was the only thing that did.

It wasn't until she approached the end of her junior year that Serena felt an ounce of validation. She signed up for a music lyrics and analysis class, designed to encourage students to analyze music—from death metal to R & B—with no boundaries, no judgment, no right or wrong answer. Her voice was finally heard, finally accepted, and those ninety minutes of freedom, of self-expression, were exactly what she needed to coast into her senior year.

She had made it through isolation, through five iodine radiation treatments, through "faker" and "liar" whispers following her down the school hallways, haunting and tormenting her.

"Your hair didn't fall out," her classmates had said when she returned to school at the end of her sophomore year. "You didn't really have cancer."

She had missed a quarter of tenth grade, undergoing radiation, keeping distance from her family—from the world—visiting the hospital for body scans, dealing with the pain and misery of being off her thyroid medication.

She had gained thirty pounds in one month, and that cruel, dead weight settled and grabbed at her muscles, pushing, pounding. She nearly buckled every day beneath its relentless strength while climbing the stairs of her school's campus, those spiteful whispers, real or imagined, pulling back at her.

She pushed ahead, to and from class, restless through lectures, pain at the forefront of her mind. Cancer had become her identity, solitude, her friend, and Darren Hayes, her musical companion. Lyrics to "Affirmation," the song that had brought peace to her when cancer first entered her life on the way to her grandfather's funeral, became part of her thoughts, her inner voice. Darren seemed to have a song for her every mood, lessons to teach, music to inspire, and he was there every step of the way.

> When the music feels like this,
> When you lose control you gotta go with it.
> Ten feet high,
> Flyin' above the sky,
> Your problems don't exist,
> When music feels like this.*

My problems don't exist, Serena thought, absorbing the words to his song "Spin." She had escaped. During all her isolation, he had taken her somewhere else—somewhere outside of that room, beyond the walls of her confinement, to a world where only words mattered.

Before, she had been engulfed with thoughts like *What did I do to deserve this? Nobody understands. I am so alone. Why me?* But

---

* From the title song on the album *Spin*, copyright © 2002. Lyrics, by Darren Hayes and Walter Afanasieffu, used by permission.

it was words from songs on Darren's album *Spin* that had guided Serena for days and weeks, pushing thoughts of *why me?* from her mind.

Serena had maintained a happy face while hiding these thoughts from her family. Beneath her smiles, she was sinking into the weight of their pull, drowning in their desperate hold. To the world, she remained strong, but facing cancer and living a life that had separated her—emotionally and physically—from that world was something that she, at the age of fifteen, could not deal with on her own. She was reminded in Darren's song, "What You Like," that he was with her as he sang about unity between people and starting over, of life's journey beginning and ending together.

Even just a voice in her speakers, Darren Hayes had become Serena's comfort, guiding her through her journey.

★ 5 ★

Serena went back to school during the last quarter of her sophomore year, and in the two years between then and graduation, she maintained friendships with others like herself who didn't quite fit in, played music, and focused on the day she would toss her green and silver cap into the air. With disapproval and accusing whispers still haunting her daily, she kept smiling, but behind that smile was pain, darkness, and a million unanswered questions.

Why did cancer choose me? What did I do to deserve it? Will it ever come back? Why won't the other kids believe me?

These thoughts and others consumed her, with moments of relief coming only from indulging in her music, those words.

Coz I don't know which way this road is gonna turn,
But I know it's gonna be fine

It's gonna be fine, she told herself as she continued to listen to Darren's "Good Enough."

> *But there are some days no matter how much I've learned,*
> *That the road gets tough,*
> *And I don't feel good enough.**

Through this song, Darren had warned that life's roads can get tough, but Serena never imagined just how tough hers was about to get.

———————— ✳

The blow came faster than lightning, a small fist, thunder cracking against Serena's head. She hardly knew the girl's name. She was a friend of a friend of a friend—one of those high school acquaintances whose paths you cross only by association. Serena had never spoken to the girl, never gave her a reason to hate.

The power of the girl's close-handed punch to Serena's forehead shot her body—weakened from radiation, easily bruised from blood thinners—back in movie-like slow motion, instant pain freezing as her mind scrambled frantically to understand what had just happened.

In that moment, every whispered threat, every blatant tease, every closed mind and judgmental stare pounded through Serena's body. Her classmates' disapproval, their haunting laughs, Serena's cries, the town's rejection, crashed into her. The emotional torment she had suffered from the time she had moved to that small town finally reached deeper than her soul, slapped harder than her outer shell could handle. This was a literal punch in the face, and Serena cracked.

---

* From the song "Good Enough" on the album *Spin*, copyright © 2002. Lyrics, by Darren Hayes and Walter Afanasieffu, used by permission.

High school, to that point, had been something she trudged through day by day, living moment to moment. It was a place of misery but never a place of fear.

As Serena sat across from the school's assistant principal, a goose egg swelling and throbbing on her head, tears choking words, she instantly knew that's what it had just become—a place of bias and fear.

"She said you wouldn't shut up," the vice principal said, a combined look of *you're wasting my time* and *you deserved this* settling into her stone eyes as they scooted from Serena's neon Converse high-tops to her jet-black pants, to her *Nightmare Before Christmas* hoodie.

Serena had already explained that, in the middle of a private conversation she was having with a group of her friends in the cafeteria, the girl—who, according to the vice principal, was "troubled with problems at home"—walked over to Serena, criticized her for an opinion she was sharing with her friends about a particular musician she no longer liked, and slugged her in the face.

Serena didn't care about the girl's "problems at home." She had plenty of her own, and she wasn't taking them out on the faces of strangers. The vice principal knew nothing of the misery Serena had been through, and mostly likely, she wouldn't care.

The vice principal had spoken to the witnesses, had heard it straight from the girl who hit her that she "rapped her on the head because she wouldn't shut up."

Rapped? Serena thought as the vice principal spoke. *Is that some sort of Midwestern slang for hitting a person unnecessarily?*

Kevin and Sedra sat beside Serena, her eyes filling with tears at the very thought that she could get punched in the face for doing nothing and feel like the accused.

Though she admitted to "rapping" Serena in the head, the girl was sent home for the rest of that school day but was back the next.

This would never happen in Tucson, Serena thought, sickened by the injustice, disheartened by the thought of facing possible bullying for the next two years while worrying about cancer's return. It seemed like too much, like more than any high school sophomore should have to deal with, but she did, and Serena made it to her senior year with bullying continuing only in the form of the judgmental stares and whispered laughs she had learned to live with before the punch she took to the head.

Regular checkups during those two years always revealed Thyroglobulin, a "tumor marker" protein in Serena's blood, but the numbers were never alarming to doctors until she and her family decided to get a second opinion.

During Serena's senior year, about six months before graduation, her new doctor didn't like the persisting levels, so his solution was a "mega dose" of radiation.

I don't want to do this again, she thought, but there was no choice, no bargaining with the inevitable. She needed this treatment, which meant another month-long, low-iodine diet and a lot of pain.

When Serena's doctor took her off of her thyroid medicine once again, the instant weight gain grabbed at her bones and joints, tugging until fatigue came to her rescue. Fifteen-hour sleep nights felt invisible, forgotten, the moment after waking, forcing Serena back into bed or onto the couch to keep from falling over with open eyes in the middle of the day.

She once heard someone say that stopping a person's thyroid medicine was like exposing them to a slow form of death—"They try to kill you, and once you're on the brink of death, they revive you"—and she concurred.

After the "mega dose," Serena was secluded to a small, corner hospital room for twenty-four hours. A week later, she was sent back to school.

As graduation approached, Serena's dad applied for and accepted a job as vice president of administration at Cochise College back in Arizona.

They were going home.

Things were looking up. Her cancer was gone. The town was about to be, too, and so were its people—gone from her life. She woke up on the day of graduation and made a very important, life-changing decision.

I need a negativity purge, she thought.

She had spent hours in the confines of her bedroom, pen in hand, letting her darkest thoughts, her greatest fears, bleed onto the pages of her hidden journal, becoming lyrics to depressing, handwritten songs scribbled within the pages:

> Holding on to shattered dreams, this life ain't what it seems.
> Holding each breath in each and every way, maybe I'll make
> it, make it someday.

The cancer was behind Serena, but the negative thoughts that had consumed her during isolation and the months following lingered. She needed them gone. She was going to graduate today, and she was leaving high school, with its judgment and its disapproval; all of its forms of cruelty would be a thing of her past in just a few short hours. She decided to rummage through her old journals and find notebooks still in hiding that contained her darkest thoughts:

> Turn on the light,
> Get me out of the dark.
> Another fright,
> Today is only the first night.

She shoved the notebooks to the back of her closet, their words to the back of her mind.

I will wake up every morning and focus on something positive, she decided, whether it was taking a moment to enjoy the simple beauty of a sunrise, internally rejoicing in the success of her favorite sports team, thinking about upcoming concerts and CD releases, or giving herself an invisible pat on the back for accomplishing a personal goal.

At the graduation ceremony, finding something positive to focus on was not a challenge—she was done with high school and she was moving home. "Pomp and Circumstance" played in the background as she walked down the aisle and across the stage toward her diploma, but the thoughts in Serena's mind overpowered its gentle drum beat, its celebratory march. *I don't have to deal with any of these people again. I'm done. I can start fresh.*

★ 6 ★

A few weeks later, Serena and her parents made the twenty-two-hour drive to Bisbee, Arizona, where they would be staying with Kevin's parents in their one-bedroom guest house for three months before moving a half hour away to the town of Sierra Vista. Kevin and Sedra slept in the bedroom, Serena and Seanza squeezed on the tiny couch in the living area.

No privacy, no bed of her own, no space to get lost in her music. But it didn't matter. She was in a place with no humidity, no cornfields, no tornadoes. She could listen to the soothing clicks of cicadas in the trees rather than worry about the sudden darkening of the sky, its collapse and uproar threatening the towns below it.

There were a handful of tornado warnings during the four years that Serena and her family lived in Nebraska, and when speakers surrounding the town had screamed their potential arrival, the family fled to the basement, waited, and watched.

Rain poured, thunder crashed, and lightning flashed across skies the color of swamp moss.

Skies the color of vomit, Serena thought during one particular tornado that flattened a town twenty miles from their Lincoln home. *Only in Nebraska.*

Lying on the hide-a-bed of her grandparent's couch at night with her sister, her parents in a tiny bedroom just steps away, the misery of their cramped living situation crept into her thoughts. She pushed them back and reminded herself, *Hey, at least we're back in Arizona. This isn't so bad.*

Serena woke up the next morning and put all of her focus—her positive energy—into starting the next phase of her life. She enrolled at Cochise Community College in Sierra Vista and signed up for classes that would begin her journey toward a degree in art.

She had turned eighteen and was starting her trek down a path that had nothing to do with disapproving classmates, cancer, or Lincoln, Nebraska, until one day, four months after returning to Arizona, a stumbling block rolled into her path.

———————— ✳

Serena and Sedra had spent the day at the Mayo Clinic in Phoenix, where Serena went through the usual routine—blood work, tests, and sonograms of her neck. When the results came back a few hours later, she sat next to her mom on a small couch in the office of her new doctor and she knew bad news was coming

"We need to get them out," said Dr. Whitaker, her endocrinologist. Her thyroid was already gone, so the only things left in her neck to remove were lymph nodes. Cancer had made its ugly return, and after receiving her "mega dose," she knew that radioactive iodine treatments were not an option—she had already received a lifetime's worth of radiation.

"Let's get you to the surgeon," the doctor said.

Serena sat with her mom in that quiet, uncomfortable room, with only one thought—*All right, I beat this once, I'll beat it again.* No more questions of *why me?* or thoughts of *I'm so alone ... nobody understands.* No more tears.

Then another thought entered her mind. *November 12—Darren will be here.*

A few weeks before, Serena had seen on Darren Hayes's website that he would be traveling through Phoenix on that date, performing a small, intimate concert at the Scottsdale Borders bookstore. The anticipation of his visit had become her positive thought every morning, but she never imagined that anything, especially cancer's return, would keep her from going.

"When will you be doing the surgery?" Serena asked her surgeon, Dr. Michael Hinni, when she and Sedra met with him shortly after their appointment with Dr. Michael Whitaker.

"We'll schedule it around November sixth," said Dr. Hinni.

Six days before Darren Hayes gets here, Serena thought. *I don't care...I am going to see him.* She had survived cancer once, and in her mind, this was just another surgery. The mere thought that this surgery would not be the cure never entered her mind. She wouldn't let it. All she had to do was go in for surgery, recover, and life without cancer would continue.

On the verge of
On the verge of something wonderful
A resurgence
On the edge of something wonderful *

---

* From the song "On the Verge of Something Wonderful" on the album *This Delicate Thing We've Made,* copyright © 2007. Lyrics, by Darren Hayes and Robert Conley, used by permission.

Resurgence—revival, recovery, rebirth, she thought. Serena knew that the rest of the world found its own meaning in Darren's music, its own interpretation, but in every song, in every word, she found something. She knew logically that Darren knew nothing about her, didn't know she existed, but she believed his music was there for a reason, for her, for others. She listened to these lyrics, the words of "On the Verge of Something Wonderful," every day until the day of her surgery. It somehow gave her hope that Darren, his concert, and his music, would be waiting on the other side.

The day of her surgery was five days before Darren arrived in town. "I'm going whether you like it or not," she told Dr. Hinni when the surgery was over.

"Sure, you can go," the doctor said, but his eyes may as well have rolled with the attitude of a teenager, as if to say, "There's no way you're going."

He thought he was safe telling Serena she could go, trying to offer the hope he sensed she wanted. He knew her mind needed something to think about, to look forward to, but, unaware of his patient's stubbornness and her spirit's determination to do what her mind gets set on doing, he was certain she would not physically be able to go.

"She won't feel up to it," Dr. Hinni later whispered to her mother, offering reassurance.

Comforted only slightly by his words, Sedra knew her daughter—if Serena was determined to go, she would go.

* 7 *

The surgery had been a smooth success of removing every lymph node from the left side of Serena's neck, but two days later, lymph fluid that should have absorbed back into her body leaked from a duct in her upper chest, resulting in an emergency surgery to repair it.

"There's no way in the world she'll be up to going now," Dr. Hinni reiterated.

Five days after surgery, on her day of discharge, Serena lay in her hospital bed watching the music video to Mary J. Blige's song "Just Fine," taking in every word she sang about the freedom of living life the way you want to live it.

Time to continue living my life, Serena thought. *My life.* This was her decision.

"Are you ready to go tomorrow?" she asked her mom when they got home from the hospital.

It was just as Sedra predicted. "Are you sure you're up to it?"

Serena didn't answer, just stared at her mom.

"All right," Sedra said, tilting her head and staring back. "But you're taking a walker."

Urgh, I don't need a stupid walker, Serena thought, but knowing her mom would not budge, she agreed.

—————✦

On the verge of
On the verge of something wonderful
A resurgence
On the edge of something wonderful...

This is something wonderful, Serena thought, pushing the walker to the back of her mind.

The words, usually coming from speakers, were flowing from the lips of Darren himself, right in front of her. Ten feet away.

Her mouth moved with every word, and she closed her eyes. Fields of yellow flashed in her mind's darkness. The sound of his voice brought her back to the highway in Wisconsin, when his music had flushed out the word *cancer* as it floated through her head in the car on the way to her grandfather's funeral.

Sitting directly in front of her, singing "Truly, Madly, Deeply," Darren brought Serena back to the hospital, white lights flashing above her, gurney bouncing, his voice filling the lonely operating room. Sitting in the middle of the crowd at Borders, lost in his music, Serena's mind became the walls of her bedroom during isolation, confined to the echoes of his voice, as he sang the last line of the song, and once again, it was just the two of them.

When Darren finished singing, Serena stood with her mom in the line to meet him. Her arms were weak under the pressure of pushing the dreaded walker, but her anticipation was stronger— the anticipation of the voice she loved becoming a person.

"Ch-ch-ch-ch-changes..." Darren sang quietly when he saw her David Bowie T-shirt, a smile on his face.

Serena laughed and thought, *Wow, he's real. And he's right in front of me.*

Darren reached for her hand. *He's shaking my hand,* Serena thought in disbelief.

She smiled and explained the walker to Darren. "I just got out of the hospital yesterday," she said.

Serena wanted to tell him that he, through his music, had been with her every step of the way, through her surgeries, her isolation from the world, her bout with self-pity, and her determination to never visit that dark place again. She wanted him to know that he was the reason she wasn't lying in bed at home that very moment.

"You're very strong for coming," he said with a smile. "And you knew all the words!"

He noticed!

Serena beamed. There was nothing more she needed. Not one more lyric, or smile, or note—until he said the next two words.

"Stay strong."

She looked straight into his eyes and knew she would. Without realizing it, that was what she needed to hear.

———✦

Over the next few weeks, Serena focused on recovering and turning her new Sierra Vista bedroom into a music haven, her walls becoming windows to her past. She hung posters of concerts she had attended, autographs she had received, album covers, vinyl, and CDs.

Forced to drop classes for the semester at Cochise, Serena had time to alphabetically organize her collection of more than four hundred CDs, lie in bed listening to music, and watch endless movies and videos of concert tours with her favorite musicians.

She traveled with Janet Jackson on her Hawaiian tour and the Backstreet Boys through Orlando. She got lost in the stories of Prince's *Purple Rain* and Pink Floyd's *The Wall,* felt immersed in the frenzied crowd of a concert scene in Michael Jackson's *Moonwalker* and, in her mind, stood among hundreds beneath the balcony as Madonna sang "Don't Cry For Me Argentina" in *Evita.*

Time passed slowly, painfully, as Serena's shoulder, sore from hardening scar tissue surrounding the doctor's incision that stretched from her ear across the front of her neck, began to heal. Her neck, stiff and tender, softened over time, and she worked daily to improve its rotation.

A week after the surgery, Serena was surfing the net, visiting different artists' websites and reading the latest music news, when she found an upcoming concert—three weeks away—of Avenged Sevenfold, Seanza's favorite band. Heavy metal bands Operator and The Confession would perform as well.

"I'm buying the tickets so we can go," Serena told her sister.

"You just got out of the hospital!" Seanza said. "We're only going if you're better. Otherwise, I'm taking a friend."

Three weeks passed, and every ounce of Serena's body, every part of her mind, screamed, *Let's go!*

⋆ 8 ⋆

The drums pounded through her, the electric guitar screeched in her head, and the raw acidity of the music pumped through Serena as Seanza guided her through the crowd, hands tightly held.

"If we get separated, you know where to meet," Seanza yelled, her breath hot in Serena's ear. "Stay out of the mosh pit!"

Yeah, right, Serena thought.

She had become addicted to the rush, the chaotic freedom found in thrashing through a frenzied mob of screaming, flailing fans when she was just twelve years old during her first mosh pit at a Good Charlotte concert in Tucson.

With ripped jeans and hair dyed the color of fire, Serena's hesitancy to jump into the crowd quickly succumbed to its raw, animal-like energy—the solitary movement of hundreds as one, pushing and shoving.

Embraced by the chaos, Serena and her sister moved with the swaying pile of bodies, arms pounding the drum's beat into the air. It was a scene, a culture, Serena had become part of and craved, and her need to fulfill that addiction resurfaced at the Avenged Sevenfold concert, where her neck was still tender and healing. Surviving another mosh pit would prove to everyone that nothing could get her down.

"I don't want to get in trouble if you have to go back to the hospital!" Seanza managed to shout before the crowd swept her away.

I'll be fine, Serena thought before plunging in.

Her internal stitches remained intact, her craving satisfied. Serena returned home with a sense of accomplishment, proof to herself that she had healed, beat cancer, and that life would continue as normal.

Still settling into their new Sierra Vista home, Serena enrolled at Cochise Community College and changed her major from graphic design to game design and creation, enjoying classes in art, coding, and artificial intelligence. Inspired by one of the first music-related video games, Michael Jackson's *Moonwalker* for the Sega Genesis, Serena wanted to join the industry and bring her creative ideas into the gaming world.

Toward the end of her first semester, she came home from school one day and checked the voicemail on her cell phone.

"Hi Serena, this is Linda from the Make-A-Wish Foundation in Phoenix."

Serena's heart folded, paused, and then pounded violently. *Is this really happening?* Back in Lincoln, before she graduated from high school, the Make-A-Wish Foundation of Nebraska had contacted Serena, told her to make a wish, and gave her the paperwork to fill out. Those piles of papers, that joyful wish, in Serena's mind, offered something undeserved.

As a child, she was the first to split her lunch with a classmate who forgot theirs. She was the one to offer half of her ice cream to a friend who ran out of money on a school field trip. She was the person who couldn't pass a Salvation Army bell ringer at Christmastime without throwing in some spare change. She was a giver, not a taker.

She had traveled the country with her family, been to Disneyland

Resort and SeaWorld, and swam with dolphins in Hawaii. How could she accept a wish that could otherwise be granted to a four-year-old who had been through much more than she had?

She pictured the wide eyes of children watching whales jump at SeaWorld, experiencing the magic of "It's a Small World" at Disneyland, holding the fin of a dolphin as it slices through ocean water—all common wishes and all experiences she'd already had.

The stack of paperwork remained blank, untouched, for more than a month before Serena convinced herself that if the foundation was contacting her, somebody must think she deserved it. She finally filled in the line that required her to list her wish: "I wish to meet Darren Hayes."

She was informed that celebrity wishes could take years to grant and in some cases, depending on the celebrity, might never come true.

If Serena ever got to meet Darren, he would be worth the wait.

She turned in the paperwork right before graduation and moved back to Arizona shortly after. She knew that the Phoenix chapter had taken over, so when she heard, "Go check your email" on her voicemail, she ran to her dad's office, quickly got online, and opened her inbox.

Hi Serena,

I just heard from our London office that Darren Hayes would like to meet with you July 19th. You and your family will spend five nights and six days in London. I'll be in touch about flights soon. Let me know if you have any questions.

Warmest wishes,
Linda

Would like to meet with you …

Darren Hayes would like to meet with you …

Serena screamed into the quiet of the house, her voice jumping from room to room, echoing down the halls, filling the silence. She got up, thought about dancing, thought about spinning, running, something …

I need to call someone.

"Mom!" she shouted into the phone. "We're going to London!"

★ 9 ★

A few months after hearing that her wish was coming true, the countdown clock in Serena's room—the one that had ticked each second, each minute, and each day away—finally stopped.

It was time.

She looked out the window on the morning of July 16, Seanza on her heels, both their hands pulling back the curtains, and in the driveway sat a long, white limousine. The closest Serena had ever been to a limousine was on the open highway, an arm's length and a lifetime away. Her eyes had always been in search of the lucky ones inside the sleek, black, and mysterious vehicle.

Now she was the lucky one.

She slid across the car's long, black seat, hand trailing behind, gliding over shiny leather, and scooted until her whole family was beside her.

The royal treatment had begun—and it continued across the ocean. On a private tour, they witnessed the world's greatest and most famous collection of jewels in the Tower of London's Jewel House. Fascinated by the colors, the glimmer, and the history, Serena went from case to case, display to display, with wide eyes and a dropped jaw. Time stood still when she stood before the Queen's Scepter with the Cross and its 530-carat diamond.

They saw Buckingham Palace, Madame Tussauds, and the Tower of London from the top of a double-decker bus—Big Ben, the Houses of Parliament, Tower Bridge, and The Crystal Palace from the London Eye, Europe's tallest Ferris wheel.

From 440 feet in the air, with breathtaking, living history below and the most exquisite scenery stretching as far as she could see, Serena's mind was a million miles away. *I am meeting Darren Hayes in a few hours*, she thought.

An afternoon of tea and scones was scheduled with Darren later that day at The Ritz London, and the official Make-A-Wish itinerary had informed Serena and her family that men were to wear jackets and ties and women were to dress "smart."

A jeans and T-shirt girl, Serena had dragged her mom and sister shopping a few weeks before, in search of something "smart." She had never been to an event with a dress code. Even during a tour of the White House on a fifth-grade field trip, the only men dressed in jackets were the U.S. Secret Service.

Serena had settled on a pair of dress pants and a T-shirt covered by a vest. Sedra wore nice pants, Seanza, a dress, and Kevin sported a jacket over a pink shirt, the same shade as the cotton candy-colored limousine that picked them up in front of their hotel before heading to The Ritz to meet Darren.

Walking through the hotel's grand entrance was like stepping into Serena's wildest imagination, her most elaborate dream. She pictured the hands of Sir Winston Churchill and Queen Elizabeth II touching the royally oriented furniture surrounding her and eating scones and drinking tea from fine china in the room she was about to enter.

She and her family glided along glossy marble floors, beneath gold-lined ceilings held by pillars reaching for the sky. They respected the hotel's quiet demeanor, its innate sophistication, with hushed voices as they made their way to the lobby.

Serena paced then sat, knees bouncing and mind spinning, as Darren and his assistant, Tracey, walked into the hotel and toward her with a smile. *He's just another human,* she reminded herself, containing squeals of excitement that wanted to burst through her smile.

"Well, you must be Serena," he said as she stood up. He embraced her like he would an old friend and kissed her on the cheek. *Darren just hugged me . . . and kissed me.*

Before being escorted to the Tea Room, a man with a deeply distinguished English accent said, "Excuse me, Sir," snapping Serena from the dream world she was about to enter. The man, dressed like a penguin, stood beside Darren, hands politely behind his back. He looked down the length of his nose at Darren's boots, then slowly to his jean-covered legs, past his vest, and finally to his questioning eyes.

"No jacket, no tie…" the butler said, somehow both politely and rudely.

"We are with the Make-A-Wish Foundation," said Gillian, the Wish coordinator who was there to oversee the wish. She showed him her Make-A-Wish badge and spoke with the hotel manager.

"Excuse me," the butler said, head down, apologetic.

He disappeared, and they were escorted to a private table outside the Marie Antoinette Suite, which they passed very quickly, momentarily, through another world. A fancy world with golden chandeliers, wall murals, tapestry drapes, pink velvet chairs, white tablecloths, crystal, and fine china. It was a room with furniture from the Palace of Versailles, a room where President Dwight D. Eisenhower, French President Charles de Gaulle, and Sir Winston Churchill had discussed war tactics during World War II—a room of privilege, class, and status.

They continued through quietly while eyes of recognition and polite whispers followed but lingered in the stuffy air behind them. They sat down at the small table, its centerpiece a four-tiered crystal plate of scones, and shared a laugh at their experience of nearly getting escorted from the Tea Room. When that finally died, uncomfortable silence danced between them, small talk hiding in the presence of strangers, threatening to submerge the rest of the conversation.

A man with a white napkin dangling from his arm brought their tea, and, determined to remain as private, as invisible as possible, they poured it themselves, the trickle peaceful yet daunting. The sound of it became laughter in Serena's mind, teasing, mocking her lack of experience in this high-class setting. Ceiling-length draperies, gold-plated everything, and furniture and ambience designed for royalty stared her in the face, waiting for her to say something equally as sophisticated, equally as proper.

Instead, Serena jumped from her seat and struck a silly pose—sporting a serious expression, she put her hands on her thighs, stuck her butt way out—while Darren threw his head back with genuine laughter.

They became instant friends.

Over the next few hours, they talked about everything from music to movies to their Zodiac signs to their dogs. Darren shared stories of growing up in Australia, and Serena talked about her hobbies and told him her plans for the future.

That was her focus now. Cancer was a thing of her past, and that's where she wanted it to stay. She never mentioned it to Darren—saw no reason to burden him with it and didn't need him feeling sorry for her. But there was one thing she wanted him to know.

"You and I have met before," Serena said. "At the Scottsdale Borders in Arizona."

Darren studied her for a moment, the faces of thousands of fans challenging his memory. "I had just gotten out of the hospital," Serena said. "I had a walker ... "

"I remember you!" he exclaimed.

He remembered me, she thought.

They continued their time together by snapping dozens of pictures, moments frozen in time for them to hold on to—pictures of high fiving, striking poses, and acting silly—documenting the beginning of a newly formed friendship.

"You know, I didn't know what to expect with meeting all of you," Darren said to Serena's family when she left to use the restroom. "A lot of fans scream and cry and carry on. You're all so normal!"

When she returned, their visit continued for the next hour or so until it was time to leave. Serena's wit, her humor and outlook, had drawn Darren to her in a deeper, more intense way than he had anticipated she would.

"I plan to stalk her until the end of time," he teased Kevin as they made their way from the hotel to the awaiting limo. And he wasn't kidding. Darren planned to surprise Serena with an ongoing friendship. As they walked, she hummed a line from Darren's song, "What You Like," a song she had repeated over and over while in isolation and found irony in its meaning—unexpectedly traveling a journey from beginning to end with the same person.

In Serena's case, Darren was that person.

He had been there from the beginning, from the first time she heard the word *cancer* on the way to her grandfather's funeral. And now, cancer-free and almost five years later, everything had finally come together and made sense—all because of this trip, all because of this opportunity.

"It was so nice to meet you," Serena said as she gave Darren one last hug. "Thank you for everything."

She left it at that.

"Everything"—his music, his lyrics, his inspiration.

Any specific thank yous she might have said, might have thought in that moment, escaped. Wrapped in the pure joy of meeting him, she wouldn't realize until later, until reality danced through the dream she was in, just how his music had driven her to a successfully positive outlook on life—how much solace she had found in his lyrics and his voice.

Darren would later learn from Serena just how his music had set her free, how he was her musical companion when cancer took her away from the world. She would tell him how he had found her in the hospital during her first surgery and prepared her for her second and how he was her reason for getting out of the hospital when it was over.

She looked at the invisible strength that stood before her and crawled into the limo after what she thought was the end of her journey with Darren.

Little did she know, it was just the beginning. She had just made a friend for life, and so her wish would last forever.

⋆ MESSAGES FROM THE FAMILIES ⋆

Tatum

WE FIRST WOULD like to thank you for taking the time to read Tatum's story. It is our sincere hope and prayer that you take from this what you need at the time of reading it. Fact is always stranger than fiction, and the fact that we experienced what most people think will never happen to them is still shocking to us. We were hit with a baseball bat to the gut and had the wind knocked out of us. We found ourselves confused with many questions and the need to redefine what life is for our family. The Make-A-Wish Foundation, along with our family and friends, helped us to make the transition from misery to the ability to have fun during trials. We find it necessary to laugh and seek out the joy in times of adversity. Laughter heals, and our friends at Make-A-Wish have made that their priority. There is no pain and there are no procedures that come with Make-A-Wish, which makes it a refuge for families. Tatum is special for reasons other than her health issues, and that is what we celebrate. We are eternally grateful for the joy we experienced through the love of so many during the most intense and difficult time of our lives.

GAYLA ANTHONY

Fifteen-year-old Tatum, her parents, David and Sherry, and her younger sister, eleven-year-old Hannah, stand in the living room of their Dallas home.

—TATUM'S PARENTS, DAVID AND
SHERRY NULL

Katelyn

Our hope for those who read Katelyn's story is to realize that life really is about choices. Kate's journey is not one we would have ever chosen, but the way we came out of it was determined by the choices we made during it. God had us walk this path for a reason, and we chose to look for every positive thread we could. We chose to never lose hope. We chose every single day to keep moving forward, never letting sadness or worry stop us. Some days, we were hanging on by a thread. It was our choice to never give up. And we are still making choices today—we choose not to let Kate's disabilities define her or us. We continue to choose to test our boundaries. God wants us to live an abundant life, not just exist. As Kate would say, "Come on, let's go jump out of a perfectly good airplane! Life is meant to be lived."

BRIAN FESTI

Katelyn Atwell and Bob Crossman, chief instructor at Skydive DeLand, pose for a quick shot before jumping from a plane flying over DeLand, Florida, in November 2011 for Katelyn's twenty-fifth birthday.

—KATELYN'S PARENTS, RAY AND SHARON ATWELL

Brittney

Brittney would have loved to know that her story would be told in a book. As she fought her battle with cancer, she often told me that she would beat it and then help other kids get through it. She had dreams of traveling and talking to kids, letting them know what they were going to face, and then helping them face it. It was her dream to spread hope and optimism to other children with cancer.

Even during the darkest moments of her fight, Brittney's dreams remained big and she never gave up. She taught me more in her short life than I could ever have taught her in a lifetime—how to

ANDY MUIRHEAD

stay strong, look at the bright side, never lose hope, and always keep laughing. She was a little girl who could have changed the world. That is why I decided to share her story. I want people to become inspired by her spirit and all that she lived and stood for. She was a true believer in putting others before herself, making nobody worry unless absolutely necessary, and keeping a smile on her face, no matter what. Together, by retelling the story we lived, we hope to spread inspiration with Brittney's motto on life—love, laughter, and no tears!

In the backyard of her San Diego home, T'Ann Wolfe holds a 2004 photo of her late daughter, Brittney, taken just seven months before Brittney passed away.

—BRITTNEY'S MOM, T'ANN WOLFE

Garrett

On a trip last year to the Czech Republic, Garrett Stuart, with his parents, Mike and Linda, pose at the Kotnov Castle in Tabor.

Life is a gift, and no matter what you are given, whether it is Dystonia or any other type of hardship, it is still a gift. It is important to stay positive and remember that if one road does not work out, there is another. Never give up! Additionally, it is amazing to see the positive impact one can have on another. While it is rewarding for the person receiving the help, it can be just as gratifying for the individual providing it. So, my message is to stay positive and realize the power of giving.

—GARRETT STUART

Meera

In May of 2012, Alex, Nita, Meera, and Zane attended the annual "Wish Night" event at the Hilton Anatole Hotel in downtown Dallas, where Meera auctioned a few of her paintings that night at a high bid.

We have always believed in logic and that our lives are governed by it. We continued to believe that way until our daughter, Meera, defied all logic and reason on the road to her recovery.

No matter how illogical life may appear, never give up hope and faith because those are the only things that can keep us sane. Our journey taught us that even the most brilliant minds cannot explain why certain events happen. They just do. We learned that these events, no matter how severe or unfortunate, are purposeful, and their intent will always be revealed. Stay faithful and you will see how much hope is in this world, and it is awe-inspiring.

—MEERA'S PARENTS, ALEX AND NITA SALAMAH

Dakota

Our family was honored that our firstborn son, Dakota, was considered for this publication. Dakota authored his own story as he lived out his faith through four years of fighting a rare leukemia with valor, selflessness, strength, and love. Through his fight, Dakota gave most of the gifts he would receive to other children fighting cancer to help brighten their day, and truly taught us that it is

Henry and Sharon Hawkins pose with their sons, Riley and Quinn, holding a picture of their late son, Dakota, in front of their Cabot, Arkansas home.

"more blessed to give than to receive." Each day he carried a gentle smile no matter how he felt. Often we are reminded that his Make-A-Wish was as unique as he was: a well-thought-out gift straight from his heart to ours that we will always cherish. He truly valued others over self and loved deeply.

—Dakota's parents, Henry and Sharon Hawkins

Tien

BEV WANLIN

Tien poses for his seventh-grade school photo at The Berkeley School in Berkeley, CA.

Tien Leou-on and his family wish to thank the many people who helped Tien on his long medical journey. If we could, we would hug each one of you: dear friends, family, nurses, doctors, medical technicians, teachers, volunteers, clergy from so many different faiths, and complete strangers. We shared the story of Tien as a light and encouragement to all who travel a difficult medical road.

—Tien's mom, Lillian Howan

Serena

There is always a brighter side to every negative in life, which I learned through a struggle that no average fifteen-year-old could ever comprehend. My battle with cancer was nothing short of an emotional civil war, and the change into a positive attitude after such a blow was not easy. I knew I had to look to something to confide in during such a negative time, hence my love of music. Just a simple melody melted all my fears and anxiety by lighting the path I needed to use to move on. Positivity is a goal that anyone can reach with the right amount of courage contained deep within. This is why I shared my story. I view my Make-A-Wish experience as a cap of euphoria and positivity to end the madness that was my struggle with thyroid cancer and other medical mishaps. In the

SEANZA BUTLER

end, I leave with a brand new friend: a truly beautiful soul by the name of Darren Hayes; he was there from the beginning and had no idea. I may be the luckiest person in the world to have a friend like him. This has only marked the beginning of my life's journey.

Twenty-three-year-old Serena poses in her Sierra Vista, Arizona, home.

—SERENA BUTLER

✴ ACKNOWLEDGMENTS ✴

I NEVER IMAGINED HOW blessed and overwhelmed with gratitude I would feel after compiling this list of thank yous. The words on these next few pages only begin to describe how special and important each and every person mentioned is in my life. This army of people has marched loyally beside me, their words of encouragement, patience, support, and optimism motivating me till the last word was written. I am forever indebted to each and every one of you for the role you have played, and will continue to play, in my life.

This book would have remained a file on my computer if it wasn't for the instant belief my literary agent, Jeff Herman, had in it. Thank you for your guidance, support, advice, commitment, and dedication to this project over the years. You never lost hope, which meant neither did I.

I am so thankful to my publisher, BenBella Books, for sharing the same belief in this book. To the staff at BenBella—Glenn Yeffeth, Debbie Harmsen, Cortney Strube, Monica Lowry, Sarah Dombrowsky, Jennifer Canzoneri, Lindsay Marshall, Adrienne Lang, Leigh Camp, Thuy Vo, and Kit Sweeney—you are a strong, united force that has offered nothing but endless support and guidance during my first-time experience of publishing a book. Thank you for sharing my belief that these truly inspirational stories needed to be told and for your vision and efforts in making my lifelong dream of writing and publishing a book come true.

A very special thank you to my editor, Marite Hart, for your creative brilliance. I felt the love and passion you had for this project the moment we started working together. Your diligent work and sincere vision helped polish and mold it to perfection.

Long before I had agents and publishers, I had editors at *The Daily Courier,* who believed in me just as much. Thank you to Karen Despain, Mark Duncan, Ben Hanson, and Tim Wieder-aenders for taking a chance on a young girl fresh out of college. For four years, you showed me the ropes, becoming the invaluable foundation for my writing career. I will always be indebted to you for that.

Frank Shankwitz, this thank you is on behalf of me, the families in this book, and hundreds of thousands of families across the globe—thank you for your role in starting the Make-A-Wish-Foundation. Your vision more than thirty years ago of fulfilling the desires of children is where it all began, and because of you and a handful of others, thousands of lives have been changed. Thank you for your partnership on this project and for believing from day one that sharing the journeys of Wish families would spread hope and inspiration to all. I am proud to call you a friend.

My most heartfelt thank yous go to my sons, Andrew and Evan, because that is where you live—in my heart. I never knew a love so true and so deep until you were born. You are reminders to me every day of just how precious life is and that nothing too big or too small should ever be taken for granted. You two are my daily inspirations and my forever loves.

Bobby—my husband, my partner, my inspiration, my best friend—thank you for encouraging me to quit my job and work full-time to write this book. You believed in my ability to do it before I even did. You have experienced every moment right alongside me, and I couldn't ask for a more loving or supportive husband.

Deepest gratitude to my parents, Joel and Debbie Bump. Your encouragement to become whatever I dreamed of becoming from the time I was a little girl is the reason I am here, able to write you this very special thank you in my first published book. Words cannot begin to describe how grateful I am for your endless love, support, and belief in me.

A big, warm thanks to my brother, Daniel—my childhood companion, my teenage rival, my adulthood best friend—for your unconditional love and support through life.

Deepest thank you to Onna, my sister (I left out the "in-law" part on purpose). You have given me endless love and support from the moment I decided to write this book. You have traveled every step alongside me, and it was your belief in me that kept me believing in myself.

A special thank you to my grandparents, Richard and Pat Twamley—Grandpa, for encouraging me to finish this book so that I can get to work on writing yours. Grandma, for being the first person to reveal the impact these stories can make by letting your tears fall. Your sincere praise and connection with this book confirmed my belief in its ability to touch people's lives so deeply.

A special thank you to Mary (Grandma) Bump, retired music and English teacher for many years, for passing along your love of literature. Thank you for the hours you spent proofreading and the lifetime of knowledge behind all those little red marks. To my late grandpa, Wallace Bump, librarian for thirty-five years, for your love of books and passion for telling great stories. I hope I made you proud.

A great big thank you to my Aunt Julie for the special role you have always played in my life. Thank you for your belief in this book from the moment the idea was born to write it, the interest you have always taken in it, and the hours you spent putting your twenty-five-year medical background to the test and editing this book.

Thank you to my Uncle Mike and Susanne for your endless love and always-uplifting words of encouragement.

A deep thank you to my husband's family, one that I am blessed to be a part of. Each and every one of you welcomed me into your family with open arms so many years ago and have shown nothing but love and support ever since.

I have shared endless conversations with each of you about the progress of this book: Paul, Danny, Dan, Jenny, Debbi, Ronnie, Rebecca, Grandma Beth, Natalie and the late George, Uncle Danny and Terry, and the Rubins (you may as well be family!)—thank you for listening.

A very special thank you to my mother-in-law, Pam, with whom I share a love of books, for your invaluable opinions and insight during the process of writing this book. Thank you for showing me the love and support you have always shown your own children.

Cindy, Karen, and Magali, you are more than my sisters-in-law, you are my friends. Thank you for your listening ears and endless words of encouragement during every step of writing this book.

A sincere thank you to all of my cousins—Anthony, Carmen, Matthew, and Alison—for the endless love and support you have given from the very beginning and every step of the way.

Heartfelt thanks to my closest friends, the best in the world, for loving and supporting me during my seven-year journey of writing and publishing this book. I love you all dearly.

Emily, thank you for listening to countless hours of me talking about this book, feeling every discouraging moment as though it was your own, praising every word in it, and loving me like a sister every step of the way.

Heather, a lifetime childhood friend is one in a million. Thank you from the bottom of my heart for your endless encouragement and support for this project. And to your parents, Bill and Suzie, my second parents growing up, for all of your love and belief in me.

Hilary, my "Partner in Believing," you have always been here for me, and I thank you for being a big part of my transition from timid newspaper reporter to someone who believed in herself enough to write this book. Yours is next!

Kristin and Brooke, years and oceans have separated us, but no matter how much time passes, we are always connected. Your friendships, nearly twenty years old, are significant parts of who I am, and I thank you for your willingness to listen to hours of my book-writing process as part of our "catching up."

Kerri, Kelly, and Shari, the hours upon hours each of you have spent sitting across restaurant tables from me on "girls' night outs," listening as I talked about this book, asking questions, caring deeply, are priceless gifts you didn't even know you were giving.

Sara, you are proof that we are never too old to make friends who will last a lifetime. Thank you for providing the same support and belief in me as those who I have known my entire life.

To Arika, Claire, and Irina—new friendships are the start of forever friendships. Thank you for the support and enthusiasm you have shown for this book.

A big thank you to Ashley, the best babysitter in the world, for your reliability and love of my boys. You made it possible in times of desperation to continue writing this book. And to Zahra Asmaytar, Angel, and your entire family, thank you for the love and exceptional care you gave to my boys for more than a year.

Since this book captures and embraces the strength, innocence, honesty, and resilience of children, I want to thank all the children in my family—Andrew, Evan, Caleb, Aubrey, Jackson, Carter, Candace, Trevor, Nathan, Audrey, Alyssa, and Jessica—for all the joy, happiness, laughter, and hope you bring to my life. You each live inside my heart.

To the families featured in this book, there aren't enough words to thank you for the hard work and dedication it took on your part to be able to share your stories with the world. You are some of the strongest people I know, with the outlooks on life I believe we should all strive for, and your stories continue to fill me with hope and inspiration, as I'm sure they will to all who read this book. Thank you from the bottom of my heart for sharing your stories with me, and in turn, the world.

Thank you so very much to the following staff members (current and former) from various Make-A-Wish chapters across the country—Robin Dunn, Jennifer Gonzales, Patricia Wilson, Elaine Kauffman, Evonne Williams, Jennifer Shuman, Berta James, Billie Milner, Julie Baron, Cheryl Unger, Suzanne Sutter, Mary Olinger, Chriss Sharer, Angela Geiss, Mark Alberts, Spring Tart, and John Wolff. If it wasn't for your vision, your dedication, and your help, this book would not exist. I appreciate you all for the work you do and for your genuine efforts and early belief in this book.

There are never too many ways to thank those who have helped us become the people we are today, and I thank each of you for the role you have played in my life; you will remain with me and part of me forever.

DATE DUE

APR 2 9 2014

NBK

NIK

PRINTED IN U.S.A.

R A‎‎ ‎st for *The*
L‎ ‎te stories
about ‎ ‎nspiration
for wri‎ ‎nce writer
for nu‎ ‎*Magazine*
and th‎ ‎*zine,* while
ventui‎ ‎ries of the
famili‎ ‎d, Bobby,
and th‎ ‎This is her
first book.